YALE JUDAICA SERIES

VOLUME XX

COMPOSITION CONCERNING RELIEF AFTER ADVERSITY

An Elegant Composition concerning Relief after Adversity

BY

NISSIM BEN JACOB IBN SHĀHĪN

TRANSLATED FROM THE ARABIC

WITH INTRODUCTION AND NOTES

BY

WILLIAM M. BRINNER

Professor of Near Eastern Studies

University of California, Berkeley

NEW HAVEN AND LONDON, YALE UNIVERSITY PRESS

1977

Library of Congress catalog card number: 49-9495
International standard book number: 0-300-01952-1

Designed by John O. C. McCrillis
and set in Garamond type.
Printed in the United States of America.

Published in Great Britain, Europe, Africa, and Asia
(except Japan) by Yale University Press, Ltd.,
London. Distributed in Latin America by Kaiman
& Polon, Inc., New York City; in Australia and
New Zealand by Book & Film Services, Artarmon, N.S.W.,
Australia; and in Japan by Harper & Row, Publishers,
Tokyo Office.

The preparation of this volume was aided by a grant
from the National Endowment for the Humanities.
The findings, conclusions, etc., do not necessarily
represent the view of the Endowment.

TO THE THOUSANDS OF JEWISH MARTYRS

WHO, INSPIRED BY THEIR FAITH AND

TRADITION, COURAGEOUSLY FACED THE

FORCES OF DARKNESS AND DEATH

EDITOR'S NOTE

Harry Austryn Wolfson, professor emeritus at Harvard University, died on September 19, 1974, the last of the three editors listed in the first volume of the Yale Judaica Series, published in 1948.

For over a quarter of a century he gave generously of his vast learning and his wise counsel to those who had a hand in the production of the successive volumes of the Series. He will be sorely missed.

L.N.

Philadelphia
December 3, 1974

CONTENTS

FOREWORD

The work of which this is a translation was written some nine hundred years ago and has ever since exercised a profound influence on Jewish piety, literature, and folklore. During the past century and a half it has become the subject of serious scholarly investigation, especially since the publication in 1933 of Julian Obermann's edition of a Judeo-Arabic manuscript which he entitled *The Arabic Original of Ibn Shāhīn's Book of Comfort*, whose text was identified as having been written by Nissim ben Jacob ibn Shāhīn, an eleventh-century scholar of Kairouan, and as being the Arabic text underlying the well-known later Hebrew work entitled *Ḥibbur Yafeh me-hay-Yĕšuʿah*. Obermann's painstaking and meticulous editorship was made especially difficult by the availability of only this single, imperfect manuscript from which he had to reconstruct a readable text. Soon after his book appeared, other scholars offered suggestions for alternate readings of some problematical words and passages in the text. In 1953 H. Z. Hirschberg published a modern Hebrew translation of the work based on Obermann's text, and in 1965 Shraga Abramson published the text of another incomplete manuscript of the Judeo-Arabic original, as well as fragments which had come to light during the thirty years since Obermann's publication, thus permitting us to reconstruct further the basic text underlying all of the versions.

The present English translation of Obermann's text cannot be definitive, in the sense that a prime desideratum for any further work with this text is a new edition of the Judeo-Arabic original, incorporating all of the additional material made available by scholars, such as Baneth, Abramson, Hirschberg, Blau, and others, who have studied the Judeo-Arabic version since the appearance of Obermann's publication. In preparing this translation I have drawn on the work of all of these scholars, but have made no effort to reproduce all the extant variant texts.

Mention must be made of the contribution of Dr. Leon Nemoy, who in his painstaking redaction of the first draft of this translation not only suggested English renditions that were in many instances more exact and more felicitous than mine, but also clarified a number of obscure passages by proceeding on the assumption that behind many difficult and problematic readings in most Judeo-Arabic manuscripts lies a copyist's misreading of careless Arabic *naskhī* or equally careless Hebrew square script. His very convincing emendations based on this assumption have been incorporated into the translation, in most instances without direct attribution. It is my pleasant duty to acknowledge his guidance and help in this respect.

Among others who have assisted me with this work my special thanks go to Professor Joshua Blau for his help and suggestions in the preliminary draft of this translation, and to my wife Lisa for her patient assistance with many aspects of the work.

Jerusalem, 1974 WILLIAM M. BRINNER

INTRODUCTION

The tale as a literary genre has evolved along various lines during the millennia-long history of Jewish literature. From the mythological and historical narratives of the early books of the Bible to the ethical and religious tales of certain later books,[1] ancient Hebrew literature presents a wealth of themes and characters, entertaining as well as instructive, that have not only persisted into later periods of Jewish literature, but served as inspiration and motifs for Christian and Muslim religious and secular literature as well.

In the course of centuries of Jewish dispersion throughout the lands of Christendom and of Islam, tales and legends became an important means of moral and ethical instruction. Tales served as a source of inspiration as well, reminding the dispersed Jews of their ancient land and of the great heroes of their past. Used by various preachers, these tales were woven into homilies for delivery in the synagogue, and were included in collections that passed from one community to another throughout the Jewish world. In this process the Jews not only absorbed themes, motifs, and entire tales from their surroundings but also served as transmitters of such materials to the cultures among which they moved. As in the field of philosophical speculation, so in the area of the tale: Jews served as a bridge between East and West, between Islam—with its borrowings from the East via India and Iran—and Christendom with its Greco-Roman and Germanic heritage.

The post-Biblical Jewish tale generally began as an elaboration, using a variety of sources and influences, of original

1. Cf. Robert H. Pfeiffer, *Introduction to the Old Testament* (New York, 1941), pp. 27–29. For example, the stories about Joseph, Samson, and Solomon, many of which contain folkloristic themes, or the semihistorical tales of Ruth and Esther. Parables, such as that of the trees choosing a king (Jud. 9), reflect the later moralistic-didactic role of the Hebrew tale.

material, often no more than an allusion, in a Biblical narrative. The Sages of the post-Biblical period themselves, however, served as a new source of inspiration and as a framework for further tale spinning. Thus Rabbi ᶜAḳiba, martyred during the futile Jewish revolt against Rome, and Hillel, the Nestor of Rabbinic Judaism, joined the Patriarchs, Moses, and other Biblical figures as heroes of the new literature. Above them all stands the mystical figure of the prophet Elijah, visible or invisible, working wonders and bringing solace and good tidings to the people of Israel.

In the course of its development, the tale came to be known as *maᶜăśeh* (plural *maᶜăśiyyoṯ*), literally "deed," and the collection of tales as *sefer maᶜăśiyyoṯ*, "book of deeds, or tales."[2] These "deeds" or "actions" (cf. the Latin *gesta*) of great men of the Biblical and post-Biblical periods served as examples to later generations not only of pious and ethical behavior but also of courage and heroism in times of adversity.

During the eleventh and twelfth centuries of the Christian era, after some four hundred years of close contact with Muslim civilization, a new Jewish cultural flowering took place, using two vehicles of expression: the Hebrew language, kept alive as a literary tongue and undergoing a steady enrichment and expansion to fill new needs, and Judeo-Arabic, the common language of the masses of Jews living in the Arabic-speaking lands from Iraq in the east to the Atlantic coast of Morocco and Spain in the west. Like other Jewish languages, such as Judeo-German (Yiddish) and Judeo-Spanish (Ladino), the vocabulary of Judeo-Arabic was sprinkled with Hebrew and Aramaic loanwords, and it was written mostly in the Hebrew script. A new stream of literary borrowings, mainly from Muslim Arabic literature, entered Jewish literature via Judeo-

2. See the discussion of this development by Moses Gaster in his translation of one of these collections, *Maᶜăśeh Book* (Philadelphia, 1934), *1*, xix ff. Gaster prefers to translate *maᶜăśiyyoṯ* as "exempla"; cf. his *The Exempla of the Rabbis* London, 1924).

Arabic, either in the form of themes and genres or—by way of translation—whole works.

The present work stands near the beginning of this process and represents one such borrowed genre—tales of relief after adversity and distress; it served as inspiration, source, and model for several later works, and was for centuries, under a variety of names, copied and reprinted in Hebrew versions in many lands. Although only a few manuscripts of the Hebrew versions remain,[3] there are several printed editions in Hebrew. In fact the work was widely distributed in manuscript and printed forms before the identity of its author became known. One Hebrew edition containing a number of tales belonging to this work, albeit in a somewhat different form than that found in what became the standard text, was printed at Constantinople in 1519 under the title *Maᶜăśiyyoṯ šebbat-Talmuḏ* (Tales of the Talmud),[4] without introduction or attribution of authorship. Only a few copies of this rare work still exist; a slightly different version was printed at Venice in 1544.

The standard printed version was first published at Ferrara in 1557 under the title *Ḥibbur Yafeh me-hay-Yĕšuᶜah* (An Elegant Composition about Deliverance, or Relief) and states on its title-page that it was composed by R. Nissim ben Jacob for "Dunash, his son-in-law (*ḥăṯano*), to speak to his heart and to console him."[5]

These two versions, especially the Ferrara one, served as the basis for all later editions, some fifteen in number,[6] the

3. For example, in Paris: Bibliothèque Nationale, Fonds hébreu, 716, no. 3; Alliance Israélite Universelle, H178; in Rome: Biblioteca Casanatense, 216, ii; Vatican, 285, 9.

4. This, or variations of it, such as *Sefer ham-Maᶜăśiyyoṯ* (Book of Tales), became a common title or subtitle for other editions of the work not necessarily based on the Constantinople edition.

5. Most printed editions include this statement on the title-page. This Dunash has not been identified, and the name of the son of Samuel han-Nagid, who married R. Nissim's daughter, was Joseph. The reading *ḥoṯno*, "his father-in-law," has also been suggested, without any satisfactory identification to accompany it.

6. Venice, 1599; Verona, 1648; Amsterdam, 1746; Zołkiew, 1799; Lemberg, 1809 (reprinted 1838, 1846, 1860, 1865); Berditchev, 1817; and Warsaw, 1883

publishers of which felt free to make changes in the text, delete or add tales, and even to give the work a new name. Individual stories made their way into other collections too numerous to list here.

Due to a printing peculiarity in two of the stories included in the work in several printed editions, the identity of the author was long in doubt. The author's father is mentioned as "my father, the Rabbi *ha-rʾš*,"[7] and "my father, my teacher, the Rabbi *ha-rʾš*,"[8] with the two letters at the end separated by the two strokes which in Hebrew indicate an abbreviation, usually of a name. On this basis some of the printed editions actually wrote out the father's supposed name as Rabbi Asher, although as noted above the subtitle clearly states that the author was R. Nissim ben Jacob, not ben Asher. S. I. Rappaport, writing in 1831,[9] showed that the word taken as an abbreviated name was in fact the word *roš*, i.e. "head" (of an academy), thus laying to rest the nonexistent R. Asher, and followed this with two conjectures, both of which were later proved correct: that the author was Nissim ben Jacob of Kairouan, and that the Hebrew text was based on a Judeo-Arabic original.

Two generations later, the conjectured Judeo-Arabic original was discovered. In 1896 Abraham Harkavy published excerpts from a manuscript which he had purchased during a visit to the Near East and which clearly contained the Judeo-Arabic source of the Hebrew versions.[10] Years later Julian Obermann published the complete text of Harkavy's then still unique manuscript (hereafter H) in complete photographic reproduc-

(reprinted 1886, 1893, 1898). A German translation entitled R. *Nissim's Legendenschatz* was published in Vienna in 1882.

7. See below, p. 88. The Hebrew MSS and the editions based on the Ferrara text have this reading.

8. See below, p. 138, n. 44.

9. *Bikkure ha-ʿIttim*, 5592/1831, pp. 58, 72–73.

10. *Festschrift zum achtzigsten Geburtstage Moritz Steinschneider's* (Leipzig, 1896), pp. 9–24. The MS eventually passed into the possession of the Library of the Jewish Theological Seminary of America in New York.

tion, accompanied by a painstaking and carefully annotated transcription of the Judeo-Arabic text into Arabic script.[11] Obermann's assumption was that H represented the basis of all the Hebrew versions, and he made copious references to them where the Arabic text was unclear or missing. In a review of Obermann's work, which offered many valuable suggestions, David H. Baneth pointed out that while Obermann's scholarly contribution was very great, his painstaking comparison of H with the Hebrew versions was of limited usefulness, for the Hebrew "translation does not bear faithful testimony to the source . . . It is more like an original Hebrew work . . . [It] did not leave a single Arabic sentence as it was, but . . . gave it a new form."[12] Later discoveries showed that even this view was too conservative and did not fully reflect the true situation.

In 1953 H. Z. Hirschberg published a modern Hebrew translation of the *Ḥibbur*,[13] based on Obermann's edition of H and taking into account the various Hebrew versions and five fragments of the Judeo-Arabic text from the Cairo Genizah—three are now at Cambridge and two at Oxford. In 1965, with the discovery of more Genizah materials and of a large fragment of a Yemenite manuscript in the possession of Rabbi Joseph Ḳāfiḥ of Jerusalem, Shraga Abramson published a masterful study of all extant fragments of R. Nissim's several works, including the *Ḥibbur*.[14] Altogether Abramson identified forty known manuscripts of the Arabic original of the *Ḥibbur*, some more or less complete, such as Harkavy's, Ḳāfiḥ's, and a manuscript (whose present location seems to be unknown) once in the collection of Solomon Skoss, while the

11. *Studies in Islam and Judaism: The Arabic Original of Ibn Shāhīn's Book of Comfort*, Yale Oriental Series, Researches, XVII (New Haven, 1933). [Obermann identified the Rabbinic sources of nearly all the tales.—LN]

12. *Kirjath Sepher 11* (1935), 350–57.

13. *Ḥibbur Yafeh me-hay-Yĕšuʿah* (Sifriyyaṯ Mĕḳoroṯ, 15), (Jerusalem, 5714/1953).

14. *Rab̲ Nissim Gaʾon, Ḥamišah Sĕfarim* (R. *Nissim Gaon Libelli Quinque*), (Jerusalem, 1965). See also the helpful review by G. Vajda, *Revue des Études Juives 125* (1966), 422–26.

remainder are fragments of one or more leaves from the Cairo Genizah.[15] But even with all this new documentation we are still unable to solve all the problems raised by the comparison of the Arabic and Hebrew texts. What does become clear is that H does not represent the original form of R. Nissim's work—it includes added stories, omits certain material, and probably reflects a reworking of the text some two hundred or more years after R. Nissim's death.

The Jews of Kairouan

During the tenth and eleventh centuries the major centers of Jewish population and Jewish traditional learning were largely, if not exclusively, located in territories under Islamic rule. The Babylonian (Iraqi) center, with its elaborate centuries-old institutions of Exilarch, Geonim, and Rabbinic academies, drawing financial support and recognition from all other Jewish communities, had been progressively declining, step by step with the deteriorating central authority of the caliphate. Meanwhile a new focal point of the Jewish diaspora was developing in Spain, with Cordova, Granada, and other cities gradually replacing Baghdad and the other Iraqi centers. At the time mentioned, while Spanish Jewry was entering into what was later to be called its golden age, it still paid some formal allegiance to Babylonia-Iraq, requesting Rabbinic decisions from the heads of that ancient community and sending contributions for the support of the academies and scholars there. Between these two centers, the declining Babylonian center and the rising Spanish one, lay the Jewish community of Kairouan, in Ifrīqiyah, the modern Tunisia, in North Africa.

The Jewish community of Kairouan,[16] situated in a great Muslim urban center founded in 670 as a *miṣr*, or garrison town, by ʿUqbah ibn Nāfiʿ, the Arab conqueror of North Africa, had soon become a magnet for Jews from Arabia, Egypt, and

15. These are listed in detail by Abramson, pp. 424–27.
16. For the history of this community see Samuel A. Poznanski, "ʾAnše Ḳayrawan," *Festschrift zu Ehren des Dr. Harkavy* (St. Petersburg, 1908), pp. 175–220. The section about R. Nissim is on pp. 211–18.

Cyrenaica. Around the year 700 some one thousand Jewish (or Copt) families were settled there at the request of the Umayyad caliph ᶜAbd al-Malik. Some time afterwards another group of Jews, from other parts of North Africa, settled there after the Berber resistance to the Arab invasion had been crushed, and quickly merged with the earlier settlers. Kairouan flourished under the Abbasids and later under local dynasties, such as the Aghlabids, Fatimids, and Zirids. The Jewish community had its synagogues, its own *kallah* or learned assembly, headed by a *roš* ("head"), as well as other necessary religious and communal institutions. Owing to the rapid rise of the larger and wealthier Spanish community, as well as to adverse political developments in North Africa, the Kairouan community did not attain the status of a major center. Nevertheless, throughout the ninth and tenth centuries, several prominent figures arose in this community, one of the most noted of whom was the *roš kallah* R. Jacob ben Nissim ibn Shāhīn (d. ca. 1006). It was his son, later to be known under the honorific titles Rabbenu Nissim and R. Nissim Gaon, who wrote the *Ḥibbur Yafeh.*

Life of R. *Nissim*

R. Nissim was born around 990—the date is quite uncertain[17]—and studied under his father and under R. Hushiel, who had come over from Italy and settled in Kairouan. R. Hushiel's son, R. Hananeel, succeeded R. Jacob, R. Nissim's father, as *roš kallah,* while R. Nissim became one of the outstanding Talmudic scholars of the city, later succeeding R. Hananeel as *roš* on his death. In his works on the Talmud, which he wrote in Judeo-Arabic, R. Nissim emphasized the systematic organization of the halakhic material to make it more accessible to his students and easier to refer to in legal decisions. This approach to the Talmud, typical of Jewish scholars in the Muslim sphere, is exemplified in his extant works, fragmentary though they are: *Mafteaḥ lĕ-Manᶜule*

17. The dates of R. Nissim are discussed by Abramson, Introduction, p. 21.

hat-Talmud (A Key to the Locks of the Talmud), *Perušim* or commentaries to various Talmudic tractates, and *Měgillat Sětarim* (Revelation of Mysteries).[18]

Although R. Nissim was honored and known throughout the Jewish world, his later years were marred by unhappy events. From references in various writings of his contemporaries[19] we know some details of his family life: he received financial support from Samuel han-Nagid, the wealthy and powerful Spanish Jewish patron of writers and scholars; his only son died in infancy; and his daughter, unhappily married to a son of the aforementioned Samuel, was eventually abandoned by her husband. Above all, however, they reveal the destruction of the world in which R. Nissim had been born and nurtured, and in which he had become a leader.

As a result of the conflicts between the local dynasty of Zirid emirs and the Shiite Fatimid rulers, who had first risen to power in Ifrīqiyah but were now established in their capital in Cairo, hordes of Bedouins of the Banū Hilāl and the Banū Sulaym in Upper Egypt began their destructive invasion of North Africa. Repeated raids and depredations by these Bedouins made life in Kairouan insecure and eventually impossible, and in 1057 the emir himself had to leave the city for the coastal town of al-Mahdīyah. Following this Kairouan was sacked, and less than three years later, in 1060, Berber tribes fell upon the city, looting and killing the inhabitants as the Arab Bedouins had before them.

During these difficult years most of the Jews of Kairouan fled to al-Mahdīyah, Sūsah (Sousse), and other coastal towns. From a letter recently published by S. D. Goitein,[20] we learn that R. Nissim resided in Sūsah in 1061, had been gravely ill, causing great concern for his life among his fellow Jews, and

18. These works were published from new manuscript finds by Abramson, pp. 3–360. Cf. also Hirschberg, pp. 33–38.

19. For these sources see Abramson, Introduction, pp. 17–35; Hirschberg, pp. 23–33; and the articles by Goitein cited in nn. 20 and 21 below.

20. S. D. Goitein, "A Letter by Labrat ben Moses ben Sighmar, Dayyan of al-Mahdiyyah, about R. Nissim, 'Renewer of the Faith'," *Tarbiṣ 36* (1966), 59–72.

had been supervising the copying of his works by a scribe for Nahray ben Nissim, a scholar formerly of Kairouan and now settled in Cairo. This information, incidentally, lends a special value to the fragments of the Arabic text of the *Ḥibbur* from the Cairo Genizah, for in Goitein's works we find several references to other documents from this same Nahray found in the Genizah, thus suggesting that at least some of the *Ḥibbur* fragments may have been examined by the author himself and eventually found their way to the Genizah. From other contemporary materials we learn that R. Nissim died in June/July 1062.[21] The contemporary letters and other writings which have survived attest to the deep sense of loss felt by the Jews of North Africa at the death of the scholar among whose honorific titles was that of "Renewer of the Faith."

Two centuries later, in 1270, Kairouan acquired the status of a holy city in Islam, and both Christians and Jews were forbidden to live in it. This ban was not lifted until after the French occupation of Tunisia in 1881.

The Title of the Work

We have seen that the problems of the identity of the author of the *Ḥibbur* and of the existence of an Arabic original were for a time subjects of scholarly disagreement and debate. Not until very recently was yet another problem resolved, that of the title of the Arabic original. Both the initial and final leaves of H are missing, precisely where we would have expected—on the title-page, in an opening paragraph, or in the colophon—to find a reference to the title of the work. The other manuscript materials, including the substantial and very helpful Ḳāfiḥ manuscript, are likewise incomplete, and in most cases mere fragments.

Over half a century ago Samuel Poznanski suggested that the title of the Arabic original was *Kitāb al-Faraj baᶜd al-Shiddah wal-Saᶜah baᶜd al-Ḍīqah* (Book of Relief after Adversity and

21. S. D. Goitein, "New Information about the Negidim of Kairouan and about R. Nissim," *Zion* 27 (1962), 18.

Ease after Anguish),[22] as found in a list of Judeo-Arabic works published by Solomon Schechter.[23] Some years later Obermann suggested that the Arabic title should be sought in the Hebrew title *Ḥibbur Yafeh me-hay-Yĕšuᶜah*, which he translated literally as *Taʾlīf Ḥasan min al-Faraj*.[24] Baneth, however, pointed out that this grammatical construction did not occur in Arabic, and suggested that the Hebrew title itself was probably influenced by European models.[25] Later Abramson found that in one of the Genizah fragments which he studied the work is referred to as *al-Faraj baᶜd al-Shiddah* [26] thus confirming the earlier conjecture of Poznanski. This title also fits in with the author's words at the beginning of the work addressed to Dunash for whom he was writing the book: "You reminded me that the Gentiles have a book composed on the subject of relief after adversity and distress." This statement indicates moreover that he was taking as his model or inspiration the Arabic literary genre of *faraj* literature.

The Faraj *Works in Arabic Literature*

When R. Nissim referred to the "relief after adversity" book of the Gentiles he probably had in mind the work *Kitāb al-Faraj baᶜd al-Shiddah* by the Iraqi scholar and judge Abū ᶜAlī al-Muḥassin al-Tanūkhī (938 [or 940]–994).[27] Although R. Nissim may have known one or another of the works of the same name written by earlier authors, such as

22. *Zeitschrift für hebräische Bibliographie*, *7* (1903), 186: "'Das Buch der Hilfe nach dem Unglück und der Weite nach der Bedrängnis.' Darunter ist wahrscheinlich das arabische Original . . . zu verstehen." Cf. also S. Abramson, *Kirjath Sepher 26* (1949–50), 83 and 86, n. 41; and S. Asaf, *ibid.*, *18* (1941–42), 274, n. 41.

23. *Saadyana, Geniza Fragments of Writings of* R. *Saadya Gaon and Others* (Cambridge, 1903), p. 79, Fragment T-S. 13-K-1.

24. *Zeitschrift für Semitistik*, *5* (1927), 43–68. [Probably rather *fī al-Faraj*; *fī* and *min* in cursive Arabic naskhī are indistinguishable.—LN]

25. *Kirjath Sepher 11* (1935), 350.

26. Abramson, p. 364, and p. 425, MS 23, T-S.N.S. 186/3.

27. Cf. GAL, *1*, 161; Suppl. *1*, 252. For a detailed study of al-Tanūkhī's work see Rouchdi Fakkar, *At-Tanûḫî et son livre: La déliverance après l'angoisse* (Institut français d'archéologie orientale, Recherches, XXIV) (Cairo, 1955).

al-Madāʾinī (d. ca. 840), Ibn Abī al-Dunyā (d. 894), and Abū al-Ḥusayn al-Qāḍī (d. 940),[28] al-Tanūkhī's work, which borrows from these predecessors and is the most famous, gave the genre its classic expression and was probably widely known in R. Nissim's time to all readers of Arabic as *the* representative of this genre.

The phrase *faraj baᶜd al-shiddah* can probably be traced back to a tradition (*ḥadīth*) attributed to the Prophet Muḥammad in which he spoke of *shiddah yajᶜal Allāh baᶜdahā faraj*, "adversity, after which God causes relief to follow." This idea is already present, though not in exactly the same words, in Surah 65, verse 2, of the Koran, "Whosoever fears God, He will appoint for him a way out, and will provide for him from whence he had not reckoned." Here the word *faraj* does not occur, and *makhraj*, "a way out," is substituted for it. The noun *faraj* has several meanings flowing from a verbal root meaning "to open (a door, a mouth), to enlarge (a thing), to spread (the legs)," with a wide semantic outgrowth including "to disperse (cares), to relieve (someone)." Hence the variety of translations, "comfort," "relief," "deliverance."

When al-Tanūkhī used this phrase as a title for his work, he was following a tradition over a century old, by borrowing not only from the earlier writers of the similarly named works mentioned above, but also from other predecessors—historians such as al-Jahshiyārī, al-Ṣūlī, and al-Ṭabarī, and anthologists such as al-Iṣbahānī—as well as by relating anecdotes told to him by his contemporaries, his father, fellow qadis, clerks in government offices, merchants in Baghdad, even Shiᶜites or Christians.

The *faraj* genre caught the fancy of the Arabic reading public, and we find numerous manuscripts and some printed editions of al-Tanūkhī's work, as well as others of the same type produced in the following centuries. At an early date al-Tanūkhī's work was translated by Lālelī into Turkish; about 1225 it was

28. Cf. the classic article on the genre by Alfred Wiener, "Die *Farağ baᶜd aš-Šidda*-Literatur," *Der Islam* 4 (1913), 270–98, 387–420.

available in a free Persian rendering by al-ᶜAwfī, and some fifty years earlier, about 1170, in a Persian translation by al-Dihistānī. Through these translations the *faraj* tales spread throughout the Muslim world.[29]

The Ḥibbur *and the* Faraj *Literature*

In his introduction to the modern Hebrew translation of the *Ḥibbur*, Hirschberg raises the question of the possible influence of al-Tanūkhī or of other Arabic *faraj* writers on R. Nissim, and compares one of the tales in the *Ḥibbur* with a similar one (also about Jews) found in al-Tanūkhī.[30] It is clear, however, from this sole possible instance of borrowing that the influence of al-Tanūkhī or of other *faraj* writers is to be sought not in the area of borrowing but rather solely in the idea of collecting tales on this theme. Although here and there some possible influence of the Koran and of Muslim thought has been detected in R. Nissim's book,[31] it must be emphasized again that the latter is a thoroughly Jewish work. The major sources drawn upon for the tales are all Rabbinic: Mishnah, Talmud, and Midrashic collections. When we find no presently known Jewish sources for certain stories, examination shows that if they were borrowed from non-Jewish tradition, the author has nevertheless given them a Jewish form and, above all, has inspired them with Jewish moral and ethical concepts and values.[32] Furthermore, from what we know of the events of R. Nissim's life, he may very well have intended

29. An interesting instance of the use in English literature of a similar title, if not of the same literary idea, without any connection with the Arabic works mentioned here, is Sir Thomas More's *A Dialogue of Comfort against Tribulation*, a debate about the proper bearing of Catholics under Turkish-Muslim tyranny, a thinly veiled reference to Henry VIII, written during More's imprisonment in the Tower of London.

30. Hirschberg, pp. 63–65.

31. *Ibid.*, pp. 62–71.

32. Cf. Baneth's review of Obermann, *Kirjath Sepher 11* (1935), p. 350: "Instead of the Islamic and secular material which fills the Arabic works, he (Nissim) used only Jewish material taken entirely, or to a great extent, from the two Talmuds and various Midrashic texts."

his work as a "book of relief" from national as well as individual adversity. This may indeed have been his intent when he wrote: "Although these stories concern individuals, nonetheless I shall not fail to mention also events that have happened to the whole nation [of Israel], and the [resulting] distress in which they found themselves but were granted relief therefrom."[33]

The Muslim and Jewish Works Compared

A comparison of the types of stories and the major themes in al-Tanūkhī's *Faraj* and in R. Nissim's *Ḥibbur* shows conclusively the slight degree of influence of the former upon the latter. It must be stated at the outset that al-Tanūkhī's work is much larger and more varied in content and that it belongs to a specific type of literature, *adab* or courtly prose, whereas the *Ḥibbur* is primarily a work of moral and ethical content.[34]

Al-Tanūkhī divides his work into fourteen chapters, each dealing with a particular theme as reflected in its title:[35]

1) What is mentioned in the Koran on the theme of relief after misfortune.
2) Mention of this theme in the Ḥadīth.
3) About those whose deliverance was foretold by omens, and those who were relieved from distress by words or by prayer.
4) About those who averted a ruler's anger by a frank remark or by an admonition.
5) About those who came forth from imprisonment to freedom.
6) About those who found relief after auspicious dreams.

33. See below, p. 6.

34. For a description of the development of the concept of *adab* as a literary form, see the article "Adab" by F. Gabrieli in *EI*², *1*, 175–76. The *Ḥibbur*, on the other hand, is classified as a work of *musar* (moral and ethical conduct) by I. Tishby and J. Dan, *Hebrew Ethical Literature* (in Hebrew) (Jerusalem, 1970); see especially pp. 41–53 which contain excerpts from the *Ḥibbur*.

35. Cf. Fakkar, pp. 61–84, where a complete outline of the contents is given.

7) About those who were released from suffocating straits by intent or by accident.
8) About those who were about to be executed but were saved.
9) About those who were threatened with death by animals but found help from God.
10) About those who were deathly ill but were healed by God.
11) About those who fell into the hands of robbers and thieves but were freed and compensated for their loss.
12) About those who fled out of fear and remained in hiding until salvation came to them.
13) About those who were unlucky in love but with God's help attained their desire.
14) A selection of poetry on the theme of relief.

This orderly and predominantly literary approach, for all of its religious content in certain stories, has no parallel in R. Nissim's work. Although we can impose some sort of order on R. Nissim's themes, he himself seems to have been aware of his frequent digressions and his inability to maintain consistently the theme of relief after adversity. There are thirty-four chapters in the Arabic version of H, with the last three perhaps not a part of the original work by R. Nissim. Hirschberg gives the following outline of the contents:[36]

1) Chapters 1–10 deal with the theme of God as a righteous judge, no matter how mysterious His ways may seem to man. Chapters 8–10 have the sub-theme of reward given for even the slightest of good deeds.
2) Chapters 11–13 (first part), deal with good and bad women and their effect upon their husbands.
3) Chapters 13 (second part)–14 deal with the duty of studying Torah and with the qualities of scholars.

36. Cf. Hirschberg, pp. 52–55.

4) Chapters 15–21 deal with children or common people who were rewarded for performing just one good deed.
5) Chapters 22–23 deal with hypocrites, people who are not what they seem to be.
6) In Chapter 24 performance of good deeds and kindnesses is likened to a deposit which is returned to its owner (R. Nissim realizes that he has strayed here from the main subject of the book).
7) Chapters 25–27 deal with the Inclination to evil and its suppression.
8) Chapters 28–31 advocate almsgiving even if the giver is himself poor.

It is thus clear that the *faraj* genre served for R. Nissim only as a point of departure. What he created was a collection of tales which at one and the same time charmed, amused, and instructed generations of Jewish readers; served as a work of ethical and moral instruction; and offered the inspiration for similar works not at all connected with the concept of *faraj*, but aimed at entertaining, instructing, or both.

The Significance of the Work

This work is important in many areas and at many levels, although our appreciation of it has undergone a change in the light of additional discoveries. It is of great interest and importance, for example, in the reconstruction of the biography and the works of R. Nissim in particular, and on a more general level, of the history of the Jewish community of Kairouan and of its intellectual life. The citations from Rabbinic sources with their variant readings from the usual texts available to us are valuable to scholars in this area.[37] While linguists have been rather disappointed in the value of the text for the reconstruction of the peculiarities of the Judeo-Arabic language of Tunisian Jewry in the eleventh century,

37. See especially the comments of Abramson, pp. 394–95.

since it has been shown that H is a later reworking of the text and perhaps not North African in origin, the several versions are still a valuable source for the study of this important Jewish language.[38]

As mentioned above, Judeo-Arabic was the form of Arabic written in Hebrew script and incorporating some conscious and unconscious borrowings and influences from Hebrew and Aramaic. Above all, like their Christian neighbors living in an Arabic-speaking environment under Muslim rule, the Jews not only developed their own dialectal features in their spoken language but, not being bound like the Muslims to the sacred linguistic model of the Koran, felt free to inject into their written literary language forms taken from their spoken tongue. Thus, while most Muslim writers strove to maintain a level of literary Arabic free from "contamination" by the vernacular, Jewish and Christian writers lacked the strict linguistic discipline and the socio-linguistic inhibitions which would have led them to avoid mixing these linguistic levels. In this area, too, the Arabic original of the *Ḥibbur* diverges from the *Faraj* of al-Tanūkhī, which maintains a strict adherence to the conventions of literary Arabic.[39]

Finally, not only did the *Ḥibbur* have wide diffusion and give rise to numerous similar collections of *maᶜăśiyyoṭ*,[40] as such stories came to be called, but it opened a new era in the publication of Hebrew tales and legends directly inspired by, or even translated from, Arabic literature. Only a century after R. Nissim's death there began to appear a stream of such works: *Sefer haš-Šaᶜšuᶜim* (The Book of Delight),[41] which incidentally contains stories from R. Nissim's work,[42] by

38. Cf. Vajda in his review of Abramson. Obermann's edition of H has been used as a source for examples by J. Blau, *The Emergence and Linguistic Background of Judeo-Arabic* (Scripta Judaica, V) (Oxford, 1965).

39. See Hirschberg's comments on the peculiarities of the Arabic of H, pp. 47–50; Obermann's comments, p. xiv; Baneth's many suggested emendations in his review in *Kirjath Sepher*; and Abramson, pp. 391–92 and elsewhere. See especially Blau's description of the emergence of Judeo-Arabic, pp. 19–50, and his comments on the peculiarities of the Arabic of H, p. 84, n. 2.

40. See n. 2, above.

Joseph ibn Zabarah (ca. 1140–1200); *Ben ham-Melek̠ wĕhan-Naz̧ir* (The Prince and the Dervish), a Hebrew version of the Barlaam and Josaphat tale ultimately derived from the life of Buddha,[43] by Abraham ibn Ḥasdai (ca. 1230); *Mišle Šuᶜalim* (Fox Fables) by Berechiah han-Naḳdan (ca. 1200);[44] a translation of *Kalīlah wa-Dimnah*[45] by Jacob ben Eleazar (13th cent.); *ᵓIggeret̠ Baᶜăle Ḥayyim* by Kalonymos ben Kalonymos (b. 1286), a translation of one of the *Rasāᵓil* of the Brethren of Purity (Ikhwān al-Ṣafā) of tenth-century Basra;[46] and finally, *Mišle Sendebar*, a translation of the *Sindabād-nāmeh*, known in the West as *The Seven Sages of Rome*.[47]

R. Nissim's work differs from all of these in two main respects: he wrote in Judeo-Arabic, in order to speak directly to his fellow Jews living under Muslim rule, and he used primarily, although perhaps not exclusively, Jewish sources. Most of the just listed works were either Hebrew translations of Arabic works or close adaptations of Arabic models. R. Nissim, although inspired by an Arabic model, wrote an original work which, after it had been translated into Hebrew, became a much loved source of entertainment, moral instruction, and inspiration to generations of Jews living in Arabic- and Persian-speaking Muslim-ruled areas[48] as well as in Christian Europe, both east and west, some of his tales becom-

41. Edited by Israel Davidson (New York, 1914); English translation by Israel Abrahams, *The Book of Delight* (Philadelphia, 1912).

42. See Davidson's comments on tales no. 4, 9, 12, and 14, pp. xlix–lxvi.

43. Edited by A. M. Habermann (Tel Aviv, 1950). English translation *Barlaam and Josaphat*, trans. Joseph Jacobs (London, 1896).

44. Critical edition by A. M. Habermann, *Mišle Šuᶜalim* (Jerusalem, 1945–46). English translation by Moses Hadas, *Fables of the Jewish Aesop* (New York, 1966).

45. Edited by Joseph Derenbourg, *Deux versions hébraïques du livre de Kalilah et Dimnah* (Paris, 1881).

46. Edited by Y. Toporovsky (Jerusalem, 1949).

47. *Tales of Sendebar: An Edition and Translation of the Hebrew Version of the Seven Sages*, by Morris Epstein (Philadelphia, 1967).

48. See for example the tales "Joseph the Righteous of Pĕḳiᶜin," "He Who Has Faith in God is Rewarded," and "A Dispute in Sign Language," in *Folktales of Israel*, edited by Dov Noy (Chicago, 1963), which were recorded from Sephardic and Oriental Jews in Israel.

ing part of the folklore of East European Yiddish culture.[49] In writing for his relative Dunash, R. Nissim "spoke to the hearts" of countless generations of Jews offering them a comforting "relief after adversity."[50]

William M. Brinner

Genizah Correspondence on *al-Faraj baᶜd al-Shiddah*

The writers of the Genizah letters usually mention books that are of a religious, liturgical, poetic, legal, or scientific character. An exception is R. Nissim's *al-Faraj baᶜd alᶜShiddah,* which must have been quite popular.

In a long letter of consolation, sent by a man named Barakāt ("blessings") to his sister Rayyisah ("leader") on the occasion of the death of their mother, he entreats her not to mourn excessively. He advises her to read the book of Ecclesiastes and sends her *al-Faraj baᶜd al-Shiddah* with the recommendation that she study it (in Arabic *tashtaghilī bihi*, "occupy yourself with it"). Obviously he was confident that the reading of this book would soothe the mind of his disconsolate sister.

(TS [Taylor-Schechter Coll., Cambridge, England] 1059, f. 1, written around 1200. Abbreviated English translation in S. D. Goitein, "New Revelations from the Cairo Genizah: Jewish women in the Middle Ages," *Hadassah Magazine*, [Oct. 1973], pp. 14–15, 38–39. Full translation in *Med. Soc.* IV [forthcoming].)

A man in the provincial capital al-Maḥallah, Egypt, writes to a *ḥazzān* in a smaller town: "I sent you the part of the book *al-Faraj*

49. See, for example, the more than twenty parallel tales in Gaster's *Maᶜăśeh Book*. Recently the noted Yiddish author Isaac Bashevis Singer published as a children's book one of the tales from the *Ḥibbur* in his *Elijah the Slave: A Hebrew Legend Retold*, translated from the Yiddish by the author and Elizabeth Shub (New York, 1970).

50. Regarding the influence of the *Ḥibbur*, it has been suggested that one of the tales of the *Ḥibbur* was the source of the Cabalistic concept of the "celestial garment" of the souls of the pious (cf. Chap. XI, The Shining Robe). See G. Scholem, "The Paradisiac Garb of Souls and the Origin of the Concept of *Ḥăluḳaᵓ dĕ-Rabbanan*," *Tarbiṣ 24* (1956), 290–306. This was followed up by David H. Baneth, who saw a Muslim origin to this concept, and as an intermediate stage, a pious tale of one of the *quṣṣāṣ*, or popular preachers in Islam, from which it may have passed to R. Nissim; see his "Ḥăluḳaᵓ dĕ-Rabbanan . . . and a Mohammedan Tradition," *Tarbiṣ 25* (1957), 331–36.

*ba*ᶜ*d al-Shiddah* which I found. Another copy [seemingly meaning: a complete one] is to be found with my nephew in al-Maḥallah. I shall go and take it and send it to you."

(TS AS 149, f. 10. Hand of twelfth cent.) Cantors in small towns often worked as copyists as well. This one might have intended making copies of the book.

A hurried note, not larger than 2 × 5″ in the hand of the court clerk and teacher Solomon, son of the judge Elijah, addressed to a relative in Alexandria, says: "My lord, R. Simḥah, may God keep you, please give *al-Faraj ba*ᶜ*d al-Shiddah* to the bearer without delay, for I am in a hurry." Approximate date, 1220.

Solomon, who was stationed in the Egyptian capital, had, while he was in Alexandria, lent his copy to his relative (who probably planned to make a copy of it). Now, about to travel home, he asked R. Simḥah to return it to him.

(TS AS 147, f. 32.)

Most likely more references may be found.

S. D. Goitein

AN ELEGANT COMPOSITION
CONCERNING
RELIEF AFTER ADVERSITY

by
Nissim ben Jacob ibn Shāhīn

[PROLOGUE][1]

My lord and friend[2]—may God keep you and protect you, may He who has created you from the womb come to your aid, prolong your life, and fulfill your desire—you have complained to me in your gracious letter about the soul's break, spirit's grief, and heart's sorrow that have befallen you upon the death of your son. May God requite you and grant you [other] sons worthy of long life.

You mentioned in your letter that it is your desire to read a book which might relieve you, cheer your heart, and remove your grief and the distress of your sorrow. You reminded me that the Gentiles[3] have a book composed on the subject of relief after adversity and distress. Because of your esteem and favor [toward me], which are cherished by me, and your great worth [in my estimation],[4] **1a** and owing to your desire for such a book because of [your] misfortune,[5] you have requested me to compose a book on this subject for you, dealing with the accounts of the most eminent and virtuous of our Sages, so that you would need to read no other book. I have hereby complied with your request, the while I give thanks to God Most High and praise Him for His kindnesses and generosity with which I have been favored. Although I have no skill in this craft nor experience therein,[6] yet my desire to fulfill your request and my longing to earn your favor and affection en-

1. From here to n. 4 lacking in H. Restored from HY; cf. Obermann, p. 1, n. 1/3. Cf. also Introduction, p. xxiii.

2. Addressed to Dunash, *ḥăṯano* (or *ḥoṯno*, perhaps simply "relative by marriage"), to "speak kindly to him and to comfort him," according to HY. Cf. Introduction, p. xvii.

3. *Minim*, literally "heretics," here clearly Muslims, non-Jews.

4. See above, n. 1. H begins here. [For *fī al-raghbah* read *wa-raghbatika*, as in HY.—LN] The numerals in heavy type indicate the foliation of H.

5. Obermann *min al-muṣībah*; HY *bĕ-diḇre Torah*; Harkavy has *min al-mathwabah*, "requital, recompense, reward."

6. i.e., in writing on this particular subject of comfort; cf. Abramson, p. 410.

courage me in this [undertaking]. I have asked for the help of God Mighty and Glorious, and have besought Him for inspiration [to walk] in the right way which leads to reward. I have placed the composition of this book ahead of my other undertakings because of your high rank and exalted station with me, **1b** and also because of the bountiful recompense and generous reward in the hereafter which I hope for from the Creator Blessed and Exalted, according as the Sages have taught us about the abundant recompense and reward which are due to one who relieves the aggrieved from his grief and the sorrowful from his sorrow, and who causes the grieving soul and the aching heart to rejoice.[7]

[R. BAROḲA AND THE JAILER][8]

The story is told that Rab Baroḳa was walking in a certain street when [the prophet] Elijah appeared to him.[9] Rab Baroḳa asked him whether there was anyone in that street who was worthy of the reward of the hereafter, to which Elijah replied, "No." While the two of them were conversing, a man passed by them wearing black boots and having no fringes on the border of his cloak, whereupon **2a** Elijah said to R. Baroḳa, "This person is one of those who are worthy of the reward of the hereafter." So Rab Baroḳa called out to him, and since the man did not answer him, went after him until he caught up with him. He asked him, "What is your occupation?", and the man replied, "My lord, I am a jailer, and it is my custom to separate the men's jail from that of the women. When night falls, I make my sleeping place between the two jails for fear that harm might come to the women from the men. And when a Jewish woman is imprisoned with me, I would risk my life to save her [from violation]. One day a Jewish woman[10] was

7. HY erroneously marks the end of the Prologue here. Cf. Obermann, p. 2, n. 31; p. 5, n. 19.

8. Rabbinic source for this story and the next: B. Ta 22a.

9. HY: "Elijah came toward him, revealed himself to him, and spoke to him."

10. HY adds: "who was married."

imprisoned, and I saw that one of the male prisoners wanted to get near her. So I took some wine dregs and gave them to her, saying, 'Smear your body with this and say, **2b** I am unclean.'[11] She did as I told her, and I thus saved her, and no man came near her." Rab Baroḳa then said to him, "I see that you wear black shoes," and he replied, "So that it would not be known that I am a Jew"—it follows from this statement of his that the custom of the Jews at that time was not to use black footwear.[12] The man continued, "I [regularly] enter[13] the palace of the king in order to hear what [mischief] they are about to set in motion against the people [of the kingdom]. If what they are about to perpetrate affects us [Jews], I hasten to inform the Sages of it, so that they may fast and pray to God Most High to annul for the Jews what they intend to do and set in motion." Rab Baroḳa then asked him, "What was the reason for your failure to answer me[14] when I first called out to you?" He replied, "I have just learned that they have gathered to set in motion [some mischief] against the people, **3a** and I was hurrying to hear it before they execute it."[15]

[R. BAROḲA AND THE TWO MEN WHO SPREAD CHEER]

As R. Baroḳa finished speaking to the jailer, while Elijah was still with him, two other men passed by, and Elijah said, "These two likewise deserve the reward of the hereafter." So Rab Baroḳa said to them, "I would like you to tell me your occupation." They replied, "We cheer the grieving soul, and when we see someone whose heart is aching, we keep on diverting him and talking to him of things that would cheer

11. i.e., menstruating.

12. On this comment and Hirschberg's explanation (Hirschberg, p. 2, n. 3), cf. Abramson, pp. 410–11.

13. For a different Judeo-Arabic version of the remainder of this story, see Abramson, p. 505.

14. [Read *lam tujibnī*, as in HY and in Abramson, p. 505.—LN]

15. HY has instead: "to inform the Sages, so that they might come before the King Lord of hosts, tc plead with Him, and to entreat Him for the remnant that is left."

him and dispel his sadness, until his dark mood leaves him."[16] I hope that you and I, too, shall be among those who are deemed worthy [of the reward of the hereafter].

[PROLOGUE—CONCLUDED]

I will recount to you in this book of mine also such other sayings of the Sages as I know of or have discovered, in the way of traditions, tales, and anecdotes about those of them who **3b** were in distress and found relief, and were in anguish and were granted easement. Although these stories concern individuals, nonetheless I shall not fail to mention also events that have happened to the whole nation [of Israel], and the [resulting] distress in which they found themselves but were granted relief therefrom, except for whatsoever is already recorded, for example, in the Scroll of Esther or the Scroll of the Hasmonaeans,[17] or in the rest of the twenty-four books [of the Hebrew Bible], about the afflictions and calamities which had befallen our forefathers[18] and predecessors and from which they were relieved, for this already exists in recorded form. I will mention therefore only that which is known and familiar only to the few.

I beseech you, my lord, and whosoever else peruses this book of mine, and I implore you by God Most High—whosoever may see any gap in it, let him fill it, or any mistake, let him correct it, **4a** for even the worthiest Sages do err.[19] Do you not see the words of [David] the saintly one,[20] *Who*

16. HY ends this episode here.

17. [The Scroll of Esther is the Biblical Book of Esther. The precise identity of the Scroll of the Hasmonaeans is uncertain; it is probably not the same as the apocryphal Books of Maccabees.—LN]

18. Beginning here, Abramson (pp. 428–502) gives, at times on opposite pages, the Judeo-Arabic text of H, and the text as found in various Genizah fragments, as well as in a large fragment (Ḳ) in the library of Rabbi Joseph Ḳāfiḥ in Jerusalem.

19. Cf. Hirschberg's comments on the influence of Saadiah Gaon and possibly al-Tanūkhī on the conclusion of this introductory section, p. 3, n. 6, and p. 108.

20. *Al-walī* (Hebrew *he-ḥasīd*) refers here to David, but is also used for Solomon, Job, and others; cf. Abramson, p. 411, referring to Hirschberg, p. 3, n. 7, and p. 108.

can discern errors? Clear Thou me from hidden faults (Ps. 19:13).[21] How much more is this true of one whose mind and ability are small! My Creator I do implore and from Him do I beg assistance in seeking His favor, that He may be of help to me and make me of help [to others]. I ask Him as did [David] His saintly one,[22] *Let Thy hand be ready to help me; for I have chosen Thy precepts* (Ps. 119:173).[23] In Him is my hope, for He Most High will not disappoint those who place their hope in Him, as He has promised—and He fulfills His promises—saying, *And Thou shalt know that I am the Lord, for they shall not be ashamed that place their hope in Me* (Isa. 49:23).[24]

21. H adds in Arabic: "that is to say, Who is there that has not erred and made mistakes? I ask Thee, O my God, to guide me." Biblical citations such as this are given in Hebrew and are, in H only, followed by Arabic translations or paraphrases. These will be translated in the notes, since they seem not to have been part of the original Arabic work; cf. Abramson, pp. 365–66, and pp. 428 ff., for comparison of H, where these translations occur, with Ḳ, where they do not.

22. Ḳ has here: "as the prophet [David] has asked and said."

23. H adds in Arabic: "that is to say, Let Thy providence be to assist me, for I have chosen Thy commandments."

24. H adds in Arabic: "that is to say, You must know **4b** that I am God, who will not disappoint those who place their hope in Me."

[CHAPTER I][1]

I say that it is axiomatic among those whose minds are free from unsound notions[2] that God Most High is true and just, and that He is neither unjust in His judgments nor tyrannical in His decrees. In addition to this being self-evident to the mind, Sacred Scriptures also make this clear, as it is said, *God is a righteous judge* (Ps. 7:12).[3] And it is also said, *For God is judge; He putteth down one, and lifteth up another* (Ps. 75:8).[4] But although He lowers this one and raises that one, He [does so] with judgment, justice, and equity. If a human creature sees someone who deserves to be raised up brought low, or someone who merits to be brought down lifted up, let him permit no blasphemous thought to pass through his mind and let him attribute no injustice **5a** to the judgments of his Creator. For this must be for a reason that is hidden from created beings and is inaccessible to their understanding.[5] This is illustrated by what the Sages have told us in a tale about one who was about to go astray when the matter was clarified to him and the cause thereof was made known to him.

[THE REWARD OF ONE GOOD DEED][6]

This is the story of two pious men who ate, drank, and studied Torah together, never parting from each other. One

1. Chapter divisions and headings supplied; cf. Obermann, p. 5, n. 19; p. 13, n. 20.

2. Reading *al-āfāt* for *al-ṣifāt*, "divine attributes"; cf. Obermann, p. 5, n. 21, [and p. xxxvi. Ḳ omits *min al-ṣifāt* (Abramson, p. 428).—LN].

3. Arabic translation here follows Biblical citation in Hebrew in H (cf. p. 7, n. 21, above) and, unusually enough, in Ḳ and some Genizah fragments as well: "that is to say, God judges with justice."

4. H adds in Arabic: "that is to say, God is a just judge, this one He lowers, and that one He raises up."

5. Ḳ continues here: "as our lord Solomon has said in [a matter] like this, *As thou knowest not what is the way of the wind, nor how the bones do grow in the womb of her that is with child* (Eccl. 11:5)." Cf. Abramson, p. 428, and p. 429, n. 13.

6. This story occurs in several Rabbinic texts: cf. P. Ḥaḡ 2, 77d; *Bet ha-Midrash*, *1*, 89. Cf. also Obermann, p. 6, n. b; Hirschberg, p. 108.

of them died, and no one attended his funeral, nor was anything done for him that should have been done. Conversely, there died on that same day the son of the tax-collector[7] of the city, and the markets were suspended and schools recessed until he was buried. This virtuous man's[8] mind was so perplexed and this terrible thing so horrified him that he exclaimed, **5b** "There is neither reward nor recompense!"

That same night, while he was sleeping, he was told [in a dream], "Do not take lightly the judgment of your Creator, nor vex yourself over the decrees of your Maker. Your virtuous companion had committed a minor transgression, for which punishment was exacted from him in this world, before he reached his grave, in order that he might arrive in the hereafter free of all sins. On the other hand, the son of that tax-collector had performed one good deed which made him worthy of what you saw, in order that he be quit of recompense and stripped of reward, and thus deserving only of punishment." He thereupon asked, "My lord, what was the lapse of which this one was guilty, and the good deed which that one had to his credit?" The [visionary] interlocutor replied, "As for your companion, he did not—God forbid!—commit a major lapse but only a minor one, **6a** namely, one day, while dressing, he put on the tefillin for the head before the tefillin for the arm. Conversely, the son of that tax-collector performed no good deeds at all throughout his life, except once, nor did he do even that one intentionally, rather he merely happened to do it by chance, yet God did not let him miss the reward for it. It happened thus: One day he gave a banquet for a certain vizier, but the latter did not come to it. The food and drink having been already prepared, the host said, 'Since he did not come[9] to my banquet, I must not let my food go to waste. Rather let

7. H: *mutaqabbil kharāj*; cf. Hirschberg, p. 4, n. 2; Abramson, p. 428, and p. 429, n. 18.

8. i.e., the one who survived.

9. i.e., the vizier. H has *lam aji*ʾ, "I did not come," which Obermann corrects, with HY, to 3 m.pl. Ḳ (Abramson, p. 430) has the correct *lam yaji*ʾ.

the needy come and eat it.' He therefore had the poor brought in, fed them this food, and thus became worthy of this recompense."

Several days later this virtuous man saw his companion in a dream reposing in the midst of paradise, beside flowing streams **6b** and [flowering] gardens. He also saw the son of that tax-collector, in dire predicament and clad in wretched garb, burning with thirst, yet unable to find anything to drink. When he awoke, the false notion that he had held previously left him,[10] and he said to himself as did the radiant master[11] Moses, *The Rock, His work is perfect, for all His ways are justice; a God of faithfulness and without iniquity, just and right is He* (Deut. 32:4).[12]

The Sages, in their interpretation of this verse,[13] have mentioned something similar to this tale, for they said that *a God of faithfulness and without iniquity* [means] that just as He defers for the righteous man the recompense for the least commandment that he has performed **7a** and the reward for the smallest good deed that he has done in this world, in order to requite him for it in the hereafter, so also does He repay the wicked man for the least commandment performed by him in this world, so that in the hereafter he might be worthy of no reward whatsoever, and deserve nothing but painful punishment and severe retribution. Furthermore, *without iniquity* [means that just as] He does not mete out punishment to the wicked man[14] in this world, not even for the slightest slip committed by him, but defers it until the hereafter, so also does he exact in full whatever punishment the righteous man deserves for all his slips, however slight and minor, so that no punishment

10. So Ḳ: *wa-zāla* (Abramson, p. 430). H has *wa-qāla*, corrected to *wa-ḥāla* by Obermann, pp. 7–8, n. 33/34.

11. For a discussion of this title, see Hirschberg, p. 11, n. 13*.

12. H adds in Arabic: "that is to say, The Creator, true in all His deeds, and upright in all His ways, there is no tyranny with Him."

13. For this exegesis, cf. B. Ta 11a.

14. [Obermann's restoration of *al-ṭāliḥ* is confirmed by Ḳ (Abramson, p. 430).—LN]

might be left for him in the hereafter, and only everlasting bliss **7b** and eternal reward.[15]

[R. JOSHUA AND THE BLIND MAN][16]

One of the kings of the unbelievers challenged this verse by inquiring of R. Joshua,[17] "Is it not written in the Torah, *For all His ways are justice* (Deut. 32:4)? Yet how can His judgments constitute justice when we see Him inflicting trials upon one who is sinless and punishment upon one who has not erred? That is to say, we see a person crippled[18] from the moment he is born out of his mother's belly—he is [born] blind, or paralyzed, or mute, or deaf, or similarly afflicted. Is this anything but injustice?"

R. Joshua replied, "As for [handicapped persons who are] believers, God does it in order to multiply their [future] reward and increase their recompense. As for them that are unbelievers, it is because of His foreknowledge, before He had created them, of their [future] evil deeds and their deliberate choice of evil in preference to good, that He created them thus. If you wish **8a** me to prove this to you, give me one thousand dinars and send along with me two men whom you regard as reliable and trustworthy." The king agreed to this, and R. Joshua went off with the two men until he passed by a man blind from his mother's belly. He said to him, "O So-and-so, know that the king has commanded that I be put to death. Take these one thousand dinars, to keep on deposit with you for me. If I escape death, I will return and take them back from you. Otherwise they will constitute a gift to you." The

15. H follows this with the Hebrew words "forever and ever, and in all eternity," probably a gloss by the copyist; cf. Obermann, p. 3, n. 12/13; Abramson, p. 431, n. 34.

16. The source of this story is SEZ, 23, 41.

17. Ḳ and HY: R. Joshua ben Ḥananiah. The source has R. Joshua ben Ḳorḥah.

18. H: *ḍarīr*; Ḳ: *ṣaghīr* (Abramson, p. 432, and n. 36). *Kal-aᶜmā* has dropped out after it (Obermann, p. 9, n. 2); in Ḳ "blind" follows "paralyzed," and "deaf" is omitted.

blind man reached out his hand and took hold of the money from R. Joshua, while the two men watched them, after which R. Joshua left him and went off.

After a while R. Joshua and the two men returned to the blind man, and R. Joshua said to him, "I would like you to return my deposit to me, and I will pay you your fee for holding it." **8b** The blind man replied, "I don't know what you are talking about. You did not deposit anything with me." R. Joshua then said to him, "Come with us to the king so that we may seek judgment [from him]." They accordingly went off, and when they entered before the king, R. Joshua set forth the evidence, and the [two] witnesses testified against the blind man to the effect that he had indeed received that same amount. The blind man, on his part, declared, "None of this is [true], I have nothing [that belongs to him]." The king thereupon ordered him to be crucified. As they were raising him upon the wooden cross, a man passed by him and whispered [in his ear],[19] "I saw your wife saying to another man, 'Look, the blind one is about to be crucified. I will then marry you and give you the gold, and we will both eat of it and enjoy it.'"

At this the blind man confessed to [having received] the gold,[20] and R. Joshua said to him, "Had I handed it over to you without witnesses, you would have surrendered none of it to me. **9a** Undoubtedly your Creator has dealt justly with you when He brought you blind out of your mother's belly."

And the king voiced his agreement: "Of a truth certain, your Lord is a just and true judge, who deals neither unjustly nor oppressively."[21]

19. Ḳ (Abramson, p. 432) adds *fī udhunihi*. [For *shāwarahu* read *jāwazahu*; Ḳ has *jāza*.—LN]

20. Ḳ adds: "and said, 'Let me down, so that I may go and fetch it.' They let him down, and he went and fetched it" (Abramson, p. 432). So also HY.

21. The manuscripts of this story contain many variations; cf. Abramson, p. 433, n. 41.

[CHAPTER II][1]

[R. JOSHUA BEN LEVI AND THE STRANGE ACTIONS OF ELIJAH][2]

Something happened to R. Joshua [ben Levi][3] which perplexed him until its meaning was revealed to him. Namely, he had fasted and prayed and entreated his Lord to let him see [the prophet] Elijah, and so one day he indeed met him on the road. Elijah asked him, "Is there anything that you desire?" He replied, "I would like to walk along with you and observe the wonders that you perform in this world." Elijah said to him, "You will not be able to endure[4] my actions as you see them, and I[5] will have to take the trouble to explain to you what made me do the particular thing." R. Joshua replied, **9b** "My lord, I will not trouble you excessively in this regard, nor will I burden you with questions. My desire is merely to observe what you do, nothing else." At this, Elijah laid down the condition that once R. Joshua asked him to explain the reasons for his actions, he would have to leave him.

And so R. Joshua went with Elijah until they came,[6] that same evening, to a poor man who owned nothing but one cow that was kept in the house where he himself was sitting with his wife. When the man saw the two of them, he received them graciously and served them whatever food he had on hand, and

1. For a discussion of this division, see Obermann, p. 10, n. 8.

2. This story, for which no Jewish source has yet been found, is strikingly similar to a story in the Koran, 18:64–80. There the protagonists are Moses and an unknown worker of wonders (according to Muslim interpreters, al-Khiḍr). Cf. Obermann's translation and discussion in "Two Elijah Stories," *HUCA 23:1* (1950–51), 387–404; Hirschberg, p. 6, n. 1.

3. Full form of the name from Ḳ, Genizah fragment, and HY; Obermann, p. 10, n. 9; Abramson, pp. 411, 432, [reading *aṣāba* for *ṣāba*.—LN]

4. Genizah fragment has *al-baṣar* instead of *al-ṣabr*, "you will not be able to behold" (Abramson, pp. 411, 434).

5. So Ḳ (Abramson, p. 434); H has "we," presumably a *pluralis maiestatis*.

6. Ḳ: *waṣalā* (Abramson, p. 434), confirming Obermann's emendation (p. 10, n. 19).

they ate and drank, the while he entertained them as generously as he could.

When morning came, Elijah arose and caused the cow to die, whereupon the two of them departed. R. Joshua, puzzled, said to himself, "Was there no other recompense **10a** for this poor man for entertaining us so generously than that his cow should die?" [He therefore asked Elijah, "My lord, why did you cause his cow to die?"][7] Elijah replied, "Did I not impose upon you the condition that whatever you see you are to remain silent? Do you want me to leave you?"

So Joshua desisted from further questioning,[8] and they went on all day long. Towards evening they stopped at the house of a wealthy man, who paid no attention to them and offered them nothing to eat. Now he had a wall that had collapsed,[9] and when morning came, Elijah arose and besought his Lord and the wall was forthwith rebuilt. Thereupon the two men departed. R. Joshua was even more puzzled by this but refrained from asking questions, and they went on all day long until that night, when they entered a synagogue and found there seats of gold and silver, each person sitting in his own seat. The people asked, "Who will show honor[10] to these poor men tonight?" To which one of them replied, "These men, their food is but bread and salt,"[11] and so they paid no attention to the two wayfarers. They slept right there, and when they arose, Elijah said to the people, "May God make all of you chiefs."

They went on from there and journeyed all day long until that night, when they stopped with some wretchedly poor

7. So Ḳ (Abramson, p. 434).

8. So Ḳ: *fa-amsaka ᶜan suʾālihi* (Abramson, p. 434).

9. Ḳ adds: "that same day"; Genizah fragments: "that same night" (Abramson, p. 434, and n. 50). See also Abramson's discussion, p. 411, [reading *fa-inᶜamara* for *fa-inᶜamada*.—LN).

10. Ḳ: *yuṭᶜim*, "feed," probably more appropriate here (Abramson, p. 434). But "show honor" may be a more polite way of saying the same thing.

11. i.e., bread and salt right here are good enough for paupers such as these, so there is no need for the customary invitation to a wayfarer to be a guest in the home of one of the members of the congregation.

people **10b**. When these saw the two of them, they received them graciously and entertained them as generously as they could, serving them an abundance of food. They ate and drank and spent the night in utmost comfort, yet when morning came, Elijah said to them, "May God grant you only one chief."

At this R. Joshua could no longer hold himself back, so he said to Elijah, "My lord, deliver me from these perplexities, even though I shall then have to leave you. I can no longer bear patiently what I observe you doing."

Elijah replied, "As for the poor man whose cow died, his wife was due to die that same day, and so I besought my Lord that the cow should die in her stead. As for the man whose wall I caused to be rebuilt, had I left him to expose[12] the foundation thereof, he would have found a vast treasure therein, and he is unworthy of it. Therefore I caused the wall to be rebuilt for him, but in a short time it will collapse [again] and will never be restored."

"As for the people for whom I expressed the wish[13] that all of them should become chiefs, that is indeed an evil wish for them, because a place in which there are many chiefs is bound to be ruined. On the other hand, those for whom I expressed the wish that they should have only one chief, are bound to prosper thereby. Do you not call to mind the popular proverb, 'A multitude of masters causes the ship to founder?'[14] And Ben Sira said, *By one discerning man a city is peopled*, etc. (Sir. 16:4)."[15]

Then Elijah said to him, "Now that we are about to part, I will charge you with some advice that will be useful to you:

12. So H; Ḳ: *yatfir*, error for *yaḥfir*, "dig up."

13. Or "whom I blessed.' Cf. Abramson, pp. 411–12 and p. 376, for a comparison of the versions of this paragraph.

14. H has the plural *marākib*, "vessels," but Ḳ (Abramson, p. 436) has *safīnah*, "ship." The singular is obviously preferable here. For this proverb, see Freytag, *3*, *1*, 435, no. 2614.

15. H adds in Arabic: "that is to say, Through the judgment of a single intelligent man the city (H has here also *marākib*, a scribal error) will prosper." Cf. Obermann, p. 13, n. 10.

If you see a wicked man advancing and prospering, do not wonder at it, for it is to his [ultimate] disadvantage. **11a** Likewise, if you see a righteous man distressed or sorely tried, he is being delivered thereby from something worse. Refrain therefore from entertaining doubts in your heart about such things." Then[16] Elijah left him and departed.

16. [See Torrey's note, Obermann, p. xxxviii.—LN]

CHAPTER III[1]

[AḤER, WHO SOUGHT FOR WHAT IS HIDDEN]

I must tell you about a man, outstanding among the Sages, who strayed[2] from righteousness and left the [true] faith in a similar manner. To wit, he observed the [goodly] promises made by God to persons who honor both their parents[3] and who release the mother bird[4] and take only the fledglings, as God Most High has said, *If a bird's nest chance to be before thee*, etc. (Deut. 22:6).[5]

11b One day he observed a man saying to his son, "My son, climb up to this nest, set the mother free, and seize the fledglings, for I crave to eat them." The boy, honoring his father and desiring to fulfill both precepts,[6] climbed up, set the mother free, and seized the fledglings. As he was hastening to climb down to the ground, the ladder broke, and he fell to the ground and died.

At this the [heretical] Sage said to the boy's father,[7] "Where

1. From here on chapter divisions are found in H, mostly without numerals; cf. Obermann, p. 13, n. 20.

2. Source of this account: P. Ḥağ 2, 77b; (variant, B. Ḳid 39b). For *ẓāla* read *ḍalla* (Abramson, p. 436).

3. In Exod. 20:12, Deut. 5:16, the reward for honoring one's parents is long life.

4. So Ḳ (Abramson, p. 436). H has, here and throughout the paragraph, "father and mother bird," although the Biblical verse requires releasing only the mother (Obermann, p. 13, n. 23). Here, too, the injunction is connected with long life. Cf. also B. Ḥul 140b.

5. H adds in Arabic: "If you chance upon a nest in which there are fledglings, take the fledglings and set the father and the mother free, so that your life may be prolonged and your life span extended."

6. i.e., the precepts of honoring one's parents and of releasing the mother bird.

7. H has *ʾbyh*, corrected by Obermann to *abūhu*, "his father said"; Ḳ (Abramson, p. 436) has "he said." Obermann notes, "possibly the word is miswritten for *ʾAbuyah* with omission of *Elisha ben* . . . cf., however, the end of the paragraph, where the name of the erring Rabbi is introduced in such a way as though it was mentioned there for the first time." To translate "his father said" (as does Hirschberg, p. 8) makes no sense in this context. Probably a scribal error for *fa-qāla li-abīhi*, "he said to his father," as translated here.

is the length of days of this one, and where is his prosperity?" This affair led him to deny the resurrection of the dead and to reject the [ultimate] reward and punishment, thus [completely] abandoning the faith. He did not realize that God's saying, *that thy days may be long* (Exod. 20:12; Deut. 5:16) refers only to the hereafter **12a**, the delights of which have no end, and *that it may go well with thee* (Deut. 5:16, 22:7) also refers to the place in which no evil will befall the righteous, as the Sages have said, "*That thy days may be long*, in a world which is uninterruptedly long, and *that it may go well with thee*, in a world which is invariably good."[8] At that same moment his good deeds were burned up[9] and a [heavenly] voice was heard proclaiming, "*Return, O backsliding children* (Jer. 3:14)—except for Elisha Aḥer,"[10] meaning Elisha ben Abuyah, the teacher of R. Meir, who was called Aḥer, that is to say, ["the other one"], after he had left the faith.[11]

It is to him that the Talmud[12] applies the verse, *Let the lying lips be dumb, which speak arrogantly against the Righteous, with pride and contempt* (Ps. 31:19). *The Righteous* spoken of here is God Most High, of whom it is said, *Righteous and just is He* (Deut. 32:4).

12b R. Meir[13] learned much from him even afterwards.[14] When the question was raised in the Talmud, how could R. Meir consider this permissible, the distinction was explained by way of comparison with a person who finds a pomegranate, eats what is inside it, and throws away the shell.

At the time of Aḥer's death, the Sages said, "We must not

8. B. Ḥul 142a. Cf. also Tos Ḥul, end of 10; B. Ḳid 39b.

9. For a discussion of this term, see Abramson, p. 412.

10. B. Ḥag̃ 15a.

11. See the conjectures of Obermann, p. 15, n. 2/3, and p. xxxix; and Hirschberg, p. 9, n. 4, and pp. 108–09, regarding the reading *ʾaḥor* in H. However, Abramson's text (p. 510), here translated, seems simpler and more logical.

12. H has "Talmud Shabbat," which is incorrect; the citation is from P. Ḥag̃, 2, 77c. Cf. Obermann, p. 15, n. a; Hirschberg, p. 9, n. 5. Abramson (p. 510) omits the two words.

13. Source for the next two paragraphs, P. Ḥag̃ 15b.

14. i.e., even after Aḥer had left the faith.

consider him among those doomed to punishment, for he was a man of great learning, but neither can we think that he is among those who deserve the hereafter, are worthy of reward, and merit recompense, for he has sinned in denying the resurrection of the dead and rejecting the [ultimate] reward and punishment." But R. Meir said, "I will no sooner be dead than you will see smoke rising from Aḥer's grave, signifying that he has been pardoned for his sins and has become worthy of the hereafter **13a** and meriting recompense." It is said that indeed, no sooner did R. Meir die, than smoke rose from the grave of Elisha Aḥer.[15]

The Sages say that R. Johanan, greatly troubled by what R. Meir had done, [said],[16] "It is tyranny and violence[17] to burn one's own teacher in the fire. [Whenever] there is among us a man who has sinned, are we not able to save him, so that no smoke would rise from his grave? Now then, I shall take hold of him with my hand, and I shall see who will [dare] take him out of my hand or lay hold of him, and when I die, I shall extinguish the smoke from his grave." And indeed, when R. Johanan died, the smoke ceased issuing from the grave of Elisha Aḥer. The mourner who lamented[18] after R. Johanan opened his eulogy thus: "Even the guardian of the [heavenly] portal could not stand up against you,"[19] meaning, "you have directly reached **13b** your Creator, and because of your great eminence and learning neither [heavenly] chamberlain nor guardian could prevent your approaching God. You entered [before the Creator] like one of the [royal] favorites who enters

15. For a Muslim parallel to this theme, cf. the citation by Ibn Ṣaṣrā, from a work by Muḥammad ibn ʿAbd al-Raḥīm al-Gharnāṭī (1080–1169), in Brinner, *Chronicle*, *1*, 257; *2*, 194–95.

16. Inserted in accordance with Hirschberg, p. 9, and correction by Baneth, *Kirjath Sepher 11* (1935), p. 355.

17. Perhaps rather "courage and strength." Cf. Abramson, p. 412. [Cross out the following *fī* as a misreading of the next word *an*.—LN]

18. Construction of the sentence unclear. Perhaps to be translated: "The mourner of R. Johanan opened [with the words], 'O thou who art lamented'"; cf. Obermann, p. 16, n. 10/11, and p. xl.

19. In Hebrew. HY and Talmudic source have "against [you,] our master."

the palace to see the king without asking leave, and is not hindered by a chamberlain. So it was with you, my master. Directly you reached your Creator and made your request of Him, and He granted you that the smoke be extinguished from Aḥer's grave. And indeed, just as he had said, 'I, whomsoever I take hold of with my hand, no one else will lay hold of him,' so did it happen, and his words came true. On the other hand, behold this [other] man, [Aḥer]—with all his great learning, he did not restrain himself in patience, with the result that he was led to such grievous heresy and such terrible punishment."[20]

Man should, therefore, **14a** think well of his Creator,[21] and should not be astonished when he sees a wicked man advance in his affairs, for this is bound to be to his disadvantage, and everlasting affliction is bound to overtake him.

Wise Solomon has alluded to this when he said, *It is not good to respect the person of the wicked* (Prov. 18:5), meaning that there is no benefit to the wicked in his advancement and prosperity in this world, for with this [transitory] prosperity he will only earn eternal chastisement, and with this [ephemeral] advancement, everlasting punishment. And the Sages have said, "There is no benefit for the wicked who are being favored in this world."[22] For with all the benefits they gain they cannot acquire a single good deed—they will only depart from this world as bereft of good deeds as when they had entered it.[23]

[TWO PARABLES]

Regarding this the Sages have propounded two parables. They said that this is similar to **14b** the case of a thief who entered the king's treasury and took some gold vessels. As he was about to leave, he found a purse full of dinars, and said, "This is better than the vessels." As he was about to ascend,

20. No division of paragraphs in MS, but this is obviously the end of the citation from the eulogy. Cf. Obermann, p. 16.

21. Cf. Hirschberg, p. 10, n. 8; meaning, be assured of God's justice.

22. B. Yoma 87a.

23. No pause in MS. HY adds here: "at their birth. *For he cometh in vanity, and departeth in darkness* (Eccl. 6:4)."

he found a larger purse, so he took it and abandoned the smaller one. Thereupon he found some jewels, and said, "This is brighter,[24] lighter to carry, and more valuable." He continued in this fashion, finding one thing better than the other, until dawn overtook him, so that he had to leave everything and depart with nothing, weeping, wailing, and saying, "I have risked my life, and have left with nothing. If only I had taken even the least valuable object!" He was thus overcome by bitter regret, but it availed him nothing.[25]

The other parable deals with a fox who saw a beautiful orchard and wanted to enter it, **15a** but could find only a small gap [in the fence] through which he could not pass. So he starved himself until his body became lean, entered by way of that gap, and ate of all kinds of fruits in the orchard, such as grapes and others. The season of the grape harvest having arrived [in the meantime], the owner of the vineyard came to harvest it, and the fox could no longer remain in the orchard, lest the owner should find him and kill him. But when he wanted to leave he was unable to do so, because he had grown fat and bulky with all that he had eaten and sated himself. So he again starved himself until he grew lean and returned to his previous condition. Thereupon he began shouting and wailing about how he had wearied and starved himself in the beginning in order to enter the orchard, yet had not benefited from it and had to leave the orchard [as hungry] as when he had come in.[26] So, too, the evildoers **15b** will be continually sorry for the chances they had missed to acquire good deeds, but this will avail them nothing.[27]

The wise one, [Solomon], has warned us not to envy them nor to be misled by[28] the prosperous state in which we see

24. [*Anyar*; probably misreading of *akhyar*, "better" (as in the preceding and following lines).—LN]

25. Obermann found no clear source for this first parable, but refers to Eccl. Rabbah 1, 10a.

26. For the source of this parable, cf. Eccl. Rabbah 5, 32a.

27. For a discussion of this popular theme, see Abramson, p. 412.

28. H has here *illā*, which seems to be superfluous. Cf. Obermann, p. 18, n. 16.

them, but rather to increase our obedience to God Most High and to study the holy Torah. Thus he says, *Let not thine heart envy sinners* (Prov. 23:17);[29] rather, *Let his delight be in the law of the Lord, and in His law let him meditate day and night* (Ps. 1:2).[30] The pious one, [David], also said, *Fret not thyself because of evildoers, neither be thou envious against them that work unrighteousness*[31] (Ps. 37:1), explaining [further] that they are like a plant which lasts but for a short while and then fades away, as he has said, **16a** *For they shall soon wither like the grass and fade as the green herb* (Ps. 37:2).

It is the same when you see a righteous man in poor circumstances, visited by calamities, struck by misfortunes, overtaken by illnesses, and dying a horrible death—all this is for his own benefit and his happiness in the eternal abode. We find many of the righteous tested by various trials. Some were tested at [the cost of] their very lives, as you learn from what befell the ten martyrs,[32] of whom one was slain by the sword, another had his flesh flayed with iron combs,[33] another was burned with fire together with a Torah Scroll;[34] among them was R. ʿAḳiba, [who was the most outstanding of the Sages].[35] When the radiant master[36] Moses asked the Creator to let him know the **16b** events that will occur after him,[37] and who will be Sage or prophet, and was shown the wisdom, excellence, and piety of R. ʿAḳiba, he said,[38] "O Lord of the worlds,[39] Thou art going to create such a one in Thy world, and yet Thou givest the

29. HY continues the citation: "*but be in the fear of the Lord all the day.*" Cf. Obermann, p. 18, n. 17.

30. H adds in Arabic: "that is to say, Devote yourself to God's Torah all of your time and labor therein."

31. Cf. the comment of Abramson, p. 412.

32. Literally "the ten executed by the state"; cf. *Bet ha-Midrash*, 2, 66 ff.

33. R. ʿAḳiba; cf. B. Ber 61b.

34. R. Ḥanina ben Teradion; cf. B. AZ 18a.

35. [So HY (Obermann, p. 19, n. 7); but not in Abramson's text (p. 510).—LN]

36. See above, p. 10, n. 11.

37. According to Rabbinic lore, Adam and Moses were shown the future; cf. Lev. Rabbah 26, 75b, and elsewhere. Cf. also Hirschberg, p. 12, n. 14.

38. For this homily, cf. B. Men 29b.

39. This world and the world-to-come.

Torah to me? Surely I must yield to a person of his qualities!" And when he learned further that the manner of ᶜAḳiba's death will be dreadful and vile, and that his flesh will be weighed on [butcher's] scales, he wept bitterly and said directly to Him, "O Lord of the worlds, is this the recompense of such an excellent and outstanding man? Is this the reward for the wisdom that he taught and the learning in the law with which he enlightened [men's] eyes?" And God answered him, "Question not My ways![40] Thus has it already been resolved in My mind."[41]

40. This part of the quotation is in Hebrew; cf. B. Sanh 111a.
41. Literally "Thus has it preceded in My knowledge."

CHAPTER IV

[NAHUM, MAN OF GAMZU]

17a Some Sages were tried in their own flesh.[1] Such was Nahum, the man of Gamzu.[2] Despite his great godliness, piety, and learning, he was stricken with diseases and illnesses, although it was he himself who had prayed to his Lord that this should befall him. The reason for this was something that had happened to him with a poor man, wherefore he asked his Lord to requite him immediately, so that no punishment would remain due to him in the hereafter. It is said of him that [as a consequence] he became blind,[3] his hands and feet were cut off, and the rest of his body became covered with leprosy. [The legs of] his bed were placed in four pots of water, so that its coolness might reach him.[4] Once he was sitting in a house whose structure had become weak **17b** and whose roof was splitting. His disciples wanted to remove him, lest it should collapse upon him, but he said to them, "Remove [first] everything that is in the house. When nothing remains in it, only then remove my bed from it, because as long as my bed is in the house it will not collapse." When they did so and finally removed the bed, the house forthwith collapsed.

His disciples asked him, "Master, since your record is pleasing to the Creator Most High, seeing that you are righteous and God-fearing to such a [high] degree, why were you afflicted by these diseases and illnesses?" He replied, "I myself invoked them upon me." They asked him, "What was the reason for it?" He replied, "One day, as I was going to my

1. The source of the following story is B. Ta 21a.

2. Actually probably pronounced Gimzo, a place in Judea. For the popular tradition about the origin and meaning of this name, see the following chapter; cf. also Abramson, pp. 395–97.

3. Arabic text has *baṣīran*, "endowed with eyesight," a euphemism for blind; HY and source have "blind." Cf. Obermann, p. 20, n. 7; Hirschberg, p. 12, n. 2.

4. In the Talmudic source, "so that ants would not reach him." Cf. Abramson, p. 396. For *qaṣrīyah*, pl. *qaṣārī*, "pot, flower pot, chamber pot," see Dozy, *s.v.*

son-in-law's house with **18a** three donkeys laden with various kinds of food, fruit, and drink, a poor man met me and said, 'My lord, give me something to sustain me, for the vehemence of [my] hunger is killing me.' I replied, 'Have patience until I unload one of the animals, and I will give you [something].' It took me a little while to unload, and then, behold, the man was dead. Great remorse overcame me, I threw myself over him, pressed my eyes to his eyes, and said, 'Let these two eyes which did not take pity on you be blinded, let these two hands which did not hasten to give you that which would sustain you be cut off, and let the same happen to these two feet!' Nor could my soul rest thereafter until I prayed for this illness to afflict the rest of my body [also]." R. ᶜAḳiba[5] said to him, **18b** "Woe is me, our master, that I see you in this state!" And Nahum replied, "[Nevertheless] the fruit thereof will be good for me and will greatly increase my [ultimate] reward."

5. The Talmudic source does not mention R. ᶜAḳiba here, and has simply, "They said." But see Abramson, p. 396.

CHAPTER V

[WHY HE WAS CALLED MAN OF GAMZU][1]

Know that the reason he was called Nahum, man of *Gam zu lĕ-ṭoḇah*,[2] was that whenever any misfortune befell him he would say, "This, too, is for good!"[3] and would not complain or become angry. Once, when the Sages of Israel[4] wanted to send a gift to the [Roman] emperor,[5] they said, "We have no one like Nahum man of Gamzu. Let us send the gift with him, for God Most High performs many wonders and miracles through his hand."

So they sent with him chests **19a** filled with costly clothes, and he took them along and set out. When he reached a place to spend the night, he set them down close by his head and fell asleep. During the night, the people of that town arose and took everything that was in those chests, filling them instead with earth. When dawn came, he took the chests and set out once more, and when he came in the presence of the emperor, he placed the chests before him. The emperor ordered them to be opened, and they were found to be filled with earth. His viziers then said to the emperor, "The Jews are making a laughingstock of you and a mockery of your royal dignity." Whereupon the emperor ordered the execution of Nahum man of Gamzu, but when they took him out[6] to be executed, he once more said, "This, too, is for good!"

At this moment [the prophet] Elijah appeared in the guise of one of the emperor's chamberlains, and said to him, "O king,

1. Talmudic source for the following: B. Ta 21a; variant in B. Sanh 108b f. Cf. also Abramson's comments, p. 396.
2. i.e., "Let this, too, be for good!" or "This, too, is for good!"
3. H adds in Arabic: "that is to say, There is good in every act of [God's] judgment." Cf. Abramson, pp. 396–97.
4. HY—all texts—has this, instead of H: "the Sages," meaning the Sages of the Talmud.
5. H: *qaysar al-malik*, literally "Caesar, the [Roman] king."
6. H seems to read *fa-akhadhahu*, "he [i.e., the emperor] took him out."

perhaps this earth is part of the earth used by Abraham the friend,[7] a little of which, when thrown in front of the enemy, turns **19b** into arrows and spears aimed at him. With it they capture besieged cities."

Now there was nearby a city which they had besieged for a considerable time but had been unable to capture. So they threw at it a little of that earth, and it turned into arrows and spears, enabling them to capture the city forthwith, at which the emperor, overjoyed, ordered the chests to be refilled with precious jewels, and also presented Nahum man of Gamzu with a beautiful robe.

On his return journey Nahum spent the night in the same town [where he had spent the night on his way to the emperor. When the townspeople saw that he had come back with honor and in safety, they asked him],[8] "What did you bring to the emperor that he found you worthy **20a** of such a great reward?" He replied, "It was the chests which I brought. When they took them, they found them full of earth, and rewarded me with this."

On hearing this, the townspeople, too, took some chests, filled them with earth, and brought them to the emperor, saying, "O king, this is some of the same earth that the Jews had sent you." The emperor ordered it to be tested, and when it was tested and nothing [of the aforementioned qualities] was found in it, he ordered them executed, and they were all put to death, down to the last one of them.

7. *Al-khalīl*, "friend, beloved," i.e., of God, occurs as Abraham's epithet in the Bible, cf. Isa. 41:8; 2 Chr. 20:7. Very frequently also in Islamic literature; cf. Hirschberg, p. 14, n. 3.

8. Not found in H, and restored by Obermann (p. 23, n. 1) from HY.

CHAPTER VI[1]

[TALES OF MARTYRDOM][2]

Know that R. Eleazar ben Simeon[3] prayed to bring upon himself many illnesses until they overcame him—the description of them would take so long that I will not undertake it.[4] Each morning he would pray for them to cease, and they would cease, **20b** and in the evening [he would pray] for their return, and they would return.

Our sainted Rabbi [Judah] was tried for five years with toothache and for seven years with dysuria. The reason for it was that he had done something for which he deserved [such a trial], and when he repented of it, he became worthy of remission of the trial. The [precise] reason was as follows: Once he was walking in the Street of the Butchers while a calf was being taken out to slaughter. It broke loose from the butchers' hands and clung to our sainted Rabbi, in the hope that he would save it from slaughter, but he seized it and delivered it to the butcher, saying to him, "Slaughter it—for this was it created." Whereupon it was announced [from heaven]: "Inasmuch as he had no pity and displayed such hardness [of heart], let these illnesses befall him." One day some time later he observed his maidservant **21a** sweeping the house, and when she saw a mouse, she was about to kill it, but Rabbi [Judah] said to her, "Don't do this! For the saintly one, [David], has said, *His mercies are upon all His creatures* (Ps. 145:9)."[5] It is said that at

1. A problematical chapter of the work. The first paragraphs, down to n. 7, appear in all the Hebrew versions. From n. 7 on the text is found only in H. Cf. Obermann's comments, p. 23, n. a, and p. 25, n. 4/17. Cf. also the discussion in Abramson, pp. 366 ff.

2. Source for following story: B. BM 84b ff. Cf. Obermann, p. 23, n. c.

3. So, and not "R. Simeon ben Eleazar," as in H. Cf. Abramson, p. 375; Hirschberg, p. 14, n. 1.

4. Reading *lā atakallaf fīhi* for *lā ikhtilāfa fīhi*. Abramson (pp. 378–79) refers to the form *lā aktalif* which does not occur, but cf. his citation on p. 379 from Ḳ: *lā atakallaf*.

5. H adds in Arabic: "that is to say, God's mercy is upon all His creatures.'

that very moment all his pains and ailments departed from him.

Were it not for his high station with his Creator, God would not have been so exacting regarding his deeds. Do you not recall the words of the saintly one, [David], *And* [*God*], *feared of all them that are round about Him* (Ps. 89:8)? And he said also, *And round about Him it stormeth mightily* (Ps. 50:3). Happy is he whom He chastises, as the saintly one, [David], has said, *Happy is the man whom Thou chastenest, O Lord, and teachest him out of Thy law* (Ps. 94:12).

The Sages **21b** have given a beautiful interpretation of this verse, as follows: If you remove the *dageš* from the letter *mem* in *telammĕdenu* (*teachest*) and the *pattaḥ* from under the letter *lamed*, it will become *tilmĕdenu*,[6] and the meaning [of the verse] will be, "Happy is the man whom Thou chastenest, O Lord, and from Thy Torah one may learn this." From [what verse in] the Torah? We say that the verse *If a man smite the eye of his bondsman*, etc. (Exod. 21:26) enjoins freedom for the slave in lieu of his eye or his tooth. Now if the Lord of the worlds, who has called Israel *My son, My first-born* (Exod. 4:22), tries a man with a trial that spreads pain over all of his body, it is all the more proper and certain that He should release him from [further] punishment and set him free from the rest of his sins . . .

[THE MOTHER AND HER SEVEN SONS][7]

22a ". . . God has said to us, *Thou shalt bow down to no other god* (Exod. 34:14)."[8] And the king slew him.

Then the king brought out the third son and said to him, "Bow down to this idol," and the youth replied, "I will not

6. Cf. B. Ber 5b. The grammar is not clear; cf. Obermann, p. 25, n. 11; Hirschberg, p. 15, n. 4. Pointing according to Abramson, pp. 412–13, based on Genizah fragment.

7. There is a gap here in H, leaving the first story incomplete and introducing the next story, with its beginning missing. This story, the source of which is Lam. Rabbah 1, 91 f., B. Giṭ 57b, and elsewhere, seems not to belong to the original, and is not included in HY; cf. the discussion by Hirschberg, Introduction, pp. 58–59. Ḳ and Genizah fragment (Abramson, pp. 440, 366 ff.) merely mention the story and refer for it to another, unnamed, work of Nissim's.

8. H adds in Arabic: "that is to say, You shall not bow down to any object of worship except Me."

do this, for God has said, *He that sacrificeth unto the gods, save unto the Lord only, shall be utterly destroyed* (Exod. 22:19)."[9] And the king slew him.

Then the king brought out the fourth son and said to him, "Bow down to this idol, or else I shall make you join your brothers." The youth replied, "I will not do this, for the Lord Most High has said, *Hear, O Israel, the Lord our God, the Lord is One* (Deut. 6:4)."[10] And the king slew him.

Then the king brought out the fifth son and said the same thing to him, but the youth would not submit to him, and replied, "God has said, **22b** *For the Lord, thy God, is a jealous God* (Deut. 6:15)." And the king slew him.

Then the king brought out the sixth son and spoke to him likewise, but the youth would not comply with his request, and replied, "God Most High has said to us, *Ye shall not make with Me gods of silver, neither shall ye make unto you gods of gold* (Exod. 20:23)."[11] And the king slew him.

Then the king brought out the seventh son and said to him, "Bow down to this idol," and he replied, "This is impossible [for me]." The king thereupon said to him, "Now I shall be merciful unto you, in that I shall throw down my seal ring in front of the idol. Bend down then and pick it up, so that my companions would think that you have obeyed my command." The youth replied, "Woe unto you! You are afraid of someone who is flesh and blood like yourself—should I not fear God Most High?" **23a** The king said to him, "Is there a God in the world?", and the youth replied, "Woe unto you! What thing have you seen in the world that is worshipped except[12] that it has a mouth but cannot speak, has eyes but cannot see, has ears but cannot hear? You yourself are like that which you worship,

9. H adds in Arabic: "that is to say, Offer sacrifices before your God alone—there is none other."

10. H adds in Arabic: "that is to say, Hear, O people of Israel, that God is the only God."

11. H adds in Arabic: "that is to say, Do not make with Me a god of silver, nor of gold shall he be to you."

12. Reading *fī al-dunyā yusjad illā*. But cf. Obermann, p. 27, n. 3.

in that you have eyes with which you do not see what can be seen, and you have [other] senses which you do not use as you should. It is as the saintly one, [David], has said, *They have mouths, but they speak not; eyes have they, but they see not* (Ps. 115:5),[13] whereas about our God [it is said], *Yea, Mine hand hath laid the foundation of the earth, and My right hand hath spread out the heavens; when I call unto them, they stand up together* (Isa. 48:13)."[14]

23b Then the king said to him, "If that is the case, why has He not saved you from my hand, as He had saved Hananiah, Mishael, and Azariah from the hand of Nebuchadnezzar?"[15] The youth replied, "Those were righteous men, wherefore God saved them, whereas we are sinners, just as you are a sinner." So the king ordered him to be slain, whereupon the youth's mother said to the king, "I adjure you by God, O king, put the sword to both his neck and mine and slay us together!" But he replied, "I shall not do so, for it is written in the Torah, *Ye shall not kill it and its young, both in one day* (Lev. 22:28)."[16] She said to him, "Woe unto you! Which **24a** of the commandments of the Torah have you observed [in the past] that you should [now] observe this one?" The king replied, "I shall be merciful unto you in this—rise and admonish him gently, so that I would not have to slay him, but would let him live for you, seeing that I have already bereaved you of your [other] children." She replied "I hear and obey."[17] Then she said to the youth, "My child, accept nothing of what this infidel tells you and you will yet meet your brothers and walk in their

13. H adds in Arabic: "that is to say, The idol of the infidels has a mouth but cannot speak, and eyes but cannot see."

14. H adds in Arabic: "that is to say, My great power has founded the earth, and the heavens have I spread out. When I commanded them, they came into being."

15. Cf. Dan. 3:26 ff.

16. H adds in Arabic: "that is to say, The ewe and its young, you shall not slaughter them both on the same day."

17. Literally "Hearing and obeying," the usual Arabic formula of compliance with a command.

company until you see an old man of splendid[18] mien, and that will be our father Abraham. Say then unto him, 'You built one altar for your son Isaac, but you did not sacrifice him upon it, whereas we have sacrificed our lives to God Most High and did not violate His command, and our mother is witness [to this] for us.'"

At this the king asked their mother, "Is it thus that **24b** I commanded you?", and she replied, "Woe [unto you]! [Had I obeyed you], I would have separated him from his brothers." Then he slew him also. When she saw [all] seven of them slain, she ascended the roof and threw herself down to the ground to her death. When the king[19] saw what the mother and her children had done, he said to himself, "If the religion of these people were not true, they would not have surrendered themselves to death in this fashion." He then ordered them to be buried in the same grave and built over them the Šěminiṯ Synagogue,[20] which was the first synagogue built after the Second Temple. It was to this story that Scripture refers in the words of David, *He maketh the barren woman to dwell in her house, as a joyful mother of children. Hallelujah* (Ps. 113:9).[21]

18. Reading *bahī* instead of *bihi*; cf. Obermann, p. 28, n. 2.

19. *Qaysar al-malik*; cf. above, p. 26, n. 5.

20. For a discussion of this interesting reference, cf. Obermann, "The Sepulchre of the Maccabean Martyrs," *JBL 50* (1931), 250–65.

21. H adds in Arabic: "that is to say, He hinted thereby how she would be left without children, like a barren woman, but promised her a [bountiful] reward."

CHAPTER VII

[TRIALS OF SAINTLY MEN]

25a Some of the Sages[1] were tried in their possessions, but when the one who was tried would repent of the act for which he had become liable to the trial in his possessions, he would be compensated. Thus it is said about R. Huna that he had four hundred jars of wine, all of which spoiled and turned to vinegar. The Sages thereupon came to him and said, "Examine your affairs and your actions; mend whichever requires mending, and abandon whichever requires abandoning." He asked them, "Am I **25b** suspected by you of having done what is not acceptable to God?" They replied, "Is our Creator to be suspected of doing something that is not right and just?" He said, "If you have heard anything [discreditable] about me, let me know what it is." They replied, "Yes, we have heard that you do not pay the monthly hired laborer[2] who works on your farm the [share of the] vines that is due him." He said, "But he steals more than is due him!" They replied, "And because he steals, do you settle the account with yourself in this manner? You are obligated to pay him his due in full, without regard to what he steals, for it is he who will be punished [by God] for that." From that day on Huna desisted from this practice. It is said that thereafter vinegar rose in price so much that it was worth almost as much as wine, so that he lost nothing.

Among the Sages there were many who were wealthy, and God tried them by taking their wealth away from them, **26a** in order that full retribution should be exacted from them in this world—I will not dwell on their stories. Anyone who contemplates these stories cannot possibly go astray, and his faith in God is bound to be strengthened.

1. The source of this story is B. Ber 5b.

2. [So H, *al-mushāhar*; Ḳ (Abramson, p. 440) has, in accord with the Talmud, *al-mushāṭir*, "the sharecropper."—LN]

[HEEDING THE COMMANDMENTS OF THE SAGES]

A person[3] may sometimes be tried for reasons that people are not aware of and about which they know nothing, as is said[4] about a scholar who had studied much [Rabbinic] lore and was very scrupulous in his faith and in most of his actions, yet died while still young. His wife took his tefillin and went with them to the synagogues and to the assemblies of Sages, [saying to them], "Is it not written in the Torah, *For she*[5] *is thy life, and the length of thy days* (Deut. 30:20)?[6] **26b** Why then did my husband die in the middle of his life?" But there was no one who could answer her.

One day one of the Sages who was her guest said to her, "Tell me, did your husband ever approach you during the period of your impurity?" She replied "God forbid! He did not approach me, not even with his little finger." He said, "What about the days of your counting, that is to say, the last seven days of purification?"[7] She replied, "Yes, he used to eat and drink with me, and sleep close to me, but no act of union would take place."[8] Thereupon the Sage said to her, "Praise be to God Most High for not being lenient with him! There is no doubt that now he must have attained a high rank, since God has already exacted punishment from him for this **27a** [venial] matter, and has been so particular with him even in the slightest of things."

The wise one, [Solomon], has alluded to this matter in the verse which I have already cited,[9] namely, *It is not good to respect the person of the wicked* (Prov. 18:5a). The Sages joined the word

3. *Al-ᶜabd*, literally "servant [of God]."

4. The source for this story is B. Shab 13a (variants in ARN 2, 2 [YJS, *10*, 16–17]; SER, p. 76).

5. i.e., the Torah; the Biblical text has *He*, i.e., God.

6. H adds in Arabic: "meaning that according as a man is dedicated to the Torah and occupies himself with it, so will she be the cause for the length of his life."

7. Reading, with Obermann (p. 30, n. 6), *lil-istiṭhār*. Cf. Lev. 15:28.

8. Ḳ has here: "but he did not approach me—God forbid!—until I completed my counting and immersed myself in the ritual bath" (Abramson, p. 442).

9. Cf. p. 20, above.

good in the first half of this verse to the second half, making [the whole verse read, "To respect the person of the wicked—no]; but it is good to turn aside the righteous in judgment," meaning that if the righteous person is tried [so sorely] that it seems to people that this is unjust to him—that is, that "His judgments [are unjust]"—this trial is better for him, for on its account he is saved from [far more] severe punishment, which is *good*, [meaning] in the world to come.[10]

It is said[11] that after God had shown to our master Moses the generations to come after him,[12] so that he saw a righteous man [sorely] tried while a sinner was at ease, He showed him also **27b** the scales of truth and the weights of justice, to let him know that all this will be done with truth, justice, and fairness.

Thus you see that when someone close to us dies,[13] we say, *The Rock, His work is perfect*, etc. (Deut. 32:4), and similarly the Sages have ordained that in the hour of trial one must say, "Blessed be the True Judge,"[14] which is taken[15] from the words of the saintly one, [David], *Righteousness and justice are the foundation of Thy throne, mercy and truth go before Thee* (Ps. 89:15), and he also said, *A psalm of David. I will sing of mercy and justice; unto thee, O Lord, will I sing praises* (Ps. 101:1).[16] The Sages have expounded **28a** [the latter verse thus]: "If it be justice, I will sing praises; and if it be mercy, I will sing."[17] Meaning, If Thou doest good unto us, and graciously bestowest Thy goodness upon us, we will render thanks; and if Thou dealest

10. The exegesis in this paragraph is from B. Yoma 87a.

11. Source for this: Lev. Rabbah 26, 75b; B. Ber 7a.

12. Cf. above, p. 22, for this theme.

13. Abramson (p. 413) cites here from a Genizah fragment the important addition: "in the middle of his life span or young in years," an obvious reference to the purpose of this work as indicated in the Prologue.

14. H adds in Arabic: "that is to say, Blessed be the One who judges with truth and justice."

15. This phrase occurs in HY but not in H; cf. Obermann, p. 31, n. 11.

16. H adds in Arabic: "that is to say, In all circumstances I must glorify the Lord and praise Him."

17. Cf. P. Ber 9:7, 14b; B. Ber 60b.

justly with us, and requitest our evil deeds with sufferings and trials, we shall likewise render thanks unto Thee for it." This is the meaning of the Sages' interpretation [quoted above]: "If it be justice, I will sing praises," [etc.].

For this reason the Sages have warned us, saying, "If you see a righteous man, and it is well with him, and an evildoer, and it is ill with him, or an evildoer, and it is well with him, and a righteous man, and it is ill with him,"[18] [etc.], meaning, [If you see such], do not think ill of your Creator, lest you forfeit your wages and cause your reward to perish.[19] It is about this that the wise one, [Solomon], has said and warned, *Suffer not* **28b** *thy mouth to bring thy flesh into guilt*, etc. (Eccl. 5:5).[20] And he said also, *All things toil to weariness*, etc. (*ibid.* 1:8), meaning that others, who have preceded you, have already wearied themselves with this [problem], such as our master Moses in his time, as the Sages have expounded his words, *Show me now Thy ways*, etc. (Exod. 33:13). And Habakkuk has said, *How long, O Lord, shall I cry, and Thou wilt not hear*, etc. (Hab. 1:2), namely when he saw by means of the holy spirit and became aware of what was to befall the ten martyrs, he said, "O Lord of the worlds, wherefore didst Thou save Hananiah, Mishael, and Azariah from the fiery furnace, while these Thou wilt not save? Yet they, too, **29a** are righteous, *Therefore the law is slacked* (*ibid.* 1:4a)." And he[21] said also, "Nebuchadnezzar the wicked clothed Daniel the righteous in purple, Ahasuerus the unclean made Mordechai the pure rule, *for the wicked doth crown the*

18. Up to here the citation is in Hebrew, followed in H by the Arabic: "The meaning of this is, If you see a righteous man who has been treated well, and a sinner from whom punishment has been exacted, or a sinner who has been treated well, and a righteous man from whom punishment has been exacted." Cf. B. Ber 7b; ARN (B) 22.

19. Obermann (p. 32, n. 15/16) refers here to Koran 3:165, "God suffereth not the reward of the faithful to perish."

20. H adds in Arabic: "that is to say, Do not speak words from which error will accrue to you, and for which you will have to go back and ask pardon, so that you will harm yourself."

21. HY: "They (= the Sages)." Cf. Obermann, p. 32, n. 36.

righteous (*ibid.* 1:4b)."[22] Our Lord Mighty and Glorious answered him, "Is it not written in the Torah, *A God of faithfulness and without iniquity*, etc. (Deut. 32:4)? Do not presume to inquire into the reason [thereof]." When the prophet [Habakkuk] realized that he had erred in his questioning, he prayed to his Lord to forgive him, as it is said, *A prayer of Habakkuk the prophet, regarding* [*his*] *errors*[23] (Hab. 3:1). As for his saying, *And holdest Thy peace when the wicked swalloweth up the man that is* **29b** *more righteous than he* (*ibid.* 1:13)—he did not say, "the man that is righteous," which would have sufficed. Hence the Sages expounded[24] this thus: "The wicked man can swallow up one who is [merely] more righteous than himself, but cannot swallow up one who is completely righteous. Therefore the prophet has said, *the man that is more righteous than he*." Asaf, in his time,[25] also asked, *Lord, how long* [*shall the wicked . . . exult*]? etc. (Ps. 94:3). For these reasons [Solomon] concluded the [aforecited] verse[26] with the words, *The eye is not satisfied with seeing, nor the ear filled with hearing* (Eccl. 1:8b).[27] Take care therefore, lest you go astray!

22. Thus understood here. The usual translation is "*the wicked doth compass about the righteous.*" H adds in Arabic: "that is to say, Nebuchadnezzar, was evil and [yet] was gracious to Daniel who was righteous, and thus [also] Ahasuerus and Mordecai, and how wonderful this is!"

23. To be understood thus here, although *šig̱yonoṯ* has been interpreted in various ways.

24. B. Meg̃ 6b, and elsewhere.

25. This psalm is not ascribed to Asaf. Obermann (p. 33, n. 16/17) read here *bĕ-rišᶜaṯo*, "in his evil," and endeavored to explain why R. Nissim would refer thus to Asaf. Cf. also Hirschberg, p. 20, n. 14. Ḳ has clearly *bĕ-šaᶜăto*, as translated here (Abramson, p. 444).

26. Quoted above, p. 36.

27. H adds an exact Arabic translation.

CHAPTER VIII

[TALES OF THOSE WHO KEPT THE SABBATH AND SCRUPULOUSLY OBSERVED THE COMMANDMENTS]

I think that I should relate [here also] some stories of those righteous persons who were granted prosperity in this world. I say that it is possible that this is granted to those who excel in honoring and revering the [divine] law, by doing something[1] for which, had they failed to do it, they would not have been liable to punishment, and that is why they are rewarded **30a** for it in this world. This comes under [the heading of] charity, as defined in the Mishnah: "These are the things whose fruit a person enjoys in this world, while the principal thereof endures for him into the next world,"[2] [meaning that] he receives the wages[3] of the income in this world, while the wages of the principal remain [intact] for the hereafter.[4]

Thus it is related about R. Ḥiyya[5] that he was the guest of a certain man on a Sabbath eve in Laodicea.[6] A table of gold was brought before him by thirteen men [who] carried it in by a golden chain skillfully ornamented with jewels,[7] and on it [were] all kinds of food. When it was set down before them, they[8] said, *The earth is the Lord's, and the fullness thereof; the world,*

1. [So Ḳ, *bi-mā* (Abramson, p. 444).—LN]
2. Cf. Peah 1:1.
3. H has *amr*, but Ḳ has *ajr*, which agrees with the Hebrew translation. Cf. Obermann, p. 34, n. 17; Abramson, p. 444.
4. This last sentence in Arabic is a paraphrase of the preceding quotation in Hebrew. It is interesting in its application of Islamic concepts to Jewish law. It occurs also in Ḳ.
5. For the source of this story, cf. B. Shab 119a.
6. Several towns founded by the Seleucids in Anatolia, Syria, and Mesopotamia bore this name.
7. Reading *jawhar* for *jafār* (or *ghafār*), with Hirschberg, p. 21, n. 2. But see Ḳ (Abramson, p. 444, and p. 445, n. 43). [Read *ghaḍār*, as in Abramson's note, "porcelain plates" (cf. Dozy); hence "skillfully set with plates containing all kinds of food."—LN]
8. [So Ḳ (Abramson, p. 444): *yaqūlūna* (i.e., the thirteen men).—LN]

and they that dwell therein (Ps. 24:1),[9] and when it was removed, they[8] said, *The heavens are the heavens of the Lord; but the earth hath He given to the children of men* (Ps. 115:16).[10]

Thereupon R. Ḥiyya said to his host, "I would like you to tell me how you attained to such tremendous wealth and ample prosperity." He replied, "I used to be a butcher, and every fat lamb that I would buy I would set aside, saying, This is to be reserved for the holy Sabbath. It was through this act that I earned the merit of this splendid estate." At this R. Ḥiyya exclaimed, "Praise be to God who has made you worthy of this affluence!"

It is also said[11] that a certain wealthy Gentile used to reside near **31a** Joseph Moḳir Šabbaṯ—meaning "he who holds precious the Sabbath." He was so named because he used to be frugal with his food and drink all week long, in order to have plenty for the expenses of the Sabbath, as he was not a well-to-do man. Now the astrologers said to the Gentile, "Know that this neighbor of yours, this Jew, will [yet] eat up all of your wealth and enjoy it." At this, alarm and fear came over him, and he took everything he had acquired, sold it, and bought with the proceeds a large jewel, which he wrapped in his kerchief, for fear of the Jew, and deposited in his sleeve, and began to scheme about [safeguarding] it.[12] One day, as he was walking along the bank of the Euphrates, the kerchief fell off of him and a fish swallowed it. That same fish was [later] caught on a Friday, and since it was a large fish **31b**, the fisherman was told, "You will find no one to buy it except Joseph Moḳir Šabbaṯ";[13] so he took it up to him. As soon as Joseph saw it, he bought it

9. H adds in Arabic: "that is to say, **30b** Blessed be God who is king over the lands and everyone in them."

10. H adds in Arabic (probably defective text; cf. Obermann, p. 35, n. 32): "and also the heavens are God's, He raised them up, and the earth He erected."

11. Source of this story: B. Shab 119a.

12. This sentence is difficult in H. Cf. Obermann, p. 35, n. 17/18. Blau suggests *kummihi* for *khummihi*. But cf. Ḳ (Abramson, p. 446), "and tied it up in his head-kerchief for fear of him, and would not leave it in his house, lest that Jew should scheme [to deprive him] of it."

13. H: *moḳer šabbe* (Aramaic).

from him, went into his house to prepare it, and found the jewel in its belly, which he thereupon sold for thirteen hundred dinars, and was thus delivered from his poverty, remaining wealthy for the rest of his life.

A story is also told[14] about a woman named Ḳimḥiṯ[15] who gave birth to seven sons and [lived] to see them all serving in the High Priesthood. The Sages came to her and asked her to tell them by what merit had she attained this [distinction]. She replied, "The ceiling of my house has never caught sight of my hair."[16] They said to her, "All[17] wheat (*qamḥ*), when ground, turns into [ordinary] flour, but your wheat, **32a** O Ḳimḥiṯ, when ground, turns into fine white flour." Observe then, O reader, what she was deemed worthy of, by reason of her fear of God and of His presence, and because of her great modesty.

It is said[18] that a fire broke out in a place where R. Huna was residing. All the houses there were consumed, but the fire did not touch the house of R. Huna nor the house of the woman who resided next to him. R. Huna thought that she was saved because of his own merit, but was told [later] in a dream, "By my life! Your merit is great, but it is this woman's custom to heat the oven in her house every day and lend it to her [indigent] neighbors, so that they might bake bread in it. It was for this attribute that she deserved being saved."

14. Source for this story: P. Yoma 1:1, 38d; Hor 3:5, 47d; B. Yoma 47a.

15. Literally "floury, flour woman," in Hebrew; or "wheaten, wheat woman," in Arabic.

16. Her modesty was so great that her head was always covered.

17. H: *kal-qamḥ*; Ḳ (Abramson, p. 446) *kull qamḥ*, agreeing with Obermann, p. 36, n. 13.

18. Source for this story: B. Ta 21b.

CHAPTER IX

[THE REWARD FOR THE OBSERVANCE OF THE COMMANDMENT OF THE FRINGES]

32b Know that a man may sometimes be consistently scrupulous in observing one particular commandment, and this [alone] may be the reason for [God's] great favor towards him and for his salvation from punishment. Because of this he may sometimes reap a bountiful reward also in this world.

Thus the Sages have transmitted[1] the story of a man who was extremely scrupulous in observing the commandment of the fringes. [Once] he heard that in one of the islands of the [Mediterranean] Sea there was a loose[2] Greek woman whose fee was four hundred dirhams. He took this amount with him and betook himself to her door. When her maidservant came out, he handed over the amount to her, and she took it in to her mistress. The latter said to her, "Tell him to return **33a** to us another time," and so he went away. When he returned, the woman gave him permission to enter, and as he came in he found the couches laid out, six of silver and the seventh of gold, while she herself was seated, disrobed, on the gold couch. As he was about to remove his wrap in [the process of] disrobing, the ends of the four fringes became twisted together and caught his eye,[3] whereupon he got down from the couch to the ground and fell on his face. When she saw him thus, she too got down to him and adjured him, [saying], "I shall not let you go[4] until you tell me what defect you noticed in me." He replied, "I have never seen anyone more beautiful than you, but we have a

1. Source for this story: B. Men 44a. Cf. Num. 15:38 ff.

2. H and Ḳ: *mutabaṭṭilah*. Source and some texts of HY have *zonah*, "harlot"; cf. Obermann, p. 37, n. 10; Abramson, p. 446.

3. Ḳ: *wa-tarāʾayū lahu kal-shuhūd*, "appeared to him as witnesses." Cf. Abramson, p. 448, and further on in the story (p. 42).

4. So Ḳ (Abramson, p. 448): *lā taraktuka*; cf. Obermann, p. 37, n. 30, and p. 38, line 4, *lā ukhallīka* (where Ḳ has again *lā taraktuka*).

commandment which our Lord had commanded us, called [the commandment of the] fringes, concerning which it is written twice, *I am the Lord your God* (Num. 15:41), [meaning, the first time], 'I shall punish whomsoever violates My commandments,' and the second time, 'I shall well reward **33b** whomsoever observes them.' When I noticed the fringes this time, they seemed to me to be four witnesses against me, and I feared the punishment and desired the reward therefor." Thereupon she swore again, [saying], "I shall not let you go[5] until you tell me your name and the name of the place where you reside, as well as the name of your teacher and the place of his residence." He gave her all this information and departed, happy at how he had overcome his desire and escaped from grievous sin.

After his departure the woman arose, divided all her possessions into three parts, giving one third to the government, one third to the poor, and keeping the other third, and set out until she reached the schoolhouse of R. Ḥiyya.[6] She then said to him, "My lord, I would like you to order someone to administer a ritual ablution to me,[7] for I wish **34a** to enter into your faith." R. Ḥiyya replied, "Begone from me! No doubt you lust after one of my disciples and desire to marry him." So she indited a letter [to him],[8] informing him of all that had happened between her and [his] disciple. When R. Ḥiyya learned these [facts], he said to the disciple, "Arise, my son, and marry her, for God has rewarded you for your fear of His punishment, and you deserve to attain her in accordance with the requirements of the holy law." He then directed that she undergo ritual immersion, and the disciple thereupon married her. And thus everything that she had laid out and prepared to come unto him unlawfully, did come unto him lawfully, and moreover there

5. See note 4, above.

6. Cf. Abramson, p. 413.

7. Literally "to bathe me," meaning the ritual immersion required prior to conversion.

8. i.e., a formal petition to the Sage.

remained [for him] the reward of the hereafter whose extent is known to no one.

We must learn[9] [a lesson] from this important commandment [of the fringes], for the numerical value of the word "fringes" (*ṣiṣiṯ*) is six hundred **34b** and thirteen, the same as the total number of commandments.[10] For if you sum up the numerical value of the letters of the word *ṣiṣiṯ*, they equal six hundred; add the eight threads and the five knots—two below and three above—and the reckoning reaches six hundred and thirteen, corresponding to the total of the commandments of the Torah.[11]

9. Source for this paragraph: Num. Rabbah 18, 152b.

10. The traditional total of positive (248) and negative (365) commandments in Scripture.

11. See the discussion of this paragraph in Abramson, p. 414.

CHAPTER X[1]

[THE REWARD FOR THE OBSERVANCE OF EVEN A MINOR COMMANDMENT]

We sometimes find that one who observes a most insignificant and slight commandment[2] earns thereby an immediate reward. Thus R. Zakkai said[3] to his disciples, when they asked him about the reason for [his][4] long life, "I have never sanctified Sabbath eve except over grape wine. One Friday I did not have any wine over which to perform the sanctification. When my mother saw that I was overcome with great anxiety and was perplexed about this matter, she sold her veil and bought **35a** me some wine over which I then performed the sanctification on that night. It was not long before she [died and] left me three hundred jugs of wine." It is said that he himself, after his death, left to his son three thousand jugs. That is why the Sages have said, "He who is punctilious in lighting the [Hanukkah][5] lamp will have sons who are disciples of the wise; he who is punctilious about [the commandment of] the mezuzah will merit a fine dwelling; he who is punctilious about the sanctification of the [Sabbath or festival] day will merit [full] jars[6] of wine."[7]

The Creator may sometimes bestow upon a righteous man a more generous boon [than he seems to deserve], according as His wisdom may deem proper, and it is not for us to ask, "Why did He favor this one and slight that one?" For I have already stated previously that all of this is [done by Him] with truth and justice.

1. From here to the end of the work chapter numbers are missing in H and are supplied by a later hand; cf. Obermann, p. 39, n. 23.
2. [Read *man faᶜala ahwana shay*ᵓ*in*; so Ḳ (Abramson, p. 448).—LN]
3. Source for this story: B. Meḡ 27b.
4. As emended by Obermann, p. 40, n. 3; confirmed by Ḳ (Abramson, p. 448).
5. So Ḳ and source (Obermann, p. 40, n. 18; Abramson, p. 448).
6. H has: *bi-ḡĕrono,* literally "in his throat." Source, HY, and Ḳ have: *zoḵeh u-mĕmalle*ᵓ *garbe yayin*. Cf. Obermann, p. 40, n. 20, and Abramson, p. 448.
7. B. Shab 23b.

[R. ḤANINA BEN DOSA]

Thus we observe R. Ḥanina ben Dosa,[8] for the sake of whose merit God supported and sustained the whole world, **35b** while he himself had no sustenance save four hundred dirhams' [weight][9] of carobs every week, with which he maintained himself from one Sabbath eve to the next, and nothing else. As the Sages have said, "R. Judah said, citing Rab: Every day a heavenly voice would go forth and declare, 'All the world is sustained only for the sake of Ḥanina, My son, yet My son Ḥanina is satisfied with one *ḳab̲* of carobs from one Sabbath eve to the next.'"

Whenever his wife saw people cooking and preparing [food] for the Sabbath, while she had nothing to make ready, she would feel in her heart shame and disgrace before the neighbors' womenfolk. She would therefore arise, light the fire, and heat the oven, in order to make them think that she had something to make ready. **36a** One Friday one of her women neighbors said to herself, "Why does this woman light the oven, seeing that we know that she has nothing [to prepare]?" So she went to look in the oven, and [behold], she found it full of bread, and she found also a kneading bowl full of dough. She then called out to R. Ḥanina's wife, "O So-and-so, come out, for the bread is ready. Hurry up and fetch something to take it out with, lest it be burned"—R. Ḥanina's wife had concealed herself out of shame before her neighbor. At this she came out with bread-baking utensils in her hand, and baked all [the dough] there was, out of what God had provided for the sake of her heartbreak.

Many were the [other] wonders that God performed for her for the sake of her prayer and her merit. Thus[10] she once mistook vessels of vinegar for vessels of oil and filled the lamp with vinegar. **36b** She then lighted the lamp without noticing

8. Source for this story: B. Ta 24b–25a.

9. Dirham here refers to a weight (today ca. 3 grams, according to *EI*², *2*, 319). The following ḳab̲ (AV: cab) is a Biblical dry measure (2 Kings 6:25).

10. Source for the following story: B. Ta 25a.

her mistake, but when evening came she noticed [that] it [was not bùrning], and was greatly upset by it. When R. Ḥanina came home and saw her so upset, he asked her what was the matter, and she told him. He said to her, "Do not distress yourself. He who has permitted the lighting of oil will permit the lighting of vinegar." It is said that with this [same vinegar-burning light] he also kindled the haḇdalah lamp[11] [the next evening].

R. Ḥanina's wife once said to him,[12] "Husband, ask your Lord to supply me with a little of what he has prepared for you in the hereafter." He accordingly asked his Lord, and was given a table-leg of gold. That same night he saw in his dream that the rest of his companions were seated before full-legged tables, while his own table was short one leg. **37a** When he woke up, he told his wife about it, and she said to him, "Pray to God that the leg be returned to its place." He did so, and his contrition was accepted. The Sages then said, "The latter [miracle] is even greater than the former." For it is not the way of our Lord to grant a request, and then take back what He has given, or as the Sages have put it, "There is a tradition: A thing once given may not be taken away."[13]

It would take too long to detail and enumerate the tales and stories concerning him, and the wonders and miracles that were wrought for him and at his hand, how no request of his was ever in vain but that it would be answered forthwith. Thus once, while walking along the highway, rain overtook him, and he said, "Should the whole world be in comfort, while Ḥanina is in distress?" At once the rain was held back. Then, **37b** having reached his house, he said, "Should the whole world be in distress, while Ḥanina is in comfort?" At once the rain came down again. Behold then the height of his rank with his Creator—[and yet] how straitened were his circumstances in his earthly life!

11. Marking the termination of the Sabbath or festival day.
12. Source for the following two paragraphs: B. Ta 25a, 24b.
13. [For a more correct text of this paragraph see Ḳ (Abramson, p. 450).—LN]

The believer should therefore take to heart all that I have mentioned, and should not feel resentful if distress overtakes him, for this distress will only increase his reward and enhance his recompense, as the Sages have said,[14] "Whosoever rejoices in [his] afflictions in this world brings about salvation in the hereafter." And they have said,[15] "They who act out of love and delight in [their] afflictions, of them does Scripture say, *But they that love Him be as the sun when he goeth forth in his might* (Jud. 5:31)." He should know that his Creator chooses for him a better thing than what he may choose for himself, and that He Great and Mighty **38a** "lavishes good upon the wicked in this world, in order that they may descend to the lowest grade [in the next], as it is said, *There is a way which seemeth right unto a man, but the end thereof are the ways of death* (Prov. 14:12).[16] And He brings afflictions upon the righteous in this world, in order that they may inherit the next, as it is said, *Though thy beginning was small, yet thy end should greatly increase* (Job 8:7)."[17]

14. Source: B. Ta 8a.
15. B. Yoma 23a, and elsewhere.
16. H adds in Arabic: "that is to say, There exists a path that appears straight to man, but its end is death."
17. The entire citation from B. Ḳid 40b. H adds in Arabic: "the meaning of it is that though his beginnings be miserable, he will be recompensed in the hereafter with ample good."

CHAPTER [XI]

[THE SHINING ROBE]

Know that I will now commence to treat of those whose beginning was small, while their end prospered greatly,[1] **38b** seeing that it is such that I intended [to discuss] in this my book.

The Sages[2] say that R. Eleazar and R. Joshua went up to Jerusalem at the time of the pilgrimage, and on the eve of the Day of Atonement were walking about in the Temple, when an angel appeared to them holding in his hand a brilliant robe which shone like the sun, but lacked a collar. One of them said to the other, "I have no doubt but that this robe is intended for one of us." So they approached the angel and adjured him [to tell them] for whom it was [meant]. He replied, "That which has been prepared for the two of you is finer and better than this. This present robe is for a person in Ascalon whose name is Joseph the gardener."

After the days of the pilgrimage had ended, the two of them left Jerusalem together in search of that man. When they arrived [in Ascalon], **39a** the most noted, great, and noble men of the town came out to meet them and bid them welcome, and asked them to accept their hospitality. But they refused all of it, and instead said to them, "We will be the guests of no one but Joseph the gardener." So they were taken to him, and looked at him, and behold, he was in the middle of the garden picking herbs. They greeted him, and he returned their greeting with the utmost courtesy. The two of them then said to him, "We have come to ask for your hospitality," whereupon he fell upon his face, bowing down and kissing their feet, and saying, "My lords, you have left people of substance and wealth and have

1. A paraphrase of Job 8:7.

2. Obermann (p. 44, n. b) found no Rabbinic source for this story. Cf., however, the article by G. Scholem in *Tarbiṣ 24*, 290–306, in which he speaks of the influence of this story upon the Zohar (p. 302), and the further study by D. Baneth (*Tarbiṣ 25* [1957], 331–36), tracing this theme in Jewish and Islamic lore.

condescended to come to me. But God is my witness that I have nothing [to eat] but two loaves of bread." To which they replied, "We will accept and be satisfied with what you have **39b** and will not trouble you to prepare anything else for us." So he brought forth the two loaves, and the two men ate, pronounced Grace after Meals, and then said to him, "You have seen that we were looking for you and not for the other people of the town, and now we wish you would tell us what is your occupation." He replied, "My lords, you behold my poverty and misery. I have no other occupation than tending this plot of land, as you have seen [me do]." They said, "Nevertheless you must tell us whether you have been on this plot of land since your childhood, or only recently." He replied, "My lords, if you wish to learn what I shall explain to you, and to be told about the rest of my affairs, I will answer your question and will gladly explain it to you. **40a** My late father was one of the most great, noted, and wealthy people of the town, but after his death all his wealth was lost and slipped out of my hand, and only a little remained for me. When the people of the town saw me in dire straits, after having been well-to-do, and knew that my wealth was gone and wasted, they drove me out of the town, and so I took refuge on this plot of land, established on it this garden, and planted in it what you see. Out of everything that I sell from it, I take one half to maintain ourselves, while the other half I spend in charity to the poor."

The two of them then said to him, "God Most Praised and High has verily prepared much good for you, for we have seen in **40b** Jerusalem, in the hands of an angel, a robe of such-and-such description, and he has told us that it was [meant] for you, but the collar thereof was missing. That is why we have come here to you, to meet you and to learn how you became worthy of it. Rejoice therefore in what God has bestowed upon you, and continue to do what you have been doing." At this he blessed them and thanked them, and then escorted them until they left him.

His wife thereupon said, "I have heard what the Sages of Israel have told you about the imperfection of your robe. Now do what I tell you, and expend in alms a sum sufficient to cause your robe to be made perfect." He replied, "I have heard your words. What you say is good and what you suggest is fine, but you know my poverty and that I possess nothing." **41a** She said, "I will advise you, and if you accept my advice, you will succeed." Thereupon he asked her, "What is your advice?" She replied, "Take me out and sell me in the market place,[3] then go and spend my price in almsgiving, and thereby you will become worthy of the completion of the robe." He said, "I am afraid to sell you, for your future master may commit a transgression because of you [by forcing you to submit to his desire], so that the robe would be lost completely, and in seeking small gain we would suffer great loss." She replied, "I pledge and swear to you with a most stringent oath that I will allow no other man to approach me, even if it costs me my life." So she swore thus to him, and he went forth and sold her, and expended her price in charity to the poor.

Now the man who had bought her conceived a passion for her and proposed to turn over to her the keys to his treasure house, but she said to him, "Master, I am not **41b** suited to being keeper of the treasure house." She continued to resist his passion for her, and refused to grant him her consent, whereat he became angry with her and handed her over to his shepherd. The shepherd, too, kept attempting to seduce her, while she kept holding him off, and he therefore embittered her life and treated her badly, but she bore her tribulations with patience. After a while her husband passed by the place [where she was living], and when he noticed her he disguised himself, drew near to her, and saw how greatly she had changed and how her body had wasted away. Thereupon he asked, "Would you like me to buy you from your master and have you marry me?" She replied, "I am a married woman, and am therefore not permitted to marry another man." He kept speaking com-

3. Cf. the story of Elijah asking to be sold, below, Chap. XXI.

passionately and gently to her, and even offered her money to make her consent, but she refused **42a** and remained firm in her oath and in her righteousness. When her husband perceived and realized that she was steadfast in her sworn promise, he revealed to her that he was her husband, and they both wept bitterly. Forthwith their cry rose up to God Most Praised and High, and a voice came forth proclaiming, "Rejoice, O man, for thy robe has been completed. Moreover the robe of thy wife is even finer than thine, for she is the cause of thy robe's completion. Now go to such-and-such a place, where there is a treasure hidden by thy father." He thereupon went to that place, dug down, and found a great treasure in gold and precious jewels, out of which he redeemed his wife from her master. Thereafter they both continued to perform acts of benevolence and charity, and lived on in far greater comfort than heretofore.

42b How bountiful is God's graciousness and how great His kindness to whomsoever cries out to Him sincerely out of distress and pain, whereupon He delivers him from it, as His saintly one, [David], has said, *Out of my straits I called upon the Lord; He answered me with great enlargement* (Ps. 118:5).[4] And if He is quick of answer to individuals out of [His] people, all the more proper and fitting for the community of His people that He will hasten to deliver them and save them from distress, as it is said, *For what great nation is there, that hath God so nigh unto them,* etc. (Deut. 4:7)[5]; and it is also said, *In all their affliction He was afflicted, and the angel of His presence saved them;* **43a** *in His love and in His pity He redeemed them; and He bore them, and carried them all the days of old* (Isa. 63:9).[6] And His saintly one, [David], has said, *The eyes of the Lord are toward the righteous, and His ears are open*

4. H adds in Arabic: "that is to say, out of distress and sore straits I called out to God, and He answered me with His mercy and graciousness."

5. H adds in Arabic: "that is to say, The other nations do not possess [anything] like the mercy of God to us and His tenderness toward us."

6. H adds in Arabic: "that is to say, In every distress He helps them and orders salvation, to help them forever."

unto their cry (Ps. 34:16).[7] And it is also said, *Thy people also shall be all righteous, they shall inherit the land forever; the branch of My planting, the work of My hands, wherein I glory* (Isa. 60:21).[8] And it is said further, *The Lord is nigh unto all them that call upon Him, to all that call upon Him in truth* (Ps. 145:18),[9] **43b** as it is also said, *Though I walk in the midst of trouble, Thou quickenest me*, etc. (Ps. 138:7).[10] Multiply therefore thanks and praise [to Him].

7. H adds in Arabic: "that is to say, God's mercy is toward the righteous, and He hears their prayers."

8. H adds in Arabic: "that is to say, All of His people are righteous forever. They shall inherit the land by the righteousness of the goodness of their deeds."

9. H adds in Arabic: "that is to say, God is near to all who call upon him in truth. He will deliver us and exact vengeance from our enemies and oppressors."

10. H adds in Arabic: "that is to say, When I am in distress, I call upon Thee, and Thou savest me from my enemies."

CHAPTER [XII]

[WHOSO FINDETH A WIFE FINDETH A GREAT GOOD (PROV. 18:22)]

Know[1]—may God vouchsafe you good [things]—that after R. Ḥananiah ben Teradion was executed, the Roman emperor commanded that his daughter[2] be made to dwell in the pavilion of harlots. Her sister Beruriah, who was the wife of R. Meir, said to her husband, "My lord, perhaps you could contrive some stratagem to rescue her from that place, for her being there is a great disgrace to me [also]." So he took with him four hundred dinars and went off, saying to himself, "If no man has yet approached her, and no transgression has been committed because of her, **44a** God Most High will surely perform a miracle for her and help me to rescue her. If, however, she has already surrendered herself to some man and has given in, she can hardly be rescued." Thereupon, having disguised himself and changed his appearance, he said to her, "Take this gold and let me seclude myself with you." She replied, "I am ritually unclean, and I have no way to do this." Whereat R. Meir said [to himself], "I have no doubt now but that she has not surrendered herself to any man and no transgression has been committed because of her." He then went to the guard and said to him, "Give me this girl, and take these four hundred dinars. Should the emperor ask you [about it], use half of it to save yourself, and the other half will be left for you. If he waxes wroth with you and [threatens] to punish you, and you see distress overtaking you from his direction, cry out, 'O Lord of Meir, save me from him!', **44b** and no evil, or anguish, or harm will affect you." The guard replied, "What proof and evidence [do you have] for this?" He said to him, "There are man-eating

1. Source of this story: B. AZ, 17b–18b.

2. According to source it was the daughter of R. Ḥananiah who was consigned to a brothel; for *ummuhu* read *ibnatuhu* (Hirschberg, p. 29, n. 1).

dogs in the treasure house of the emperor. Let me enter among them, so that I may prove this to you." So the guard let him in to them, and when they sprang at him to devour him, he cried, "O God of Meir, save me!", and the dogs forthwith desisted from him and did not harm him. Thereupon the guard handed over the girl, having been convinced of the sure certainty [of the promise], and took the gold, while R. Meir went off with her. When the emperor heard the story, he ordered the execution of the guard by crucifixion, but when they drew near to him to put him to death, he cried out, "O Lord of Meir, save me!", and no one was able to come at him to do him harm. So they said to him, "Tell us the story," and he told them everything that had happened to him. They then said to him, "Draw for us **45a** a likeness of this man upon the gate of the city," and he did so, whereupon the emperor issued a proclamation, [saying], "Whosoever has seen a man resembling this likeness, let him bring him to the king." One day R. Meir was recognized, but fled from his pursuers and entered the Street of the Harlots, whereat they let him go, saying, "No one described as possessed of such virtues would enter such a place." R. Meir then took his wife and all that he possessed and moved to Iraq.

Observe then this righteous woman, how having preserved her virtue, God Most High permitted her to be rescued. It was of such persons that the wise one, [Solomon], said, *Grace is deceitful, and beauty is vain; but a woman that feareth the Lord, she shall be praised* (Prov. 31:30).[3] **45b** Righteous women should pattern themselves after such women and should learn from them and from their like, and should not be among those women of whom it is said, *But a woman among all those* [*which my soul sought*] *have I not found* (Eccl. 7:28b).

[THE PERFIDIOUS WIFE][4]

When Solomon said, *But a woman among all those have I not found*, he noticed that this [saying] dismayed the Sages of the

3. H adds in Arabic: "that is to say, Beauty and grace are delusions, but the woman who fears the Lord is the one who is praised and described [as having good attributes]."

Sanhedrin, so he said to them, "Do not be amazed at this. I shall prove it to you and make it evident." He thereupon ordered his menservants to seek out for him a man who had a wife of comely appearance and outstanding beauty, and they reported to him, "We have found that So-and-so has a wife of beautiful countenance," whereat he replied, "Bring her husband to me." His command was obeyed, and the husband was brought before him, whereupon the king said to him, "I have been told about the excellence of your deeds, which made me desire **46a** to have you near me. I therefore wish to have you marry my daughter, following which I will grant you my favor, increase your dignity, and raise your rank." The husband replied, "Master, I am the meanest of your servants in rank, and the least in importance," to which the king retorted, "This plea of yours is one more instance of your laudable qualities. But now go and kill your wife tonight, and bring her head to me in the morning; I shall then carry out my promise to you, and you will attain the highest rank and noblest position with me." The husband thereupon departed and came to his wife, meditating about how he could [bear to] kill her, who was possessed of such a degree of beauty and grace, all the more so as she was the mother of his children—he had two children by her. She said to him, "My lord, I see you pensive and worried this evening." He replied "[It is] because I am heartbroken." She then set **46b** a meal before him, but he would eat nothing, while she ate and went up to sleep. The husband resumed pondering in his heart, saying, "How can I kill my wife when I have little children by her? Is there anything more shameful and foul than this?" Whereupon he turned his mind away from this idea, but then bethought himself of the king's promises, and his attention turned back to the high station and elevated rank that he would attain, and the matter became easy in his mind, so he took hold of a sword that he had, drew it,

4. No direct Rabbinic source is known for this story, which belongs to the vast genre of tales about Solomon. But cf. a similar tale in *Bet ha-Midrash*, *4*, 26–30 (where it is told about a king of Arabia).

and approached her in order to cut off her head. But when he uncovered her, he found her sleeping, with the younger child lying on her chest and nursing at her breast, while the other child rested his head on her shoulder. He then resumed addressing himself, saying, "O my soul, how can I kill this wife of mine as well as my children, and thus lose both this world **47a** and the next? Moreover, it is possible that none of the king's promises will be fulfilled for me." Whereupon he sheathed his sword, saying, *The Lord rebuke thee, O Satan!* (Zech. 3:2). But then once again he reverted to his thought and remembered the king's promises, so he arose once more, drew his sword, and approached [her], and found her hair loose and shading the younger child. Again he said, "By God, I will do nothing of the kind! May God bless neither the king's daughter nor her riches!" So he sheathed his sword [a second time] and slept until the break of dawn, when behold, the king's messengers were at his door. They took him to the king, who asked him, "What have you done of that which I had commanded you?" He replied, "Master, thus-and-so happened to me, and I was unable to do this. Be not hard on your servant in this matter, **47b** for it is distressful to me." So the king let him go.[5]

Several days later the king sent for the man's wife, had her brought into his presence, and said to her, "I have heard of your high repute, your beauty, and your grace. I therefore desire to marry you and raise your rank above all my other wives, so that you will be their mistress. But I find no way to do so while you have a husband. Go then and kill your husband tonight, and bring his head to me in the morning"—the king knew that she would kill him and would have no mercy on him as he had had mercy on her—"I shall moreover give you a fine sword with which to kill him." He then gave her a sword made of tin—that is to say, [soft] lead—which he had polished for her to look [like an iron sword], though it was not so in reality.

5. HY has instead of this sentence: "So the king said, *Therefore now flee thou to thy place; I thought to promote thee unto great honor* (Num. 24:11)"; cf. Obermann, p. 53, n. 7/8.

So she took it and went off, without giving any further thought [to the matter], **48a** to her house and hid it.

When her husband came in in the evening, she met him with a deceitful heart, kissed his eyes and his head, and asked him, "My lord, what has kept you until now?" He replied, "Some business that came my way," and sat down, happy and at ease, while they ate. She then said, "Master, I would like to drink with you tonight, so that we might have some pleasure and enjoyment," to which he replied, "I grant your request and your desire." So they drank and enjoyed themselves, while she plied him with drink until he fell drunken upon his couch and slept. She then seized the sword and struck him with it, secure and trusting in what the king had told her, but the husband was awakened by the violence of the blow, to find her standing [over him] with the drawn sword in her hand. When she saw that he was awake and that the blow had not affected him at all, **48b** she fell to the ground in a faint. He rose to her [assistance] and said to her, "What made you do this?", whereupon she told him the whole story and what had passed between her and the king.

Next morning the king's messengers lost no time in coming for them and taking them to the king—the Sages of the Sanhedrin were already in his presence—and when the king saw the couple, he laughed and said to them, "Tell me all that has happened to you two." So the husband related all that had happened to him first, and then the wife related her own story. The king thereupon said, "I knew that she would have no mercy on you as you had mercy on her, and that is why I gave her the tin sword." Whereat the Sages realized and understood the truth of his words, *But a woman among all those have I not found*[6] (Eccl. 7:28b). **49a** Observe, then, [O reader], how much difference there is between the behavior of this one,[7] [the husband], and that one, [the wife].

6. H adds in Arabic: "that is to say, I have not found a woman who is as perfect as she should be."

7. H has pl. *ulāʾika*, and so does Ḳ (Abramson, p. 457), but the sing. *hadhā* seems to be required by the context.

Therefore have the Sages said,[8] "Rabba said: Come and see how excellent is a good woman, as it is written, *Whoso findeth a wife findeth a great good, and obtaineth favor of the Lord* (Prov. 18:22).[9] And," he continued, "how evil is a bad woman, as it is written, *And I find more bitter than death the woman whose heart is snares and nets* (Eccl. 7:26a)." And this is the explanation of this saying: How excellent is the woman whose deeds are commendable, and how evil and difficult is the woman of reprehensible qualities. As for the good woman, it is as the saintly one, [Solomon], has said, that he who has been **49b** vouchsafed a good woman has been vouchsafed a boon. If the [true] meaning of this verse is the literal one, how good is she whom the saintly one has extolled and Scripture has praised! If, on the other hand, what was intended [here] was the study of Torah, he who has been vouchsafed the learning thereof has [certainly] been vouchsafed a [precious] boon. "Woman" is thus used [in the latter case] in a metaphorical sense, and the best of the virtuous persons whose name has been used as a metaphor for Torah is thus the good woman; and this goodness which is praised lies in her deeds, not in her appearance, unless indeed she is both virtuous in behavior and lovely in appearance. She is most virtuous and best, however, if she has also a pleasant disposition. Contrariwise, how vicious and bitter is a bad woman, as it is said, *I find more bitter than death*, etc., the explanation of which is, "I have found her, the bad woman, more evil than death." If **50a** the explanation of this verse is literal, how evil is she whom the saintly one condemns and whom Scripture describes as more bitter than death! If, on the other hand, this verse is to be understood as referring to Gehenna, it should be sufficient for you that [Scripture] likens her to, and compares her with, Gehenna, and praises him who endeavors to escape from her. There is no doubt that it is he whose misdeeds are many and whose sins are great who will stumble over her and

8. The Rabbinic source for the following paragraph: B. Yeḇ 63b.

9. H adds in Arabic: "that is to say, Whosoever finds a good wife and is benefited through her, is as benefited as by performing the commandments."

will be ensnared by her, and will find no escape from her. Care and caution are required to escape from Gehenna and from anything resembling it.[10]

This is especially true if, in addition to [all] this, the bad woman's dower is large, and it is of such a case that it is said, *The Lord hath delivered me into their hands, against whom I am not able to stand* (Lam. 1:14),[11] and the Sages also speak of[12] "a bad woman the amount of whose marriage-writ is large." **50b** Among her characteristics is that as she sets the table [for her husband] she also sets her tongue for abuse and curses, or as the Sages put it, "She has ready for him both the dining tray and her mouth."[12]

Some[13] of the Sages were afflicted with wives of unsavory natural and moral qualities. Among them was Rab, whose wife contradicted everything he commanded her and everything he said to her. If he told her, "Cook small peas," she would cook lentils; and if he told her, "Cook lentils," she would cook small peas. When his son Ḥiyya grew up and saw her contradicting his father in everything he said to her, he would, when his father told him, "Ask your mother to prepare lentils for us," say to her, "My lord tells you to cook small peas," whereupon she would cook lentils **51a**, as his father had desired; and similarly everything that Rab would request him to ask her to prepare, he would tell her the opposite thereof, so that in contradicting his words she would in fact be doing what his father wished. One day Rab said to him, "My son, I see that your mother's disposition has improved, and her contrariness has been mended." He replied, "By your head, my lord, her nature has not changed, nor has she turned from her [former] ways. It is only that I tell her the opposite of what you say, so that as she turns your words around, she prepares what you

10. This is an expanded exposition by R. Nissim of the simile of the Talmud: a good woman = Torah; a bad woman = Hell. Cf. SER, 18, 92; B. Yeḇ 63b.

11. H adds in Arabic: "that is to say, I have fallen into a difficult situation, which I cannot endure."

12. B. Yeḇ 63b.

13. The following stories are found in B. Yeḇ 63a–b.

wish." Whereat his father said to him, "Your thoughtfulness and intelligence are admirable, and I rejoice at your insight, for this is what is meant by the saying, 'Out of your own loins comes forth he who teaches you wisdom.' However, do not continue to do so henceforth, lest you should become accustomed to untruth and set in it, as it is said, *They have taught their tongue* **51b** *to speak lies, they weary themselves to commit iniquity* (Jer. 9:4)."

R. Ḥiyya's wife likewise used to irritate and distress his heart, yet whenever he found anything [that might please her] he would hide it, in order to give it to her in the evening. Rab asked him, "[Why do you bring her gifts?] Do you not complain about her that she distresses your heart?" He replied, "Yes, but it is enough for me that she raises our children and saves us from the sin [of fornication]."

In the Land of Israel[14] they used to ask the bridegroom, "Are you *findeth* or *find*?"—[*findeth*] referring to *Whoso findeth a wife findeth a great good*, etc. (Prov. 18:22), and *find* referring to *I find more bitter than death* [*the woman*], etc. (Eccl. 7:26a).

The Sages have said that the remedy for a bad wife is that a man should take a co-wife in addition to her, if he can afford [to support] a co-wife, or as they have put it, "A bad wife, the amount of whose marriage-writ is large, should be given a rival at her side, as people say, **52a** '[Restrain her] with her rival, not with a thorny stick.'"[15] And they have also said, "A man cannot arouse [his wife's] jealousy except with her rival's thigh,"[16] that is to say, the co-wife is harder for her to bear than blows. This remedy is suitable for a wife whose marriage-writ amounts to so much money that her husband is unable to pay it. If, however, he is wealthy enough to afford the writ's amount, he should divorce her and be rid of the burden of [her] evil, as

14. *Bil-Shām*, literally "in Syria", but here, and usually, the Land of Israel.

15. B. Yeḇ 63b. The translation of this citation is based on the reading of the Aramaic in the Talmudic source and in Ḳ (Abramson, p. 459) rather than in H. The meaning of the saying is, "Let her be punished by having a rival, rather than by being beaten."

16. Cf. B. Meḡ 13a. For variants cf. Obermann, p. 58, nn. 6–8.

it is said, *Cast out the scorner, and contention will go out* (Prov. 22:10).[17] Ben Sira also has said,[18] *A good wife is a good gift, and shall be given into the bosom of him who fears God* (cf. Sir. 26:3). [And the Sages continued], "A bad wife is a plague on her husband. What is the remedy for her? He should divorce her and thus be cured of his plague."

Ben Sira has also explained this further, *A daughter is a deceptive treasure to her father; for fear about her he sleeps not at night* (cf. Sir. 42:9–10). **52b** That is to say, while she is little, he fears that she might be seduced. While she is growing up, he fears[19] that she might not mature nor develop the tokens of womanhood, inasmuch as she might turn out to be an *ʾaylonit̲*, meaning a dried up woman,[20] one who does not have protruding breasts, does not menstruate, has a deep voice indistinguishable from a man's, and feels pain whenever her husband goes in unto her. When she does mature, her father fears that she might not find a husband; [if she does marry], her husband fears that she might not give birth; and if she does give birth, he fears that when she grows old, she might turn into a witch and become one of those who destroy the world.[21]

[THE STORY OF YOḤANI BAT REṬIBI][22]

This is explained by the saying of the Sages, "A maiden overfond of prayer, or a gadabout widow,[23] brings destruction upon the world, [for example, one] like Yoḥani[24] bat Reṭibi." Now **53a** this woman was a widow who flaunted her piety, but

17. H adds in Arabic: "that is to say, Drive evil away from yourself."

18. Cited in B. Yeb̲ 63b; Sanh 100b.

19. [Read *yakhāfu* (so Ḳ, Abramson, p. 459).—LN]

20. Arabic *shaṭūr*, a woman with one breast gone dry; cf. Hirschberg, p. 35, n. 13. The explanation of *ʾaylonit̲* is from B. Yeb̲ 80b.

21. This entire Section, using Talmudic materials as indicated above, seems to be the author's exposition of Ben Sira, 42:11–14.

22. Cf. B. Soṭ 22a; variant, P. Soṭ 19a (cf. 18c). Cf. also Rashi to B. Soṭ 22a, *s.v.* Yoḥani bat Reṭibi.

23. Cf. the discussion of these two types by Lieberman, *Tarbiṣ 5* (1933), 101. He interprets the epithets as meaning "a fasting virgin and a gadabout widow." [Literally "sanctimonious widow," influenced by the next sentence.—LN]

24. H: Yoḥano; Ḳ: Yoḥana (Abramson, p. 461); but cf. Rabbinic sources.

was secretly a witch and used to cast spells upon every pregnant woman [to make her delivery difficult]. Whenever she learned that a woman's confinement was near and that her pains were growing strong, she would go to her and say, "Let me go and pray for you, and you will forthwith give birth." [She would then go home and revoke the spell, and the pregnant woman would be immediately delivered],[25] while [all] these [pregnant women] went on thinking that she was a righteous woman whose prayers were accepted [in heaven, and would befriend her so that she would pray for them].[26] One day she went out and left a boy in her house to watch it. The boy heard a [sound of] movement inside the house, but seeing no one, got up to search for it and found in the corner of the house a covered jar. He uncovered it, and behold, there in the jar was her magic. All of it, [having been exposed], became ineffective, and thereafter the pregnant women repeatedly gave birth without any need of her. **53b** Thus her situation became exposed and known, and the people of the place gathered together, condemned her to exile, and drove her out of their locality.

That is why the Sages have forbidden a man to teach his daughter Torah, or as the Mishnah puts it, "R. Eliezer said: Whosoever teaches his daughter Torah is as though he had taught her wantonness."[27] According to the conception of the Talmud, this is bound to lead her to corruption, manifold deceits, and spite,[28] or as the Sages have put it, "What is the reason for R. Eliezer's saying this? He interpreted the word *ᶜormah* (prudence) in *I, wisdom, dwell with ᶜormah* (Prov. 8:12) as 'cunning,' that is to say, whenever wisdom enters into a man, so does cunning enter into him." That is why Ben Sira has said, *A daughter is a deceptive treasure to her father*, etc. (cf. Sir. 42:9).

There are,[29] however, some women whose contrition is

25. H omits this sentence which occurs in HY and in Rashi (cf. Obermann, p. 59, n. 27), and also in Ḳ (Abramson, p. 461).

26. So Ḳ (Abramson, p. 461).

27. Soṭ 3:4.

28. Cf. B. Soṭ 21b.

29. Source for this paragraph: B. Soṭ 22a.

sincere, as R. Johanan has said, "We have learned **54a** the fear of sin from a maiden, and the earning of reward from a widow." Regarding the maiden he said, "I saw her fall upon her face after completing her prayer and say, 'O Lord of the worlds and Lord of lords, Thou hast created Paradise, and Thou hast created Hell-Fire; Thou hast created saints and sinners. I ask Thee[30] and plead with Thee, for the sake of Thy great Name, spare me from causing misadventure, or sin, or liability to punishment, to any creature.' And on another day I saw a widow who went at nightfall to the synagogue in my neighborhood to pray, although I knew that there was a synagogue in her own neighborhood. So I asked her, 'Why did you leave the synagogue in your neighborhood and come here?' And she replied, 'My lord, in order to gain recompense and earn reward **54b** for the additional steps from that synagogue to this.'"

A man should seek out the virtuous ones among women and keep away from the evil ones. Accordingly the Sages have commanded us [to endeavor] to marry a daughter of scholars, or else someone only slightly inferior to her, if we are unable to find the former. For they have said in the Talmud, "A man should always sell everything he has in order to marry a daughter of scholars. If he cannot find a daughter of scholars, let him marry a daughter of the great men of the generation. If he cannot find [such a one], let him marry a daughter of the heads of synagogues. If he cannot find [such a one], let him marry a daughter of alms collectors. If he cannot find [such a one], let him marry a daughter of teachers of infants. He should not [marry] a daughter of the unlearned, for they are [as detestable as] forbidden animals, and their women are [as unclean as] crawling things."[31]

And they have said also, "A man should sell everything **55a** he has in order to have his daughter marry a scholar, because marrying her off to an unlearned person is the same as if he had

30. So Ḳ, *fa-asʾaluka* (Abramson, p. 461).
31. B. Pes 49b.

tied her up and placed her before a lion."[32] And they went to such extremes in praising a person who marries off his daughter to a scholar, or[33] causes a scholar to gain some benefit at his hand, that they said, "All the prophets have prophesied only for the sake of him who marries off his daughter to a scholar or causes a scholar to gain some benefit from his wealth. As for the scholars themselves, *Neither hath the eye seen a God beside Thee, who worketh for him that waiteth for Him* (Isa. 64:3)."[34]

32. Cf. B. Pes 49a–b.
33. [Obermann's emendation (p. 62, n. 1) *wa-man* is confirmed by Ḳ (Abramson, p. 461).—LN]
34. B. Ber 34b.

CHAPTER [XIII]

[SOME STUDY TORAH IN POVERTY, SOME IN WEALTH]

I will now explain, in keeping with the purpose of this book, a tradition which reflects this theme, concerning the virtue of a woman, daughter of wealthy and eminent parents, whose own desire, and whose father's **55b** desire, was that she marry someone possessed of learning. Know[1] that [our] trustworthy forefathers have transmitted a tradition that a certain rich man in the Land of Israel was called Ben Kalba Śebuᶜa, a name derived from his generosity, for whosoever came to him hungry, be it even a dog (*kalb*), left him sated (*shabᶜān*).[2] R. ᶜAḳiba was his hired man, tending his flocks. Now Ben Kalba Śebuᶜa had a daughter, of goodly appearance and pleasing disposition. She came to R. ᶜAḳiba and said to him, "Marry me." He replied, "Very well," and betrothed her lawfully,[3] whereupon she left him [and went home]. When her father heard the story, he swore an oath that he would not give her any of his property, seeing that she had chosen for herself someone unsuitable **56a** for her. [Nevertheless she went to live with her husband].

Now R. ᶜAḳiba had nothing except a little straw which he spread out under the two of them, and they slept on it and used it for a pillow, for he had said to her, "You will have to be content with this; if I had anything [better], I would have made for you a [crown][4] of gold." While they were sleeping, someone knocked on their door, saying, "My lord, I have a wife who is about to give birth, but she has nothing to be delivered upon. Perhaps you have something." R. ᶜAḳiba replied, "We have nothing save a little straw." The man said, "Give me then some

1. Rabbinic source for this story: B. Keṯ 62b; B. Neḏ 50a; also found in *Mafteaḥ*, 36b.
2. For this etymology, cf. B. Giṭ 56a.
3. i.e., wrote out the *kĕṯubbah*, or marriage writ, and handed it to her.
4. Missing in H. Restored from Ḳ (Abramson, p. 463).

of it." So they gave him some of it, and R. ᶜAḳiba said to his wife, "We are still better off than others. Here is this one—he didn't even have any straw." Some say that this [poor] man was [really the prophet] Elijah.

After a while R. ᶜAḳiba's wife said to him, "If you will take my advice, go and study [Torah]." He followed her advice and went off to pursue his studies under R. Eliezer **56b** and R. Joshua for twelve years, upon the completion of which he returned home with twelve thousand disciples. When he arrived, he heard someone say to his wife, "I fully approve of what your father has done to you, inasmuch as you had married someone unsuited to you. Moreover, here he has gone off and left you for twelve years, the widow of a man still living."[5] She replied, "I wish he would continue away for another twelve years." When R. ᶜAḳiba heard this from her, [he said], "Since this is her wish, I will be guilty of no sin on her account [if I extend my absence]." So he returned to his place [of study] and stayed there another twelve years, whereupon he came home with twenty-four thousand[6] disciples. Apprised [of his arrival], the people of the city went forth to meet him, and he entered **57a** with great acclaim.

His wife, too, wanted to go out to meet him, but she had only one shabby garment, so a woman neighbor of hers said to her, "Take [this] pretty garment [of mine]; do not go out to meet him in this raggedy thing." She replied, "*A righteous man regardeth the life of his beast* (Prov. 12:10)"[7]—she meant, "My husband knows that I have nothing." So she went forth to him, and when she reached him and his retinue of disciples, she bent down to kiss his feet. Just as one of his disciples was about to push her away from him, R. ᶜAḳiba said to him, "Let her be! All that I have learned [of Torah], and all that you have

5. H: *armalat al-ḥayāt*; cf. 2 Sam. 20:3: *ʾalmĕnuṯ ḥayyūṯ*.

6. [So Ḳ (Abramson, p. 463). H has "a throng of disciples."—LN]

7. H has here "*The righteous considers the cause of the poor* (Prov. 29:7), [meaning] the judgment of the needy." Cf. Obermann, p. 64, n. 14/15. The translation here is based on Ḳ, which follows the Talmudic account; cf. Abramson, p. 463, and p. 464, n. 13.

learned from me, this woman is the cause of it and the root thereof." When her father Ben Kalba Śebuʿa heard that a great and learned man had come to the city, he said, "Let me go **57b** and ask him for a legal decision—perhaps he will find[8] a release for me from my vow, so that I may give my daughter something to live on, for the straitened circumstances in which I see her make by heart ache." So he entered in R. ʿAḳiba's presence, [without recognizing him], and told him about his vow, whereupon R. ʿAḳiba asked him, "For what reason did you do this?" He replied, "Because she married someone who could not read and had neither knowledge [of Torah] nor wealth." R. ʿAḳiba then asked him, "What if he had done as well as I?"[9] He replied, "My master, could he but read just one chapter, I would give her most of my wealth." At this R. ʿAḳiba said to him, "I am her husband!" Whereupon her father arose, kissed him upon his head, and gave her half of his wealth, [out of which] R. ʿAḳiba made for her a crown of gold, as he had told her and promised her. And thus were they delivered from their poverty, their hardships ceased, and their **58a** well-being increased. Observe then, [O reader], what he did attain through his great learning, despite his poverty.

Know[10]—may God vouchsafe you good works—that Hillel the Elder was a poor man, who labored all day long for half a dirham,[11] out of which he sustained himself with one quarter-dirham, and paid the other quarter to the academy watchman, so that he would let him enter the academy to hear the words of the living God from the mouths of Shemaiah and Abtalion.[12] It is said that one day, when he could find no one to hire him, he went to the academy, but the watchman would not let him enter. So he climbed to the roof of the academy and stuck his head in a dormer window, in order to hear the lecture. The day

8. So Ḳ, confirming Obermann's conjecture (p. 64, n. 26); cf. Abramson, p. 463.

9. i.e., in knowledge of Torah.

10. Rabbinic source for this story: B. Yoma 35b.

11. So Ḳ (Abramson, p. 465). Missing in H. HY: *zuz*.

12. A favorite story in the era of R. Nissim; cf. Schechter, *Saadyana*, *I*, 195 f.

was cold and snowy, and because of his concentration on listening, though the snow covered him, he was unaware of it and did not feel it, **58b** so intense were his eagerness, attention, and desire, until evening, when everyone left the academy. [By that time] he was unable to free himself from the snow, nor could he move from his place, but had to remain there until morning. When morning came, Shemaiah said to Abtalion, "What is the matter with our house[13] today that it is so dark, and there is no light in it as on other days?" So they climbed up to inspect it and found Hillel near death. They forthwith took him down, removed his [frozen] clothes, put dry clothes on him, and lit a fire before him until he got warm.

That is why[14] the Sages say that even a poor man has no excuse before his Lord for failure to pursue Torah. If therefore he uses his poverty as an excuse, he should be asked, "Are you more destitute than Hillel the Elder?"—to which he can find **59a** no answer. Likewise a rich man, if he says, "I was too busy with my wealth," should be asked, "Are you wealthier than Eleazar ben Ḥarsom?" Eleazar's father had left him many estates and gardens, and besides them ships at sea, yet not once did he go to inspect them, but rather left this to his servants, while he himself sat in pursuit of the knowledge [of Torah]. To this query the rich man, too, can put forth no argument. So also a rake, if he excuses himself on the ground that his lust [had overcome him and distracted him][15] from the pursuit of Torah, should be asked, "Were you more [sorely tempted] than the righteous Joseph, of whom it is said that[16] his master's wife not only was very beautiful but would also adorn herself for him every day with all kinds of ornaments and would wear clothes of different colors? **59b** Yet he, though himself young and handsome, would not respond to her nor give in to his passion"—thus the rake, too, can find no argument or [valid]

13. So Ḳ (Abramson, p. 465). H has *mā labithnā*, emended by Obermann (p. 65, n. 35) to *mā albathanā*, "How late we are!"

14. Cf. B. Yoma 35b.

15. Supplied from Ḳ (Abramson, p. 465).

16. [Read, with Ḳ (Abramson, p. 465), *fīhi anna*.—LN]

excuse to put forth. "Therefore," [conclude the Sages], "we find that Hillel the Elder obligates the poor, Eleazar ben Ḥarsom obligates the rich, and the righteous Joseph obligates the wicked."

Nor is there any excuse for the sons of the unlearned to fail in the pursuit of Torah on account of their parents, for this is not something that is received by inheritance from one's parents.[17] Parentage counts only when added to learning and good works—otherwise parentage is of no use, as R. Dosa[18] has said when the Sages announced to him, "Our lord, R. Eleazar ben Azariah, who is of the tenth generation from Ezra
60a the Scribe, is standing at the door." He replied, "Why did you bother [to mention] this [genealogical] specification? If in addition to this parentage and this descent, he possesses also learning and good manners, he has reached a doubly high station. If, however, despite this descent, he lacks learning, may God burn him in [Hell-]Fire!" Indeed learning without descent is preferable [to descent without learning].[19]

[DESPISE NOT PROSELYTES]

Thus we see that Shemaiah and Abtalion, notwithstanding their virtue and great learning, were proselytes, for they were descendants of Sennacherib, as it is said in the Talmud,[20] "Descendants of Sennacherib gave public lectures in Torah. Who were they? Shemaiah and Abtalion."

It is said that in the days of the Roman emperor,[21] a certain High Priest left the Sanctuary after the completion of the worship, and the crowd went out [after him] **60b**, but when they met Shemaiah and Abtalion, they left the High Priest and followed them. The High Priest became sorely vexed at this,

17. Cf. B. Neḏ 81a.
18. Cf. B. Men 53a. But see Hirschberg, p. 40, n. 7, for variant reading.
19. Supplied from Ḳ (Abramson, p. 467).
20. Cf. B. Giṭ 57b.
21. Source for this story: B. Yoma 71b. HY and Talmudic source have here instead: "that on the Day of Atonement," as does Ḳ (Abramson, p. 467). [In what follows, Ḳ confirms several emendations suggested by Obermann.—LN]

and when he parted from Shemaiah and Abtalion he said to them, "May the descendants of Gentiles come in peace!", wishing to reproach them for being of heathen stock. Their reply to him was that he who is of heathen stock but does good works is better than he who is of Aaron's stock but does not do the like of Aaron's works, or as the Sages have put it, "May the descendants of Gentiles who do the like of Aaron's works come in peace!" The Mishnah, in the Section dealing with the saving of life and the return of lost property, states expressly,[22] "A bastard who is a disciple of the wise has precedence over a High Priest who is an unlearned man."

There is also a tradition concerning Onkelos the proselyte,[23] he who laid the foundation of the Targum of the Torah[24] and taught it **61a** to the people. Namely, it is said that when he became a proselyte, the Roman emperor sent messengers to him to fetch him, but he did not cease reciting to them verses from Scripture and entertaining them with tales of the [Biblical] forefathers, until he caused them, too, to become proselytes. So the emperor sent other messengers to him and ordered them not to speak to him, out of fear that he might do with them as he did with the first ones. When they reached Onkelos, he said to them, "Listen to just one question from me—no more." They replied, "Ask [it]." He said to them, "It is well known that the tax-collector bears the torch before the general officer, the general officer before the vizier, and the vizier before the emperor. Does the emperor bear it before anyone?" They replied, "No." He continued, "Yet see what God has done for the Children of Israel, **61b** as it is said, *And the Lord went before them by day in a pillar of cloud* [*. . . and by night in a pillar of fire*], etc. (Exod. 13:21). Accept [therefore the true faith] from me, and become proselytes." So they, too, accepted [the Jewish faith]. The emperor then sent still other messengers and gave them the strictest orders to say not one word to him nor to reply to

22. Hor. 3:8.
23. Source for the following story: B. AZ 11a.
24. The Aramaic translation (or paraphrase) of the Pentateuch. Cf. B. Meg̃ 3a.

anything he might say, and so they went forth and seized him. As they were traveling along the road, he saw a door bearing a mezuzah, put his hand over it, and stopped, saying to them, "Is it not the emperor's custom to dwell within the castle, while his servants stand guard over him at the gate, or do they dwell within the castle, while the emperor stands guard over them?" They [could not help] replying, "No, the servants stand guard over the emperor." He continued, "Yet God Most High does not act thus with the Children of Israel. Rather they dwell within their houses, while He **62a** watches and stands guard over them from without, as it is said, *The Lord is thy watchman*, etc. (Ps. 121:5)." So they, too, became proselytes. When the emperor saw this, he sent no more messengers to him. Observe then, [O reader], the greatness of his learning, his virtue, his faith, and his piety, notwithstanding that he, too, was a proselyte.

Neither parentage nor descent are of any use to a man unless there is added to them learning [in Torah] and good works. That is why, when the son of a Sage asked his father, who was on the brink of death, to commend him to his colleagues and disciples, he replied, "Your own deeds can cause you to be far [from them], and your own deeds can cause you to be near to them."[25] And the Sages have said, "Beware of the sons of the unlearned, for out of them may come forth Torah."[26]

[THE UNLEARNED AND THE DISCIPLES OF THE WISE]

I must, however, mention something of their[27] [negative] characteristics, so that we should not exaggerate their worth. **62b** It is typical of [some of] them that when they acquire a little knowledge, vainglory overcomes them, and they waste the little that they have learned [by associating] with people who do not ask them [about matters of learning]. As the Sages have

25. Ed 5:7.
26. B. Sanh 96a.
27. Meaning the unlearned, particularly such as have let a little knowledge inflate their self-esteem.

said,[28] "*In the heart of him that hath discernment wisdom resteth* (Prov. 14:33)—this is a scholar the son of a scholar; *but in the inward part of fools it maketh itself known* (*ibid.*)—this is a scholar the son of an unlearned man. ʿUlla said: As people are wont to say, A coin in an [empty] pitcher makes rattle-rattle."[29] They are likened in this vainglory of theirs to a coin inside an [empty] pitcher; when the pitcher is shaken, the coin rattles, whereas if the pitcher were full, the coin would not have rattled. Indeed, if scholars and men of high rank are seated together, and are asked a question to which such a one happens to know the response, you see him rush forward to answer it in their presence. **63a** This is the manner of boors. Only fools and rogues rush forward to speak and hurry to answer concerning a matter without self-restraint, deliberation, and reflection. As the Sages have put it,[30] "*And Memucan answered before the king and the princes* (Esther 1:16)—from this [we learn] that a boor jumps out [in front]," for these were a company of learned men, while he was the least of them in rank, since he is listed last, as Scripture says, *And the next unto him was Carshena*, etc., [*and Memucan*] (Esther 1:14). Therefore, because of his rushing forward to answer, he is called a boor.

It is proper for such [boors] to answer only in a place where there is no scholar, and where the people[31] are inferior to them in learning and knowledge—only there is it proper for them to speak up, as the Sages have said, "In a place where there is no man, there be thou a man."[32] Among those who do not understand [learning], **63b** they occupy a high station, but when they speak up in the presence of one who is more intelligent than they, and he demolishes their arguments and exposes their error, those [who had previously respected them] begin to look at them with a disparaging eye.

How becoming is silence, yea, even to scholars! As the Sages

28. B. BM 85b.
29. i.e., an ignorant man makes too much of what little he knows.
30. Cf. B. Meḡ 12b.
31. [*Huwa* seems to be a misreading of a cursively written *al-qawm*.—LN]
32. B. Ber 63a.

have said, "Silence is becoming to Sages—all the more so to fools,"[33] and they have also said, "A word is worth one *sela*ᶜ,[34] silence is worth two."[35] They have said further something that is even more expressive than this, "Silence is the universal medicine."[35] However, in places where [speaking up] is proper and suitable, especially if it serves to improve and benefit people, there scholars are obligated **64a** to speak profusely and in detail, or as the Talmud puts it,[36] "R. Isaac said: What is the meaning of the verse, *Indeed in silence speak righteousness* (Ps. 58:2a)? What should be a man's guideline in this world? He should act like a mute, [and keep silent]. Should he perhaps act thus also in regard to matters of Torah? [No indeed], for the verse says expressly, *speak righteousness*;" and Scripture says also,[37] *And my tongue shall speak of Thy righteousness* (Ps. 35:28) [—in both instances righteousness stands for Torah].

I say that this is why Hillel pursued learning notwithstanding his extreme poverty and destitution; and additionally [he did so] because of his great piety and his noble disposition. True tradition has consequently stated[38] that the rule in every disputed case is according to the School of Hillel rather than according to the School of Shammai—students will find [the few exceptions to this rule] there, [in my commentary on the first chapter of the Talmudic tractate Yĕḇamoṯ].[39] The Talmud cites several stories [about Hillel] which ought to instruct us how **64b** to conduct ourselves, as the Sages have put it,[40] "A man should always be as humble as Hillel, and should not be as intolerant as Shammai."

33. B. Pes 99a.

34. A weight and a coin in Talmudic times, equal to one sacred or two common shekels.

35. B. Meḡ 18a. Followed in H by Arabic paraphrase.

36. B. Ḥul 89a.

37. Read *wa-qāla* here, and add *aqūlu* at the beginning of the next paragraph (Abramson, p. 470).

38. Cf. Tos Yeḇ 1:13; P. Ber 3b.

39. Confused text in H (Obermann, p. 72, n. 16/17), clarified by Abramson, p. 470.

40. B. Shab 30b.

CHAPTER [XIV]

[THE VIRTUE OF PATIENCE]

Know[1]—may God Most High guide you aright—that two men made a wager that whichever of them would [succeed in] enraging Hillel the Elder and leading him to anger and fury, would win from his friend four hundred dirhams. One of them then went on a Friday evening to Hillel's door and shouted, "Is Hillel home?" Hillel, [who was bathing], replied, "Yes, my son," put on his robe, and came out to him, saying, "Come in. Do you perchance want anything?" The man replied, "Yes, [I have] a question I came to ask." Hillel said, "State your question." The man then asked, "Why are the heads of the people of Baghdad elongated and not round?" Hillel replied, "My son, you have indeed asked **65a** a difficult question. The answer to it is that their midwives are unskilled, and at the time of birth they do not know enough to tie up the [newborn infant's] head, so their heads remain [long] like this." The man went away, but after Hillel had re-entered and resumed bathing, he came back and shouted, "Is Hillel home?" Hillel came out, asking, "Did you perhaps forget something?" The man replied, "Yes. Why are the eyes of the people of Damietta bleary and small?" Hillel said, "Because they live in a sandy region, and there are [strong] winds there; so they keep their eyes [almost] shut because of the sand. Eventually they become [used to] keeping their eyes [almost] shut, and that is how their eyes come to [seem] bleary." Again the man went away, then once more returned, and when Hillel came out to him, asked him a similar question. Finally the man himself became disgusted with the [repeated] going and coming, while Hillel grew neither **65b** angry nor furious. When the man saw that he could not enrage Hillel, he asked him, "Are you the one who is called the dean of the people of Israel?" Hillel replied,

1. Rabbinic source for this story; B. Shab 30b f.

"Yes." The man exclaimed, "May God Most High not multiply such as you among men! You have caused me to lose four hundred dirhams." Hillel said to him, "My son, beware of your temper. Many a [wagered] dirham has been lost in this manner, yet I was never moved to fury." And so the man [finally] went off and weighed out the four hundred dirhams. There are many other stories concerning Hillel which I will not deal with, for it is impossible to retell them without the book becoming too long and the reader becoming weary of it.

I will say, however, that a man should master his disposition
and expand his bosom, so as not to succumb to anger nor **66a**
constrict his disposition, for this is reprehensible and its result is blameworthy, as the wise one, [Solomon], has said, *Therefore remove vexation from thy heart, and put away evil from thy flesh*, etc. (Eccl. 11:10). And the Sages have said,[2] "R. Samuel bar Naḥmani said, citing R. Jonathan: Any man who loses his temper is exposed to all the torments of Gehenna, as it is said, *Therefore remove vexation from thy heart*, [*and put away evil from thy flesh*], etc. Now *evil* can mean only Gehenna, as it is said, *Even the wicked for the day of evil* (Prov. 16:4b)." Indeed, anger leads him to disbelief in God Most High, as the Sages have said,[3] "Rabbah said: Any man who loses his temper will show no deference even to the Divine Presence, as it is said, *The wicked, in the pride of his countenance*, [*will not seek* (*God*); *God is not in all his thoughts*], etc. (Ps. 10:4). R. Jeremiah of Difti said: Anger makes him even forget his learning, as it is said, *For anger resteth in the bosom of fools* (Eccl. 7:9b). Rabbah bar Ḥanah said: It even
66b increases foolishness, as it is said, *But a fool unfoldeth folly* (Prov. 13:16b)." A man should know that his evil qualities are more numerous than his good qualities, for the Sages have said,[3] "Rab Naḥman bar Isaac said: It is certain that his sins outnumber his merits, as it is said, *A wrathful man aboundeth in transgression* (Prov. 29:22b)." And if, in his fury, he rends his garments, he is also a fool, [as the Sages have said], "Who is a

2. B. Neḏ 22a.
3. B. Neḏ 22b.

fool? He who rends his garment in his fury,"[4] or as they have said in another place, "He who smashes his vessels in his fury."[5] Even if the damage caused [by his fury] is only to his own body, a man should refrain from it—all the more so if it corrupts his mind and his faith, and causes him to forfeit his [ultimate] reward. May God protect those who fear Him from such [faults] as this!

[TITLES BORNE BY THE SAGES]

We may ask a question at this point, by saying, Why are the greatest and most virtuous **67a** of the forefathers called by their proper names [alone], while those who were inferior to them are not,[6] some being styled Rabban, some Rabbi, and some Rab? What then is the significance of this one being styled Rab and that one Rabbi or Rabban? Our reply to this question is as follows: There is a tradition reaching back to our forefathers, stating, "He who is higher than Rab is styled Rabbi, and he who is higher than Rabbi is styled Rabban, and he who is higher than Rabban is called by his name [alone]." The earliest ones, who were the greatest and most prominent, such as Simeon the Just, Antigonus of Socho, Shemaiah and Abtalion, Hillel and Shammai, and others like them, are the ones referred to in "he who is higher than Rabban is called by his name [alone]." Indeed the prophets—Isaiah, Haggai, Zechariah, Malachi, Ezra, up to our shining master [Moses]—are called by their names [alone], without [the prefixed] Rab, Rabbi, or Rabban. **67b** We say "Moses Rabbenu [our master]" to glorify ourselves in him, whereas "Rabbenu Moses" would be to glorify [the title] "Rabbenu" rather than his name. If such were [the intention], we would have said "Rabbenu Moses."[7] This is a principle which should be kept in mind.

4. Cf. B. Ḥag 3b.

5. B. Shab 105b.

6. For full discussion of this question, which was asked of R. Sherira Gaon, see his *ʾIggereṭ R. Sherira Gaon*, p. 106 f.; cf. also *ʿAruḳ*, *1*, 4 f., *s.v.* Abbaye; cf. also *Yuḥasin*, 83b ff.

7. The meaning seems to be that "Moses our master [Rabbenu]" stresses *our* pride in that he was our teacher, whereas if we wished to honor Moses with the

As to why the remaining ones were variously styled Rabban and Rabbi, I say that Rabban is used for those who served as princes (*nĕśi'im*), that is, the descendants of Hillel[8] who was related to David through his mother, though not through his father. That is why they were styled princes and not exilarchs—such were Rabban Gamaliel, Rabban Simeon, and Rabban Johanan ben Zakkai; all these were princes. As for those styled Rabbi, they were the scholars of the Land of Israel and the leaders thereof, as the Sages have said, "Ordination is effected by the conferring [of the degree]: the candidate is designated Rabbi and given the right to adjudicate **68a** cases involving fines."[9] Our sainted Rabbi [Judah] said to R. Eleazar ben Simeon, "They have made you a Sage, have spread a gold-trimmed cloak over your head, [and have called you Rabbi], and yet you say, 'I am going back to my town.'"[10] It is also said about him that he was anxious to have his physician Samuel[11] Yarḥina'ah ordained [as Rabbi], but was unsuccessful in this; as the Sages have said, "Rabbi [Judah] exerted himself to have him ordained, but the matter was not vouchsafed support."[12] Finally Samuel said to him, "Do not trouble yourself. I have come upon the Book of Adam,[13] and in it it is written, 'Samuel Yarḥina'ah will be styled Sage but not Rabbi, and Rabbi [Judah]'s cure will be effected through him.'" The headman among them was thus the one who was styled Rabbi.[14]

---

title Rabbenu, it would have come before his name; cf. Hirschberg, p. 45, n. 4. [Abramson's text (p. 474): "... in him, in that he is our master, not to glorify him, for in the latter case we would have said 'Rabbenu Moses.' That is why you see us calling him by his name alone, Moses, to which we postfix 'Rabbenu,' to glorify ourselves thereby," seems more logical.—LN]

8. Cf. P. Kil 32b; Gen. Rabbah 33, 306; Tosafoṯ to B. Sanh 5a (*s.v. dhb'*).

9. B. Sanh 13b.

10. B. BM 85a.

11. H: Ishmael; but cf. HY and Rabbinic sources (Obermann, p. 77, n. 9).

12. B. BM 85b.

13. A no longer extant apocryphal work occasionally referred to in the Talmud, cf. *JE*, *1*, 179–80. [Here probably meaning a heavenly book recounting the genealogy and history of mankind. Cf. *Enc. Jud.* (German), *1*, 789.—LN]

14. Cf. Obermann, p. 77, n. 17/18, interpreting this as a gloss explaining why one could be called Sage and yet be denied the title of Rabbi.

While the headmen of the Land of Israel were styled Rabbi, **68b** the headmen of Babylonia were styled Rab, to distinguish the ones from the others, or as stated in the tradition, "Everyone styled Rab is from Babylonia, and everyone styled Rabbi is from the Land of Israel."[15] The exilarchs, who were related to David in the male line, were styled Rabbana, as we read in the Talmud, "Rab Ḥisda took Rabbana ʿUḳba bar Nehemiah around."[16]

As for [the Sage called] Rabba, his actual name was Abba; Rabba thus stands for Rab Abba, which was then shortened to Rabba. The same is true of [the Sage called] Rabbah,[17] whose actual name was Abbah, to which was prefixed the letter *reš* to signify an abbreviation of Rab Abbah. The same is true of Abbaye, whose actual name was Naḥmani, as the Sages have said, "The rule follows Naḥmani,"[18] referring to the immediately preceding "Abbaye." The reason why he was called Abbaye is given by Rabbenu Sherira as follows:[19] **69a** He was the son of the sister of Rabbah bar Naḥmani as well as his disciple. Now since his name was the same as that of Rabbah's father, Rabbah did not deem it right to call him constantly Naḥmani—Rabbah's father's name—so he called him Abbaye, which in Aramaic means "my little father."

I have given here no more than a concise and abridged answer to this question. By my life, it could stand a far more detailed exposition, but this little should be sufficient for scholars.

[THE STORY OF NAḲDIMON BEN GORION]

I will now return to what I was discussing, in line with the purpose of this book. I say that the Rabbis have a tradition[20] that there were three wealthy men in the Land of Israel whose

15. Cf. Sherira, p. 106 f.; STwA, 252a; Rashi to B. MḲ 25b.
16. Cf. B. Beṣ 29a.
17. Cf. Rashi to B. Pes 40a.
18. Cf. B. Giṭ 34b top (and Rashi *ad loc.*).
19. *Aruḳ*, *1*, 9a (*Yuḥasin*, 85b; Sherira, p. 127). [Presumably read *wa-ammā sabab ismihi.*—LN]
20. B. Giṭ 56a.

names were derived from deeds or events which happened to them. One of them was Ben Kalba Śebuʿa, whose story has already been cited.[21]

The second was Naḳdimon (Nicodemus) ben Gorion, whose name too was derived **69b** from an incident that occurred at his hand,[22] namely, as the Sages have stated, "the sun rose prematurely on his account," meaning that for his sake the sun hastened to rise after having set. It happened one year, during the pilgrimage season, that a multitude of Israelite pilgrims came up, and there was not enough water for their needs. So Naḳdimon ben Gorion went to one of the Roman emperor's officers who was in charge of them, and asked him to let him have an advance of twelve [cistern] steps[23] of water, repayable at a specified time. Should rain fall, he would be repaid in [water; if not, he would receive][24] one hundred and twenty thousand[25] silver dirhams. The officer did so for him. When the day which marked the expiration of their agreement to wait came around, the officer sent a messenger in the morning to Naḳdimon, to say, **70a** "Either return the water, or pay the sum stipulated between us." Naḳdimon replied to the messenger, "Tell him, at noon." Noon came, but there was no rain. The messenger returned, and Naḳdimon said to him, "Give me the remainder of the day. When the sun sets, if no rain has fallen, I will weigh out for you one hundred and twenty thousand silver dirhams, as stipulated between us." The officer said to himself, "It is most unlikely that there will be rain between now and evening, for here is the sun shining." The fool was unaware that[26] God's deliverance takes but the twinkling of an eye, as it is said, "His salvation cometh in the

21. Cf. above, Chap. XIII.

22. Cf. B. Ta 19b–20a. [Naḳdimon is here derived from *niḳdam*, "preceded."—LN]

23. *Darajah*, probably meaning the volume of water represented by one of the several steps in the traditional cisterns of the Land of Israel. Cf. Hirschberg, p. 46, n. 13.

24. Missing in H. Restored from HY. Cf. Obermann, p. 79, n. 11.

25. Literally "twelve *badrah*" (1 badrah = 10,000 dirhams).

26. Translation based on HY. For Obermann's comments see p. 79, n. 32b. [Presumably read *fa-ghafala al-jāhil anna faraj*. Cf. Ḳ (Abramson, p. 478).—LN]

twinkling of an eye."[27] Thus the officer rejoiced greatly in his expectation to receive the money, and went to the bath to kill the rest of the day. [At sunset] Naḳdimon ben Gorion went to the Temple to pray to his Lord **70b** and to beseech Him, saying, "O Lord of the worlds, it is not hidden from Thy omnipotence that it was not for my benefit nor for my own sake that I took this water, but for the sake of Thy people, the Children of Israel, who have come up here seeking Thy mercy and Thy favor. I feared that they would perish of thirst, yet they have come seeking [Thy] reward." Immediately clouds rose up and rain poured down, and before the officer could leave the bath the rain covered twelve [cistern] steps of water and rose above them. As the officer was leaving the bath, Naḳdimon ben Gorion met him, himself having just left the Temple, and the officer said to him, "I have no doubt that God did not cause these events to pass in His world in such a short time except for your sake. **71a** But it still remains for you to make the sun rise [again now], in order to make it a fact that the rain had fallen on the day stipulated by you, or else you must weigh out the silver according to the agreement." So Naḳdimon returned to the Temple and prayed again to God Praised and Most High, saying, "O Lord of the worlds, just as Thou didst not disappoint me in the beginning, even so do not disappoint me in the end." Forthwith the clouds opened up and the sun rose, and that is why he was called Naḳdimon ["he who made (the sun) rise prematurely"] ben Gorion.

The third man was [Ben] Ṣiṣiṯ hak-Keseṯ, for whose name two derivations are given.[28] One of them is that his ritual fringes (*ṣiṣiṯ*) used to trail over chairs, that is to say, as he was sitting in the chairs; the second is that his chair was set in the midst of the greatest and most exalted [Roman][29] notables.

27. No Biblical source is found for this quotation; cf. Hirschberg, p. 47, n. 14, who refers to an article by Abramson in *Minḥah li-Yĕhudah* (J. L. Zlotnik Jubilee Volume, Jerusalem, 1949), pp. 27–38, which gives occurrences of this maxim in liturgy, poetry, and prose.

28. Both derivations in B. Giṭ 56a; variant ARN 6 (YJS, *10*, 44).

29. So in the Talmudic source; cf. Obermann, p. 81, n. 8. Abramson, p. 478, has *al-Rūm*.

CHAPTER [XV]

[SECRET SAINTS]

It is said[1] about a certain **71b** scholar who had attained a high degree[2] of piety, godliness, and righteousness, that he asked his Lord to tell him who in his time was worthy of the same reward as his, and was to occupy an equal rank and stand next to him in the hereafter. So he fasted for many days and prayed much in an effort to find this out, until [finally] he was told in his dream, "Thy rank in the hereafter shall be the same as the rank of So-and-so, the butcher." He awoke from his sleep hurt in spirit and sick at heart at what he had seen, and resumed fasting, praying, and weeping, until he was told once more, "I have already told thee that thy rank shall be the same as that of So-and-so, the butcher." At this his hurt increased, and his weeping grew more intense and profuse. Thereupon he heard a voice calling from heaven, "Were it not that thou art a virtuous man, great in learning and zealous in **72a** piety and godliness, thou wouldst have surely perished. Wherefore art thou weeping? Dost thou know what So-and-so, the butcher, has done, or dost thou know what his rank shall be in the hereafter? Pay no heed to the lowliness of his condition in this world, and to his being smeared with blood, for he shall not be thus in the hereafter."

So the man arose and went to the butcher, and greeted him, whereat the latter returned the greeting. The scholar then said to him, "I wish you would tell me what good works you have performed in this world." The butcher replied, "My lord, observe my condition—I am as you see me. Howbeit, whatsoever[3] I slaughter each day, I spend one half thereof in alms, and I sustain myself and my family with the other half." The scholar said, "Many a man spends more than this in alms. But

1. Source for this story: Tanḥuma Introduction, p. 135 f.
2. [So Ḳ, *bi-manzilah* (Abramson, p. 478).—LN]
3. [So Ḳ, *falladhī* (Abramson, p. 480).—LN]

tell me, **72b** have you done some great thing which no one had done before you?" The butcher set himself to thinking for a [considerable] period of time, then replied, "My lord, I call to mind something that happened to me[4] a while ago." The scholar asked, "What was it?" He replied, "My lord, one day, as I was carrying on my work, a caravan passed by containing several captives, among them a girl who lagged behind weeping bitterly. So I too began to weep at her weeping, and following her I asked her, 'Why are you weeping when no one else in the caravan is doing so?' She replied, 'My lord, I am a Jewess, and having been taken captive I fear for my religion at the hands of these unbelievers. I was wishing I would reach a place where there are Jews who might redeem me.' My heart ached **73a** at her words, and I said to her, 'Keep silent, and be of good cheer, for I will redeem you.' I then went to her master who had captured her, and bought her from him for a very high price, weighing out for her most of my money."

"The girl not yet being of age, I took her to my house, outfitted her with clothing, and maintained her honorably [until] she reached maturity.[5] Now I had an only son twenty years old, so one day I took his hand and spoke to him affectionately, saying, 'My son, accept from me what I am about to advise you, and you will be happy both in this world and in the next.' He replied, 'Father, I shall not disobey you.' I said, 'Marry this girl, and I will provide you with whatsoever bedding, clothing, and jewelry both of you need.' He agreed to my words, whereat my joy **73b** and happiness waxed great, and I executed the marriage contract and prepared everything that was necessary for them."

"When the time of the wedding came around, I set out a great banquet to which I invited everyone, without exception. Among the invited guests were many poor and indigent persons,[6] and since I did not wish to set them apart from the

4. So Ḳ (Abramson, p. 480), *fī amrin jarā lī.*

5. [Torrey's emendation (Obermann, p. xlviii) confirmed by Ḳ, *ḥattā adrakat* (Abramson, p. 480).—LN]

6. Reading *wal-masākīn* with Ḳ (Abramson, p. 480).

[other] people, lest their hearts should be hurt, I made them sit at the table[s] and plied them with much food. All the people ate and rejoiced, except for one of the tables from which as much food was removed as was originally served on it, the guests at it having eaten nothing. So I asked them, 'Brothers, why are you acting thus and spoiling our rejoicing? Have you seen some fault in our food?' They replied, 'We have seen no food more delicious or better served than this. **74a** But this poor man whom you have placed among us—ever since he sat down and until now, he has been weeping bitterly, and we have wept at his weeping and could not enjoy the food.' So I took his hand[7] and led him out of the house, and I said to him, 'Brother, you have spoiled our rejoicing for us. Tell me, why you are weeping? Let me know your story, explain it well, and hide nothing of your affair from me. If you are in debt, I will pay it, and if you need money for expenses, I will give it to you.' He replied, 'I am not in debt, nor do I need to have anything. My weeping is due to this girl whom you wish to join in matrimony with your son. She hails from such-and-such city, and so do I. I had affianced her to me **74b**, so that she is betrothed [to me]. But she was taken captive, and later I too was taken captive. And here is her writ of betrothal in my hand.' He showed it to me, whereupon I asked him, 'Do you have any mark to identify this girl therewith?' He replied, 'Yes, I caught sight [of her] one time in her father's house, and she has a mole on her private parts,[8] the shape of which is such-and-such.' His words were truthful to me, as I knew for certain that what he said was indeed so, whereat I bade him be calm and patient, and said to him, 'Remain here[9]—you shall have what you seek.'"

"I then called my son and said to him, 'My son, you accepted my advice in the beginning. Accept [again] now what I am

7. Ḳ: *bi-yadihi* (Abramson, p. 480), as Obermann suggests, p. 84, n. 3.

8. Following Ḳ: *fil-mawḍi*ᶜ *al-fulānī* (Abramson, p. 480); H: *fī ba*ᶜ*ḍi aṣābī*ᶜ*ihā*, "on one of her fingers."

9. [For *tataghayyar* read *ta*ᶜ*bur* (? or *tataḥarrak*?). Ḳ has *aqif* (!) *makānaka* (Abramson, p. 480).—LN]

about to advise you, for I desire nothing but your happiness.' He replied, 'Father, I did not disobey you in the beginning, and I will not disobey you now.' I said to him, 'This girl is betrothed to another man, and here **75a** is her husband in person. I have examined her marriage writ, and she is now indeed forbidden to you. I want you to give me back all that I made for her in the way of jewelry and clothing and other things, so that you might hand it to her. You will acquire merit thereby and attain a great reward, and I will marry you off to someone even prettier than she, and do for you double what I did for her.' He agreed to this, and we cleared the house [of guests]. Thereupon the best men arose, pronounced the nuptial benedictions, performed the wedding, and led the bride to her betrothed husband. Not one grain was left in the house—rather I gave him everything that I had prepared for my own son, so that he might make a handsome appearance among the people."

"The two of them stayed with me for some time, joyful and rejoicing, having forgotten all the misery that had befallen them, and having been comforted **75b** after all the distress that had overtaken them. When they decided to depart for their own locality, I set aside for them a valuable and handsome gift which I gave them, and escorted them [part of their way]. I did not cease inquiring about them until I was informed that they had reached their city safely."

The scholar thereupon said to him, "You have relieved my concern and my anxiety. I no longer question the greatness of God Most High and my rank in the hereafter, since you are one of my companions."[10]

It is said also of Abbaye[11] that he was pained when he heard a voice calling out to him as well as to a practitioner of cupping who resided in his vicinity, and greeting [both] him [and his neighbor] from heaven every Sabbath, but when he was

10. Ḳ (Abramson, p. 482): "There can be no doubt that your rank in the hereafter is as exalted as mine, and that you are one of my companions."

11. Source for following story: B. Ta 21b. [For *li-rajul* read *wa-ilā rajul* (Abramson, p. 482).—LN]

informed of the reason, his mind was set at ease. That is to say, he was told **76a** in a dream, "This man has such good works to his credit—wherewith he has earned this distinction—as you would not be able to perform." He asked, "What is it that he has done?" The reply was, "He has set aside a separate place for the women, so that they would not have to uncover in front of the men. He has also a gown with holes[12] marking the location of the veins used for blood letting, so that when a woman comes [to him], he makes her put it on, and takes her blood from these [marked] places, in order to avoid uncovering any other part of her body. Furthermore he has a place outside the office in which he sits, whereinto everyone may throw his fee, so that whosoever has nothing to pay him with may enter without suffering any embarrassment or shame. For if the practitioner were in a position to look into the place where his fee is deposited, **76b** the patient who has nothing would feel ashamed, which is why he put it out of his sight, so that he who can pay and he who cannot might be equal, and he himself would not know who did pay him and who did not. Before nightfall he would go out to see how much silver there was in that place, which he would take and be content with it. If he saw a poor man, he would give him [alms] out of what he had, and if that man had a disease which he himself could not treat, he would [also] give him money to obtain treatment [from someone else]. It is with these works that he has earned this distinction."

12. Ḳ: *fīhi thuqūb* (Abramson, p. 482).

CHAPTER [XVI]

[THE CHILD TAKEN CAPTIVE WHILE HOLDING A SCROLL OF THE BOOK OF GENESIS]

The Sages tell the story of a man in Israel who had an only son.[1] When he reached the age of three, his father had [a scroll of] the Book of Genesis made for him and sat him down in the synagogue before the teacher. One day an army[2] entered **77a** the city and took its inhabitants captive, including the boy who was taken holding the Book of Genesis in his hand. They took him to the city in which the king resided and imprisoned him together with the other prisoners, while his Book was deposited in the king's treasury. One night [thereafter] the king, finding himself unable to sleep, ordered that any books that were in his treasury be brought up, so that they might be read to him and provide entertainment for him. The Book that belonged to the boy was found [among them], but none of the chiefs and scholars[3] knew what was in it. One of the king's servants then said, "There is a Jewish boy imprisoned here. Perhaps this is in their script, and he may know it and be able to read it." So the king ordered him to be summoned, and when he was brought in the king's presence he was given the Book to read. But when the boy saw it he wept **77b** bitterly, whereupon the king asked him, "Do you know what is in it?", to which the boy replied, "Yes, master." The king said, "Read it to us," and the boy recited to him from *In the beginning* (Gen. 1:1) to *And the heaven and the earth were finished* (Gen. 2:1).[4] Thereupon the king said to the boy, "Interpret it," and the boy did so. When the king heard this interpretation, he rose to his feet [from his couch] and knelt down[5] upon the ground for a whole

1. Source for this story: SEZ, 17, 21 f. *Bet ha-Midrash*, *1*, 77 f.
2. Missing in H (Obermann, p. 87, n. 19), and supplied by Ḳ (Abramson, p. 482).
3. Ḳ: *ʿulamāʾ al-Rūm*, "Roman scholars" (Abramson, p. 482).
4. i.e., he covered the entire first chapter of Genesis.
5. Ḳ: *wa-sajada* (Abramson, p. 484); H has *wa-jalasa*, "and sat."

hour. Then he said, "Blessed be God Most High, creator of heaven and earth."[6] He then ordered the boy to be clothed in a handsome robe, seated him beside him, and asked him for his story. The boy replied, "Master, I am an only child to my parents and was taken captive while I was reciting from this Book before my teacher. Now I know the distress my parents are suffering on account of me, and their weeping **78a** and worry." The king said, "I have no doubt that God had caused this sleeplessness [of mine] tonight solely for your sake. So be of good cheer, for I am going to order that you rejoin your parents, and let your heart rest easy." The next morning the king ordered the boy to be given some money and clothing and to be conveyed in a litter until he reached his family. All this was done for him, and he [finally] reached his parents with his heart at ease. When they asked him, "Son, how did you attain this favor, and how did you return to us? We had already given up hope for you," he recounted to them all that had happened, and they gave thanks to God Most High for His favor in reuniting them with their son after they had despaired of him, he being their only child. And even though the custom is for our children to begin their recitation of **78b** the Torah with the Book of Leviticus, yet this man was inspired by God Most High to begin teaching his son with the Book of Genesis, so that it might cause his salvation.

6. Cf. Koran 43:85, and elsewhere.

CHAPTER [XVII]

[THE PURE SHOULD BUSY THEMSELVES WITH PURE THINGS]

When I was young I asked the Chief Elder, my father, the Chief Rabbi,[1] as I was reciting before him the section beginning *And God called unto Moses* (Lev. 1:1), "Master, why is it our custom for a child to begin recitation of Torah with Leviticus, skipping Genesis which is the first Book of the Torah? Is it right for one who wishes to read a book to begin reading it from its middle, skipping its beginning?" He replied, "May God make His countenance shine upon you! You have asked a good question, showing your intelligent effort to understand it, notwithstanding **79a** your tender age"—he used to be greatly delighted, overjoyed, and pleased whenever[2] he was asked questions, especially good questions, being ever so much eager, quick, and penetrating in [answering] them—"The answer to your question, my son, is that God Most High has ordained for us the offering of sacrifices in order that they might atone for our sins, and that through their acceptance [by Him] our transgressions might be forgiven and our errors pardoned. But after the Temple was destroyed and the sacrifices were discontinued, our forefathers have ordained for us that we make our children commence their recitation with Leviticus, because the sacrifices are mentioned in it, so that the recitation of [the ordinances concerning] them may be reckoned for us by God Most High the same as sacrifices [actually] offered, and so that many of our sins **79b** may be pardoned thereby."

I have seen, however, another explanation of this by the Sages, as follows: "R. Jose said: Why do they make children commence with the Priestly Code? Should they not commence rather with Genesis? Children, however, are pure, and should

1. H has *ha-rab̤ ha-rišon*, but cf. Hirschberg, p. 52, n. 1, and Abramson, p. 363. Ḳ omits *ha-rišon* (Abramson, p. 484, n. 13).

2. H: *kamā*, but cf. suggestion of Obermann, p. 90, n. 6, *kullamā*. [Read *bimā*?—LN]

therefore occupy themselves with pure things."[3] Another Sage, on the other hand, has given the same explanation[4] as I have quoted from[5] my lord [father], and both explanations are equally to the point and true, neither contradicting, nor detracting from, each other, for this ordinance was [probably] given to us for both of these reasons together.

3. Lev. Rabbah 7, 22a.

4. Source unknown. Not B. Ta 27b, as Obermann (p. 90, n. b) and Hirschberg (p. 53, n. 2) thought. Cf. Abramson, p. 418.

5. [For ᶜ*alā* read ᶜ*an*.—LN]

CHAPTER [XVIII]

[THE TWO CHILDREN SAVED FROM A COLLAPSED WALL]

I say further that one of the Sages[1] had two male children born to him in his old age. Because of his great anxiety concerning them, they never went to the synagogue nor returned home without him, nor **80a** did he feel safe enough to entrust them to anyone else. One Sabbath day the two boys set out for the synagogue with him, and on their way they brushed against a leaning wall which [forthwith] collapsed over them. [Nevertheless] their father went on to the synagogue to pray and give thanks to God Most High, and heap praise upon Him, while he bore [his misfortune] with steadfastness.

When he returned home without the boys, their mother, trembling, asked him, "How could you leave them, when it is your custom not to leave them with anyone else?" He replied, "Woman, you are right; howbeit, I have entrusted them to someone with whom they are as [safe as] with me." She asked, "Who is he?", and he replied, "So-and-so, the Sage, asked me to leave them with him to share his meal. At the end of the **80b** day I will go and fetch them." After the parents had eaten, the time of the afternoon prayer having come, the father went [again] to the synagogue to pray, still steadfast before God Most High, while the boys' mother kept hoping that he would return with them. When he came back again without the two boys, she no longer doubted but that they were both dead, and that her husband had hidden it from her out of solicitude for her, lest she should go out of her mind and perish. So she said, "My lord, I would like to ask you something," to which he replied, "Ask me about anything that may have occurred to

1. Source of this story: Yalḳuṭ Prov. 31, 1002b. Cf. also Hirschberg's comments, Introduction, p. 69; and cf. the Muslim story in Ibn Saᶜd, *Ṭabaqāt*, *8*, 315 f. Cf. also Abramson's comments on this version of the story, p. 417 f.; in some of the sources it is the mother, and not the father, who knows of the tragedy and tries to comfort the other.

you." She said, "A man had left something on deposit with me, and yesterday he came back asking for it. Shall I give him his deposit, or shall I withhold it from him?" He replied, "God forbid that you should withhold his deposit from him! On the contrary, make haste to give it back to him, and do it soon." She then said, "Should I feel a loss when he takes it back?" He replied, "How could you feel a loss or be regretful about it? **81a** Did you mean to keep it for yourself, or to deny that the deposit is his [property]?" She said, "The Creator Most High had entrusted two deposits to me, and now He has demanded them from me, and has come and taken them back. Why should I feel a loss or be regretful, inasmuch as Job has said, *The Lord gave, and the Lord hath taken away; blessed be the name of the Lord* (Job 1:21)?[2] One should bless the name of God Most High in any event." The man thus found for himself some slight consolation in the steadfastness of his wife, her laudable faith, and her clear conscience, as well as in the manner in which she had justified the judgment of the Creator Most High upon herself and had accepted it willingly.

When evening came, the wall was cleared from over the two boys, and they were found alive and were taken to their parents. As the parents were conversing with each other, **81b** behold, their two sons approached. They fell upon them, weeping copiously, and asked them, "What was it that saved you?" The boys replied, "The wooden beam of the wall formed a roof over us and made a brace between us and the stones and earth, and when [all] this was removed from over us, we came out safely." They then thanked God Most High for their safe escape and for His great kindness to them. Moreover the reward for their steadfastness[3] and the recompense for their firm confidence in Him remained reserved for them in the hereafter.

2. H adds in Arabic: "She meant [to say] that God Most High had given and granted, and has now taken back again."

3. [Probably cross out *wa-thawābuhumā* as tautological.—LN]

CHAPTER [XIX]

[THE YOUNG WOMAN OF JERUSALEM AND THE OPPRESSOR]

Know—may God vouchsafe you righteousness—that there has been transmitted [to us] the true story of one of the kings of the unbelievers, a confirmed tyrant, who laid siege to Jerusalem with two hundred thousand warriors.[1] He continued besieging it for some **82a** time, so that Israel was in great distress and sore straits. Now there was in Jerusalem a girl of the daughters of the prophets, and when she saw the distress, the straits, and the siege afflicting the people, she dedicated herself to God to strive to save them. She then went forth with her maidservant until she reached the city gate, and said to the guards, "Open up for me and let me out. Perchance God will work a miracle at my hand, so that I may slay this unbeliever, and so that the deliverance of this [people][2] may come to pass through me." They replied, "We will not open up, for we fear that you intend to trick us, seeing that you may lust after one of these unbelievers." She said to them, "God Most High forbid that I should do such a thing! On the contrary, I trust in God Most High and hope **82b** that He will graciously aid me to slay this unbeliever and deliver the people." And after she swore an oath to them about this, they opened the gate for her.

She then went forth and walked on until she came before the king—she was blessed with great beauty and charm—and when the king saw her, she found favor with him. He asked her, "Who are you, and whence do you come?"[3] She replied, "Master, I am one of the daughters of the prophets, and I have heard from my father that you will capture this city and take possession of it. I have therefore come before you to ask you to

1. This story, based on the apocryphal Book of Judith, differs in many details from it. Cf. the Book of Judith, and its later versions in *Bet ha-Midrash*, *1*, 133 ff. Cf. also Hirschberg's comments, Introduction, p. 77, and text, p. 54, n. 1.

2. So HY, Talmudic source, as well as Judith; cf. Obermann, p. 94, n. 6/8.

3. So HY and Judith 10:12; cf. Obermann, p. 94, nn. 26–28.

grant protection to me and to my family when you shall have captured the city. My heart will then be at ease in the assurance that you will spare us and will do us no harm." He said, "I will fulfill your desire regarding what you have requested, and I hereby give you [my] promise that I will do no harm to you or to **83a** anyone of your brothers or family, but only on condition that you marry me." She replied, "Master, were it[4] one of your menservants [who wanted to marry me], I would have accepted him and been content. How much more so when it is my master the king!" He said, "I desire you for no one but myself." She replied, "I would not refuse the least of your menservants anything he might desire;[5] [how much more so yourself]. However, I must inform the king that his maidservant is unclean,[6] and this day completes her period of uncleanness. What I would request of my master the king, is that he let me be until this evening, so that I may go off, purify myself, and come back. Let the king therefore order his menservants that when they see two women at the spring in the evening, they are not to approach them nor challenge them." The king so ordered, rejoicing greatly as he observed her beauty and the grace of her appearance. He also ordered at the very **83b** same time that his viziers and generals be summoned and that food and drink be brought, and they ate and drank. When evening drew near, they saw that the king had become intoxicated, so they all withdrew. As the girl then came into the king's presence, God caused deep slumber to overcome him, and he lay upon his couch so dead asleep that he did not know where he was because of his intense intoxication. Then did the righteous woman dedicate her intention before her Maker and pray to God Most High, whereupon she seized the king's own

4. H has: *wa-lā*, "and not," miswritten for *wa-law*; cf. Obermann, p. 94, n. 38 (misprinted 39).

5. Read *yashtahīhi*. HY has instead: "Behold, I am as one of your maidservants. Do what is good in your eyes." Cf. Obermann, p. 94, n. 39, referring to Rabbinic source and to Judith 12:14.

6. That is, menstruating.

sword, cut off his head,[7] put it inside her wrapper, and went off with her maidservant towards the spring—none of the king's menservants challenged her, since he had forbidden them to approach the two women—until they reached the city gate. The girl said, "Open up **84a** for me, for God Most High has helped me against this unbeliever. I have slain him, and here is his head with me." But the guards would not believe her words and would not trust her.

It is said that one of the king's generals had urged him to fear God, saying, "This people have a Master who will not forsake them nor let them out of His hand. Cease therefore making war against them, which is more fitting for you. Observe rather the kings who have preceded you, what happened to them and what was their end. He who harms this people or opposes them has never prospered. Be warned then by [the fate of] those who came before you!" Whereat the king ordered him to be crucified, but he fled, and it was he who was [among those] on guard [at the city gate]. When she saw him, she said to the guardsmen, "This is the general who was almost[8] crucified; he will identify the head of his master." When this became known [to the guardsmen], the gate was opened **84b**, and they came out and asked him—the [refugee] guard—"Do you recognize the head of the king?" He replied, "Yes, this is he," and having ascertained [this] he raised his eyes to heaven and said, "Praise be to God who has delivered him into your hands and has relieved you of him." Immediately the news spread throughout the city, and the young men of the townspeople assembled, seized their swords, and went forth shouting loudly and saying, *Hear, O Israel, the Lord our God, the Lord is One!* (Deut. 6:4).

When the soldiers of the king saw them, they went to the king's tent and found him lying [there] slain. They forthwith abandoned all their belongings and fled headlong, and the young men of the townspeople pursued them until they caught

7. So emended by Obermann (p. 95, nn. 29–30).
8. [For *rāda* read *kāda*.—LN]

up with them in Antioch; some they killed and some they took captive.

The elders of the townspeople [in the meantime] assembled and entered **85a** the Temple to pray and give thanks to God Most High for His grace and favor, in that He had not denied them His mercy. They continued thus until the young men returned laden with booty, rejoicing, and safe, whereupon their joy increased and their thanksgiving and praise grew manifold to their Creator who had fulfilled for them what He had promised them, *And yet for all that, when they are in the land of their enemies, I will not reject them, neither will I abhor them, to destroy them utterly, and to break My covenant with them; for I am the Lord their God* (Lev. 26:44). It is He who in His mercy and compassion deals with us in times of our distress just as He had dealt formerly with our forefathers.

CHAPTER [XX]

[DESPAIR NOT IN THE MIDST OF MISFORTUNE]

The Sages say[1] that a certain very wealthy man, **85b** considering the great riches that had come to him, meditated in his heart, saying, "When the time comes for my departure from this world, will the great wealth that I possess avail me, or will rather ample beneficence and lavish charity save me?" He was told that it is charity that earns its reward, whereas wealth is the easiest and quickest thing to disappear; and it was in a similar vein that the saintly one, [Solomon], has said, *Wilt thou set thine eyes upon it? It is gone. For riches certainly make themselves wings*, etc. (Prov. 23:5).[2] So the man swore an oath that he would give alms only to those who have lost hope in this world and wish for death.

He then went forth until he found a poor man cast upon a dungheap **86a** outside the city, clad in rags with which he covered himself. The rich man said to himself, "Undoubtedly this man has no more hope in this world and is wishing for death, for whosoever has reached such a state of distress and wretchedness has nothing left to hope for in this world." So he took one hundred dinars and gave them to him, but [instead of thanking him] the poor man asked him, "Why did you bestow this one hundred dinars upon me instead of the rest of the poor and indigent people who are in the city?" The rich man replied, "I swore an oath that I will give alms only to those who have lost hope in this world." The poor man retorted, "Only fools, ignoramuses, and unbelievers lose hope in this world.[3]

1. No source for this story has been found in Rabbinic literature.

2. H follows with Arabic paraphrase: "that is to say, Material gain flies away as with the flight of an eagle."

3. The whole sentence is missing in H; restored by Obermann from HY. One text of HY, however, has instead, "The poor man said to him, 'Take your money, you ignorant fool! You are the one who has lost hope in the good things of this world.'" Cf. Obermann, p. 98, n. 24.

As for me, I rest my hope in my Creator who generously sustains all His earthly creatures, great and small. Have you not read in Scripture, *He raiseth up the poor* **86b** *out of the dust, He lifteth up the needy from the dunghill* (1 Sam. 2:8)?[4] You must know that God Most High has the power to free me from dependence upon His creatures, and to deliver me from this straitened state. Abandon therefore this ignorance in which you find yourself, for this is better for you." The rich man then asked him, "Is there no reward due from you to me, seeing that I took pity on you, save that you should reproach me?" The poor man replied, "If you imagine that you were exercising pity upon me, the matter is not as you indicate. On the contrary, you have as good as made me dead, since only the dead have lost all hope in this world." Whereat the rich man said, "Since the matter is so, I might as well go and bury this [one hundred dinars in] gold in the cemetery with the dead," and went home [and did so].

Before long, while he **87a** still was so minded, all of his [other] wealth vanished, and he had nothing [of it] left. So he began thinking about the [buried] one hundred dinars and went to dig in the cemetery in order to recover the money. The watchman found him, and thinking that he was exhuming the dead, seized him and brought him before the king. And who was that king but the same poor man—it is said that he was a scion of noble and eminent stock, and when the people of that city assembled they chose him to be king over them—and when he saw the prisoner he recognized him. The watchman said to him, "O king, we found this man exhuming the dead." The king asked the prisoner, "How dare you do such a shameful thing?" The man replied, "Master, I was not exhuming the dead at all; what [really] happened was such-and-such." The king then asked him, "Do you recognize me?", and the man replied, **87b** "How can the manservant fail to recognize [his

4. H follows with Arabic paraphrase: "that is to say, He raises up and re-establishes the miserable from the dust, and from the dunghill the poor and destitute."

master]?"[5] Whereat the king said to him, "I am the man you thought had lost all hope in this world!" He then arose and embraced him, ordered him to be given [the buried money, as well as] additional money out of the treasury, and appointed him superintendent over one of the towns of his kingdom and its tax revenue.

And so the man abundantly praised and glorified God who lays low and raises high, who makes man rich and poor, as it is said, *For He hath torn, and He will heal us; He hath smitten, and He will bind us up* (Hos. 6:1),[6] and further, *After two days He will revive us, on the third day He will raise us up, that we may live in His presence* (Hos. 6:2). That is to say, God looks at the righteous and remembers for their sake His convenant with the patriarchs, Abraham, Isaac, and Jacob; He raises high those that are broken and restores them, as it is said, *He raiseth up the poor out of the dust*, etc. (1 Sam. 2:8).

5. Meaning "Certainly I recognize you as the king."
6. H follows with Arabic translation.

88a CHAPTER [XXI]

[ELIJAH THE PROPHET AS BUILDER][1]

The Sages tell the story of a poor man who had several children and a wife. Life was very straitened for them, and they did not have enough to sustain them even for one day. His wife said to him, "Cousin, arise and go to the market place—perchance you will find there something to sustain us, else we shall perish of hunger." He replied, "Sister, where shall I turn, and to what place shall I go? I have no relative to whom I might go and to whom I might turn, nor do I have a friend. I have no one but God Most High." Whereat she desisted from him, but as the children's hunger grew so fierce that they wept and screamed, she spoke to him again, saying, "So-and-so, go out—perhaps something will come your way, or else you will die wheresoever you go, which is better **88b** than that we should expire one in front of the other." He replied, "But how can I go out naked?" Now she had on a worn-out gown, so she clothed him with it, and he went forth, but when he stepped outside, he hesitated in bewilderment, not knowing which way to turn, right or left, and he wept profusely. Then he raised his eyes to heaven and said, "O Lord of the worlds, Thou knowest that I have no one to whom to turn, nor one to whom I might complain of my poverty and destitution. Here I have come forth, yet I know not whither to turn. I have neither brother, nor relative, nor friend, nor can I think of any stratagem, yet my children are small, their hunger is fierce, and they will accept no excuse from me. Thou hast created us—turn therefore

1. No Rabbinic source has been found for the Elijah story in Chap. II or for this story. Both are discussed by Obermann in *HUCA 23:1*, 387–404. Abramson, p. 418, points out that HY and the Sabbath hymn *ʾIš ḥasid hayah*, "There was a pious man," composed by Jesse bar Mordecai in the twelfth or thirteenth century, mention five sons. Hirschberg (p. 58, n. 1) indicates that this story is probably the source of the hymn.

to us in Thy mercy, or else take away my soul quickly, so that I may find rest!"

89a As he walked on a little way, weeping and perturbed, [the prophet] Elijah met him and asked him, "What is the matter with you, Sir?" He told him all about his circumstances and the predicament he was in, whereupon Elijah said to him, "Come, go and sell me, and use my price to relieve yourself and your family." The man replied, "My lord, how can I sell you when people know that I am a poor man and have neither bondsman nor manservant?"[2] Whereat Elijah said to him, "Never mind. Listen to what I am about to advise you, and no mischance will befall you. When you receive my price, give me one dinar out of it, and I will return it to you. But be careful to sell me only to the person whom I will point out to you, and do not accept any bid higher than what this person will offer." So the man took Elijah to the market place, and whosoever asked, "Is this your master?", he would reply, "No,[3] he is my bondsman," and when they asked Elijah **89b** about it, he would say, "Yes, what he says is true." [At that moment] one of the king's viziers happened to pass through the market place, and seeing a young man of comely form and handsome countenance, desired to buy him, and waited until the young man was called up for sale. When the price bid by the vizier for him reached eighty dinars, Elijah said to the man, "Sell me," and although several other persons raised the bid by several hundred dinars, the man did not accept it, but honored the vizier's bid, out of which he gave Elijah the single dinar, which the latter returned to him as promised. Then Elijah said to him, "Go and sustain yourself, your family, and your wife, and no want will ever befall you again." So Elijah went off with the vizier, while the man who had sold him went to the [food] market and bought bread, meat, olive oil, wheat, and other cereals, as well as everything else that he desired, and took it all to his house.

2. [HY adds: "I fear people will say that you are the master and I am the servant," which seems to conform to what follows.—LN]

3. [As emended by Obermann (p. 102, n. 15), *lā* for *naʿam*.—LN]

When he came in, he found **90a** his children about to perish of hunger, but they [forthwith] ate until they were satisfied. His wife then said to him, "Tell me your story," and he told her everything that had happened to him, whereupon she said, "What do you think now of my advice to you? Had you failed to go forth, both you and we would have perished." Later on he acquired great wealth beyond count, and never saw want again.

It is said that the vizier went off with Elijah until he brought him before the king. Now the king had been planning to build a castle outside the city and had bought many menservants to transport the stones, the timber, and all the other materials necessary for building. When Elijah entered before the king, the latter asked him, "Do you have a trade?" Elijah replied, "Yes." "Which one?", asked the king. Replied Elijah, "I am a builder." The king said, "Fortune has favored us in purchasing you. I want you **90b** to build me a castle outside the city, to such-and-such specifications." Elijah replied, "Very well, I shall respond to your wish, and [do] even more than you choose." The king then said to him, "I would like speed in building it, so that it might be completed quickly. If it is completed within six months, I will free you from bondage and give you a generous reward." Elijah replied, "Command your menservants to prepare all the materials for it." The king so ordered, and when night fell, Elijah arose and entreated [God] Most High to perform a miracle for him, so that the castle might be built in the form desired by the king. God Most High accepted his prayer, and no sooner had day dawned than the castle was completed, whereupon Elijah went off on his way. The king thought it wonderful and awe-inspiring, and rejoiced greatly at the fulfillment of his desire **91a** to build the castle. He searched for the man, but not finding him, thought him to be one of the angels.

Some days later the [formerly] poor man who had sold Elijah met him and asked him, "My lord, how did you make out with the king?" Elijah replied, "I could have freed myself from him immediately, but I did not want to break my word and do him an injustice. I had made him a promise, and I was bound to fulfill my promise. So when he told me, 'Build the castle, and I will set you free,' I built it for him and then left, for I did not want him to regret having bought me and to grieve over the gold he had weighed out [for my purchase price]. I therefore did work for him worth many times what he had paid [for me]." So the man thanked him for it and said to him, "Master, you have given us [new] life," to which Elijah replied, "Give thanks to God Most High, who brought this about for you." He then departed.

CHAPTER [XXII]

[BEWARE OF HYPOCRITES]

A certain scholar said:[1] **91b** Once I journeyed to Iraq and reached a certain city on a Friday evening. I had with me some money which I had saved at the cost of great hardship, and found no one I could trust with whom I might deposit it.[2] So I entered the synagogue and found a man standing in front of the ark and praying, with tefillin upon his head. I said to myself, "I shall find no one [else] like this man to entrust [my] money to." I therefore greeted him, and he returned the greeting, after which I said, "My lord, I am a stranger. Evening is upon us, and I have found no one to whom to entrust this money. I would like you to hold it with you for me, since I trust you." He took the money from me and went with it to his house. The following Sunday I went to him and said, "My lord, I want **92a** the deposit which I handed over to you, as I am about to continue my journey." He replied, "I never saw you [before], nor do I know what you are saying to me. Get away from me!" I nearly died because of my great distress [at his words], and spoke to him again imploringly, but he did not answer me, so I departed, saddened, dejected, and despairing of the money. I sat down weeping, at my wit's end over my condition—how was I to support myself, and what was I to live on? And I wept [some more] over my [sudden] destitution.

When night fell, I entered the synagogue and stood praying to God Most High, saying, "O Lord of the worlds, not in this man did I place my trust, nor upon him did I put my reliance; rather in Thy great and glorious Names which I had seen [inscribed upon the tefillin] on his head did I place my trust. Therefore do I ask Thee to deliver me." And I wept **92b** before

1. Source for this story: Pesiḳta Rabbati, 22, 111b. Cf. Abramson, p. 418.

2. So he would not have to carry it on his person during the Sabbath, which is forbidden.

God Most High until sleep overcame me, and I slept right where I was, and [dreamt that] I saw Elijah standing over my head. He said to me, "Do not be distressed. In the morning go to the man's wife and say to her, 'Your husband tells you [through me]: Give me the purse which I brought [home] on Sabbath eve and which I ordered you to hide. And the countersign between me and you is that on Passover eve we ate leaven, and on the Day of Atonement we ate that particular food.'"[3]

The narrator then awoke[4] from his sleep, and early next morning went to the man's wife and said to her what he had been told to say. When she heard it and verified the countersigns, she hastened to give him the purse, and he went off joyful and rejoicing, having thus been delivered from his anxiety, but still wondering about the behavior of this man.

Now when the man returned to his house in the evening, **93a**
his wife asked him, "Why did you reveal our mutual secret?" He replied, "What secret?" She said, "A man came [here] and mentioned such-and-such to me, so I gave him the purse." He replied, "I sent no one, nor did I tell [him] anything. But now that our secret and our actions have been revealed, it is best that we return to our [previous] religion." For behold, they were Christians who had become proselytes, and so now they returned to their original faith.[5]

That is why the Sages have commanded us to beware of those in Israel who are of this type, who vaunt [their] faith, piety, and austerity, displaying them ostentatiously, while their deeds are not acceptable and their inner disposition is not upright. Rather it has been said [in the Baraita] about such, ["There are seven kinds of Pharisees who are as guilty as if they had][6] destroyed

3. The former is forbidden, and the latter is a double sin: not only did they eat food on the holiest fast day, but the food itself was of a forbidden kind; cf. Hirschberg, p. 60, n. 2.

4. Note that the story continues in the third person.

5. The source does not mention their previous religion. R. Nissim, living in a Muslim environment, makes them Christians (Hirschberg, p. 61, n. 3). Abramson (p. 418) points out, however, that the source, probably pre-Islamic (cf. YJS, *18:1*, 26), might have regarded their Christian origin as self-evident.

6. Cf. B. Soṭ 22b; P. Ber 9, 14b; B. Mak 11a. H has a gap here, filled by HY.

the world. The first of them is the Shechemite Pharisee, meaning one whose behavior is like that of [the people of] Shechem," **93b** that is to say, he vaunts his faith, piety, and devotion for his personal gain, in the hope that someone will hand him something as a gift or as a deposit, like the people of Shechem[7] who submitted to circumcision, yet their circumcision was [inspired] not by faith but by self-interest. As one of them was quoted saying,[8] "Shechem wishes to marry Jacob['s daughter]—if he wishes to marry, let him cut off his [own] foreskin." They did [submit to] this [circumcision] only out of respect and fear of the king, namely Shechem['s father, Hamor].

The second kind is the knocking Pharisee, meaning "one who knocks his feet together," that is to say, he walks with his feet knocking against each other until they become swollen, whereupon he comes back and says, "I had to walk to a distant place to get willow branches for the sukkah and the lulab," or "I had to walk **94a** to a distant place to attend the performance of the commandment of circumcision and to pronounce the benediction over it." Had his motive been [pure] faith, he would not have knocked his feet together.

The third kind is the bleeding Pharisee,[9] meaning "one who drips blood on walls," that is to say, he brushes so [closely] against the walls as he walks that the dust thereof rubs off on him, out of fear that some [lay]man might pass near to him and render him unclean, thus keeping himself away from such people, as though he were shunning them and were not one of them.[10]

The fourth kind is the pestle Pharisee, meaning "bent over, as if [he were using] a pestle," that is to say, he walks bent over like a man pounding something with a pestle,[11] to suggest that

7. Cf. Gen. 34:20 ff. Hirschberg (p. 61, n. 6) considers the text from "that is to say" to here as a superfluous duplication.

8. Gen. Rabbah 80, 304b (cf. B. Mak 11a).

9. P. interprets this as "the calculating Pharisee," who performs a good deed and an evil deed, setting one off against the other.

10. HY has: "he thinks that he is more pure than anyone [else]."

11. [Hirschberg (p. 62) translates "in a mortar," thus emending the difficult *min* into *fī*, and interpreting *midaqq* as "mortar" rather than "pestle."—LN]

his piety, devotion, and austerity are so [intense] that he is unable to raise his head.

The fifth kind [is the Pharisee who asks, "What further duty is there for me to do?"], and the remaining two kinds[12] are Pharisees out of love **94b** and out of fear [of God], meaning that [they are inspired by] their desire to reach the [affection of the] people and to be called pious, [or] they do this in order to earn a reward from God Most High, that is to say, they are afraid to relinquish their [present] poverty and [to seek][13] wealth. Nevertheless Abbaye and Rabba have said[14] to the Tanna, "Remove [from the list of hypocrites] those who are Pharisees out of love and out of fear [of God]" for they are not destroyers of the world, because they sometimes end up well, and are led to act thus for the sake of God Most High, as the Sages have said, "Through [engaging in the study of Torah] not for its own sake, he will eventually come [to engage in it] for its own sake." The former [four] kinds, [however], are destroyers of the world, and Rab Naḥman bar Isaac has said, "What is hidden is hidden, and what is revealed is revealed. The Great Tribunal will exact punishment from those who rub themselves **95a** against the walls."[15] That is to say, what is within is hidden from us, and what is without is revealed to us. The Judge who is in heaven will exact vengeance from those who brush against the walls as they walk and display outwardly what is not within them, but you are safe from them.[16] [As Yannai the king said to his wife], "Do not be afraid of those who do not practice austerity and whose behavior is obvious to you, but beware of those who are dyed"—that is to say,

12. For *wal-aṭrīyūn* read *wal-ākharayn.* Cf. B. Soṭ 22b.

13. There is obviously something wrong with the text here. Cf. Hirschberg, p. 62, n. 9; Obermann, p. 109, n. 42. [Presumably read *wa-yaṭlubūna ḥāl al-naᶜmah.*—LN]

14. Cf. B. Soṭ 22b.

15. So B. Soṭ 22b, explained by Rashi as "who wrap themselves in their cloaks." Hence H has "who cover their heads with lies" (a reader's gloss?).

16. This is not in keeping with the following warning. Text obviously corrupt. [For *āmin* presumably read *iḥdhar*: "Beware therefore of them." Cf. *iḥdhar* in the next sentence.—LN]

those whose exterior is dyed to make it pretty, but whose interior is not like their exterior—"for they do the works of Zimri but demand a reward like that of Phinehas."[17] As the Sages have said, "King Yannai said to his queen consort: Fear neither those who are Pharisees nor those who are not Pharisees, but only those who dye themselves to resemble the Pharisees,
95b for their works are like those of Zimri though they demand a reward like that of Phinehas."

17. See Num. 25.

CHAPTER [XXIII]

[THE STORY OF KIDOR]

Something resembling the aforementioned story happened to several Sages, namely, R. Meir, R. Judah, and R. Jose.[1] They left the Land of Israel[2] on a journey, entered a certain town on a Friday evening, and sought hospitality from one of its inhabitants. When they asked him his name, he replied, "My name is Kidor." R. Judah and R. Jose deposited their purses with him [over the Sabbath], while R. Meir did not deposit anything with him, but instead went off and buried his purse at the cemetery. They spent the Sabbath with Kidor, and when Sunday came and they desired to continue their journey, R. Judah and R. Jose asked for their purses, but Kidor replied, "You did not give me anything." They spoke imploringly **96a**
to him and even offered him part of the money, but he would not admit anything at all to them, and they could not find any way to make him relent. Distressed and anguished, they asked R. Meir, "What was your motive in refraining from depositing your purse with him?" He replied, "When we asked him his name, and he replied 'Kidor,' I said, *For they are a very froward generation* (*ki dor*),[3] *children in whom is no faithfulness* (Deut. 32:20b), and I felt afraid of him and had no confidence in him." The two Sages said to him, "If only you had told us this, so that we might have been on guard against him!" He replied, "How could I warn you of something of which I was not certain, and which occurred to me merely as a matter subject to doubt?" So they went forth and leased a house [in the town] and invited Kidor to be their guest, in the hope that they might thus induce him to return part of their money. He came to them before

1. Source for this story: B. Yoma 83b.
2. *Al-Shām*, literally "Syria." Cf. below, p. 118, n. 2.
3. The first two words of this quotation in Hebrew are omitted in H, possibly due to scribal error.

nightfall, and having previously supped on lentils[4] without thereafter washing **96b** his hands, some lentils remained stuck to his hand. When they saw this,[5] one of them arose and went to Kidor's wife, and said to her, "Your husband says to you, 'By the countersign of what we have eaten this evening, namely lentils, let me have the purses that I gave you on Sabbath eve.'" She accordingly gave him the purses, and he took them and came back to his companions, joyful and rejoicing, and informed them of this, but not Kidor. In the morning they went on their way, while Kidor returned to his house and asked his wife about the purses. She replied, "A man came and took them, by authority of such-and-such a countersign from you." At this he drew his sword and cut off her head.

That is why the Sages have warned us to be particular concerning the washing of hands.[6] Indeed [failure to wash his hands before eating] caused a man of Israel to eat of swine's flesh, **97a** just as failure to wash after eating caused the slaying [of Kidor's wife]. The former event was mentioned without explanation in its proper place,[7] but was [later] explained in another place.[8] I will, however, recount it to you here and tell you what caused it. The reason for failure to wash the hands before the meal causing the eating of swine's flesh is as follows: A man of Israel was the guest of another Israelite, who placed bread before him. When the host saw the guest eating it without washing his hands, he thought that he was not a Jew, so he served him next food which is not permitted [to a Jew]. Observe therefore what befell this man because of his disregard of the least and smallest ordinance, and it is for this reason that

4. H has "both (Kidor and his wife) having . . . supped."
5. Literally "saw him," with lentils stuck to his hand.
6. HY adds: "before and after eating." Cf. B. Ber 53b; Ḥul 105a.
7. Cf. B. Yoma 83b; Ḥul 106a.
8. Cf. Num. Rabbah 20, 174a; Tanḥuma Num., 145. Hirschberg (pp. 63–64, n. 5) says that the story is unclear in HY. Whereas the source states that the Jew was a pork merchant, so that it was not known that he was a Jew, HY omits this detail, perhaps because of Christian censorship.

the Sages have said, "Be as particular about a minor ordinance as about a major one."[9]

It is said that afterwards, whenever the [aforementioned] two Sages[10] heard a name **97b** similar to Kidor, they would not accept that person's hospitality. Thus the Sages say that another would-be host was named Balah, and [upon hearing his name] the two Sages recited the verse *Then said I of her that was worn out* (*lab-balah*)[11] *by adulteries* (Ezek. 23:43), and turned away from him.

[OUR SAINTED RABBI JUDAH AND ANTONINUS][12]

The Sages in many instances derived names from [various] things in a similar manner, and often spoke of things by way of allusion or performance of an act from which one might understand their intention, as in the case of our Sainted Rabbi [Judah] with one of the emperors of Rome named Antoninus.[13] This emperor used to honor our Sainted Rabbi highly and would initiate nothing in ruling his empire without the latter's advice. The emperor used to come to the Rabbi's house in disguise, unbeknownst to anyone, accompanied by two slaves,[14] one of whom he would slay as he reached the door, **98a** and the other as he returned to the door of his own residence, lest they should spread word of this about him. He would also command our Sainted Rabbi to have no one else with him when he came to him. One day, however, the emperor entered the Rabbi's house and found R. Ḥanina ben Ḥama sitting with him, whereupon the emperor exclaimed, "[Did] I [not] command you to have no one with you when I arrive?" Our Sainted

9. Aḇ 2:1.

10. i.e., R. Judah and R. Jose; the story, interrupted by the preceding paragraph, is concluded here.

11. Some texts of HY give the person's name also as Labbalah.

12. Source for the following paragraphs: B. AZ 10a–b.

13. H has "Antiyonus," but cf. HY and source. For a discussion of the possible identity of Antoninus and his son Severus (Asverus in the text), see Soncino Talmud, AZ, p. 50, n. 3.

14. H: *al-ṣaqālibah*, a reflection of the use in the Western Islamic world of Slavic slaves from Eastern Europe.

Rabbi replied, "Do not be afraid. He is not like all the other people, and will assuredly not reveal a secret." The emperor then said to R. Ḥanina, "Get up and go out to the door, and bring us the slaves who are standing there." R. Ḥanina went out, found one of the two slain, and said, "What stratagem am I to use? What shall I do? [If] I return to him and tell him that I found the slave slain, [the Sages have said], 'One should not bring back bad news[15] [to a king].' And if I leave **98b** without bringing an answer to his request, it is not right to contemn a ruler, for he who contemns[16] him is given no thanks." So he directed his intention and prayed to his Lord to resurrect the slave and revive him, and God Most High wrought a miracle for him, and the slave rose to his feet and went with him to the emperor. The latter then said, "Verily even the least amongst you can revive the dead! Nevertheless I still do not wish to find anyone at all with you when I come to you."

The Sages say that the emperor used to say to our Sainted Rabbi, "Let me bend over for you, so that you might climb on my back and thence to your couch," but our Sainted Rabbi would reply, "It is not permitted to treat you with contempt—on the contrary, it is one's duty to treat you with honor and respect."

One day Antoninus said to the Rabbi, "Would that I were part of your sandal in the hereafter!", [to which the Rabbi replied, "Fear not, for you will be one of the inhabitants of Paradise in the hereafter"].[17] "But," asked Antoninus, **99a** "is it not written, *And there shall not be any remaining of the house of Esau* (Ob. 1:18c)?" The Rabbi replied, "This refers to those who do the works of Esau; as for you and the likes of you, not so." The Baraita puts it thus:[18] "*And there shall not be any*

15. B. AZ 10b.

16. [For *wal-tahāwun* read *wal-mutahāwin*.—LN]

17. The bracketed sentence is missing in H. Restored from HY and source; cf. Obermann, p. 114, n. 3; Abramson, p. 487, n. 13. [For "sandal" (*madās*) the source has "mattress."—LN]

18. B. AZ 10b.

remaining—could it refer to everyone? [No,] for the text goes on to say expressly, *of the house of Esau*, that is to say, he who does the work of Esau." Antoninus then asked, ["But did not the prophet say],[19] *There is Edom, her kings* (Ezek. 32:29)?", and the Rabbi replied, "It says *her kings*, not 'all her kings'"—the Baraita puts it thus: "It says *her kings*, not 'all her kings,' that is to say, except for Antoninus, son of Severus."

One day Antoninus said to the Rabbi, "I wish to make Severus, my son, emperor in my place, and to grant Tiberias a full year's exemption from the land-tax,[20] but it is our rule not to introduce two new enactments at the same time. What is your opinion in this matter?" In reply our Sainted Rabbi commanded one man[21] to be mounted on the neck of another, and gave **99b** the mounted man a bird, saying to him, "Set it free!" The king [immediately] understood what he had meant to advise him thereby—namely, he was advising him to make his son succeed him as emperor, and to command him to order the remission of the land-tax for a year.

[On another occasion] Antoninus said to the Rabbi, "The chiefs of my government, my viziers, and the noblemen of my empire have grieved my heart[22]—what is your opinion?" In reply the Rabbi entered the garden with him and picked for him one radish a day, day after day,[23] whereat the emperor understood what he wished to tell him thereby, namely, that he should put them to death at the rate of one per day, and not execute all of them [at once] on the same day, so that no disorder would ensue in his empire.

Antoninus had a daughter named Gilah. One day he sent to our Sainted Rabbi by messenger some watercress, the name of

19. Missing in H. Restored from HY and source; cf. Obermann, p. 114, n. 10.

20. Obermann's emendation (p. 114, n. 16/19) *wa-uᶜtiq* is confirmed by Abramson (p. 487, n. 16).

21. [Abramson (p. 487, n. 17): "The Sainted Rabbi replied, 'Command one man,'" etc., which seems more logical.—LN]

22. Or "have prepared my overthrow," as proposed by Obermann, p. 115, n. 7/8.

23. [Cf. Abramson, pp. 487–88, nn. 17–18.—LN]

which in Aramaic is *gargila*ʾ, and our Sainted Rabbi sent him in return some coriander, the name of which in Aramaic is *kusbarta*ʾ. **100a** Antoninus replied by sending him a leek, [called in Aramaic *karaṯa*ʾ], and the Rabbi sent him back some lettuce, which is named *ḥasa*ʾ in Aramaic. [The meaning of this exchange was as follows]: As for *gargila*ʾ, Antoninus meant by it that his daughter, whose name was Gilah, had committed fornication, because the word for fornication in Aramaic is *gar*—as in the Talmud,[24] "Whosoever writes a bill of divorcement should not write ʾ*iḡraṯ* [without *yoḏ*: 'writ'] with a *yoḏ*, lest it should be read ʾ*i ḡart*, meaning 'if thou hast committed fornication.'" When our Sainted Rabbi replied by sending coriander, *kusbarta*ʾ, he meant *kus barta*ʾ, that is to say, "kill the daughter!" When Antoninus then sent him a leek, *karaṯa*ʾ, he meant that [at that time] he had no other [child] beside her—should he cut off (*kĕraṯ*) his line? [This use of the verb "to cut off" being] the same as in the verse *That soul shall be cut off* (*wĕ-niḵrĕṯah*) (Gen. 17:14)—this was before a son was born to Antoninus. Whereto the Rabbi replied by sending him some lettuce, *ḥasa*ʾ, that is to say, "Have mercy (*ḥus*), and do not kill [her]!" When our Sainted Rabbi was asked why he refrained **100b** from saying this in explicit and clear words, he answered, *For a bird of the air shall carry the voice, and that which hath wings shall tell the matter* (Eccl. 10:20), meaning "you cannot be sure but that the birds of the air and every [other] winged thing might report your words."

[USE OF ALLUSION BY THE SAGES][25]

In the Talmud the Sages have often spoken in this [allusive] manner. Indeed, even their servants used to grasp what they said by way of riddle, finger-pointing, or hint, and would reply to them in the same manner. For instance, the maidservant of our Sainted Rabbi said to him one day when he had guests, "The ladle is knocking against the jug—will the eagles fly to

24. B. Giṭ 85b.
25. Source for the following: B. Er 53b.

their nests, or [shall I remove] its companion's crown from it?" By this she meant to say, "The cup with which we draw wine has reached the bottom of the jug and is knocking against it"—in other words, nothing remains in the jug—**101a** "Will the guests be going home, or shall we remove the crown of the jug's companion?"—meaning, shall we open another jug? At times he would then tell her [to open another jug], and at other times he would tell her that the guests were leaving.

So also R. Jose ben Yasin[26] would say to the members of his family, "Make me some ox of justice with mountain of the poor man," meaning, "[Let me have some] beets with mustard," for in the [Aramaic] language of the Sages beets are called *tĕraḏin*, which when split into two words, *tor din*, means in Hebrew "ox of justice," while mustard, called in Hebrew *ḥardal*, [if split into two words, with *h* substituted for *ḥ*, *har dal*, would mean the same as] the Aramaic *ṭur misken*, ["mountain of the poor man"].[27] There are so many such instances in the Talmud that if a whole book were written on this subject, it would be worthy of it. Perhaps the Creator Greatly Praised will help me to compose such a book and explain all this. [In fact] I have hinted at the explanation of many such expressions in my book entitled *A Key to the Closed Doors of the* **101b** *Talmud*.[28]

[A DEPOSIT RETURNED SEVENFOLD]

[To resume our discussion of deposits], he who deposits something with the virtuous and the good does not fare as badly; rather he gets back his original property, and sometimes even more, as you may learn[29] from the story of the two scholars who owned a *qafīz*[30] of wheat. When they decided to set out on a journey, they deposited it with a certain most virtuous man

26. So Abramson (pp. 420 and 489); H: ben Joseph.
27. Cf. Abramson, p. 489, n. 25, on this passage.
28. Cf. Abramson, pp. 420, 1–90.
29. The source of the following story: Deut. Rabbah 3, 210a; P. Dem 1, 22a. Cf. the story of the three Jews who were saved from destruction because of good deeds, in al-Tanūkhī, *Faraj*, *1*, 28.
30. A dry measure of varying content; cf. *EI*², *s.v. ḳafīz*.

and departed on their travels. That year the rains were plentiful, the harvest was abundant, and everyone prospered. The bailee waited for the two bailors to come and claim their deposit, but when neither of them came, he feared that the grain would spoil and lose its value, and was grieved on their account because of the loss that would befall them. So he took it on his own responsibility to plant the wheat, and [in due time] harvested many qafīz of it and stored them **102a** for a period of time, until [eventually] the owners returned from their journey. When one of them said to the other, "Let us go and ask the man for the qafīz of wheat which we had deposited with him," the other replied, "Let it be—the wheat must have wasted away after so long a time." They therefore let the matter rest, and stayed for a while in the town until they had occasion to travel [again], when one of them met the bailee and said, "I would like to ask you about the qafīz [of wheat]. Is it still in existence?" The bailee replied, "Yes, I have done thus-and-so [with it], my lord, and the grain is on hand. Bring some pack animals and haul it away." The scholar then went to his companion and informed him of this, and they collected the wheat, thanked the bailee profusely, blessed him, and departed on their journey, marveling at his **102b** good deed and praising God Most High for the greatness of His works. It is of such virtuous men that Scripture says, *Israel, in whom I will be glorified* (Isa. 49:3b).[31]

31. For the theme of this chapter, cf. Koran 3:68: "Among the people of the Book are some, to one of whom if thou entrust a thousand dinars, he will restore them to thee. And there is of them to whom if thou entrust a dinar, he will not restore it to thee, unless thou be ever instant with him."

CHAPTER [XXIV]

[ABANDON NOT YOUR FATHER'S FRIEND]

The Sages say[1] that a man of Israel, who was well-to-do and had ten sons, vowed one day that after a certain period of time he would give each one of them one hundred dinars. At the termination of that time, however, most of his wealth had disappeared, and he had but nine hundred and fifty[2] dinars left. So he gave nine hundred dinars to nine of them, leaving out the youngest one, who said [to him], "Father, I am left with nothing!" The father replied, "My son, I had made my vow in the hope that I would remain in my previous circumstances. I could not violate **103a** my vow. However, fifty dinars remain, so I will set aside out of them thirty dinars for what I shall require at the time of my death, and I will give you the [balance of] twenty dinars, since I have nothing more. I have moreover ten friends, and I will give them to you, for they are better for you than one thousand dinars." So he handed him the gold and gave him instructions concerning his friends. After the man died, each one of his sons went about his own business, while the youngest son kept spending his share until he had only one dinar left, and his circumstances became straitened. So he began to think about what he should do, and in his perplexity he said, "What shall I do, and how shall I make use of my father's friends, of whom he said that 'they are better for you than one thousand dinars?'" After meditating upon his situation, he decided that it would be best to invite his father's friends **103b** and spend the remaining dinar in entertaining them. So he went forth and invited them to his house, and after they had eaten and drunk, they said to each other, "Do you not see that

1. No Rabbinic source has been identified for this story.

2. H: 550; HY: 950, which is needed for the proper division. Cf. Baneth, *Kirjath Sepher, 11* (1935), p. 356; Abramson, p. 490, n. 28. Obermann (p. 119, n. 12/13) assumes that the original number of sons was six and was later confused with the ten friends.

So-and-so, who has invited us, has kept up his father's friendship [with us], unlike his brothers? We must repay him for this act of his." So each one of them presented him with a pregnant cow. Then one of them said, "We must add to this for him," and they did so, and [each] one gave him some of the money that they had with them. [In due time] these cows gave birth, and [the calves] grew up, whereupon he sold them for a large sum of money, and before long he amassed a fortune double his father's, whereat he said, "I no longer doubt my father's words that friends are more precious and more beneficial for me than gold."

One should preserve **104a** one's friends, for Solomon has said, *Thine own friend, and thy father's friend, forsake not*, etc. (Prov. 27:10),[3] rather multiply them. But be close to only a few, as Ben Sira has said, *Many be they that seek thy welfare; reveal thy secret only to one of a thousand* (Sir. 6:6).[4]

3. H adds in Arabic: "that is to say, Your friend and your father's friend do not abandon."

4. Cf. B. Yeḇ 63b; Sanh 100b. Cf. also Hirschberg's comments (p. 68, n. 2) indicating that the negative ʾ*al* is due to a scribal error.

CHAPTER [XXV]

[R. MEIR AND THE PERFIDIOUS WOMAN]

The Sages say[1] that at the time when R. Meir went from [his place in] Syria[2] on a pilgrimage [to Jerusalem], he had [an acquaintance] in Tiberias, a man named Judah, who had a righteous and chaste wife, doer of good works and zealous in deeds of loving-kindness. When R. Meir stayed with them, she would stand before him and serve him, prepare bountiful food for him, and show him much honor and respect. He grew fond of them, and they of him, **104b** and he felt comfortable in staying with them, and each year, going and coming, he would be their guest. One year Judah's wife died, and he married another woman. When the time for R. Meir's arrival approached, the man instructed his [new] wife, saying, "Know that we have a man of whom I have grown fond, and it is his custom to stay with me during his passage on pilgrimage and on his return. Should he arrive while I am not [at home], hasten to make him welcome and prepare for him whatever he may need in the way of food and service, for this is the customary manner in which we treat him. His name is R. Meir. Observe therefore my instructions, and beware of any neglect or failure in regard to him." She replied, "I will carry out your desire in full according to your preference, and your wish according to your choice."

105a Several days later R. Meir arrived in town and came to the house—meaning Judah's house—according to his custom. He knocked on the door, and a woman came out whose voice he did not know.[3] He asked, "Is Judah at home?" She replied,

1. The probable source of this story may be found in *Bet ha-Midrash*, *1*, 81 f. Abramson (p. 420) discusses the names Meir and Judah and concludes that in this story the reference is to persons other than the Tannaim of these names.

2. *Al-Shām*, here clearly meaning Syria and not Palestine. The source makes clear that the pilgrimage was to Jerusalem, hence he must have started from Syria and had to travel via Tiberias (Abramson, *ibid.*). Cf. above, p. 108, n. 2.

3. [Obviously she wore a veil while speaking to a stranger, hence he could not see her face.—LN]

"No." He asked, "And where is his wife?" She replied, "She died, and thereafter he married me. If you are the one called R. Meir, please enter into the house, for my husband has instructed me, saying, 'Should So-and-so come, let him enter into the house, and serve him and make him welcome until I come [home].'" When R. Meir heard this from her, he had no doubts about what she had communicated and said to him, so he entered and sat down until the end of the day. At that time the master of the house, Judah, came in and embraced and kissed him, and the two of them sat eating and drinking, until **105b** Judah fell asleep in his place and R. Meir in his, both being [somewhat] tipsy. The woman then approached R. Meir, took his clothes off of him, and lay down close to him, [expecting him] to help her to satisfy her desire, but he was not aware of her. When morning came, she woke them up, brought them water to wash their faces and feet, whereupon they said their prayers, and her husband went off to ply his trade, while R. Meir remained seated in the house. She then arose and served him food, and began frolicking with him, but he would not raise his eyes to look at her. When she came near him, he said to her, "Desist from drawing near me!" She retorted, "What will your keeping away from me avail you, seeing that you have done such-and-such a thing yesterday?" At this he exclaimed, "God forbid! Do not do [such a wicked thing]![4] You are lying **106a** and committing a [grievous] sin." She replied, "[In proof of what I am saying], there is such-and-such a mark on your body," and she proceeded to describe to him the shape of the birthmark, whereupon R. Meir became suspicious of his own self. He therefore arose, fleeing from the place, and went back to his home, bewildered, distressed, and perplexed. On his way a Gentile met him and asked him, "What is the matter with you, R. Meir?" He replied, "While I was on my way back to [my place in] Syria, robbers overtook

4. Obermann (p. 122, n. 21) suggests, "I did not do [such a wicked thing]," but cf. Baneth, *Kirjath Sepher*, *11* (1935), p. 357, who suggests "Do not say [such a wicked thing]."

me and took everything I had with me, leaving me with nothing." Finally he reached his house, saddened, worried, and weeping about how this terrible thing could have happened to him, and began to lament over himself, saying, "I have forfeited my [share in the] hereafter, woe is me!"[5] A certain Sage then questioned him, adjuring him to disclose the matter to him, so he told him what had happened to him, whereat the Sage remarked, "Perhaps the woman had merely noticed this mark on you **106b** while you were asleep, and you had done nothing, and [are guilty of] neither an unintentional lapse nor an intentional sin. Why then have you brought upon yourself this great distress?" R. Meir thereupon fasted for three days and prayed to God Most High to let him know the true facts of this matter. He then saw in a dream a [person] who said to him, "Do not be distressed, O Meir, nor let your heart be troubled. You have committed neither an unintentional lapse nor an intentional sin or transgression. The wicked woman had lied. Rest easy therefore and compose yourself, and remove all [worry] from your mind. You will receive great reward and recompense for this." He awoke from his sleep joyful and rejoicing, all the doubts that he had felt having ceased, and returned to Jerusalem, joined the pilgrimage, and never again passed by that place.

5. From here on the story has a longer and different ending in the source. For a discussion of some of the apparent difficulties here see Abramson, p. 421.

CHAPTER [XXVI]

[SUSPECT NOT INNOCENT MEN]

The Sages say[1] that a certain scholar **107a** killed himself for a similar reason. One day, about to enter a public lavatory in order to relieve himself, he left his tefillin outside, and a [loose] woman, passing by, seized them and exhibited them to the people, saying, "Look at what So-and-so has given me as my fee!" The scholar thereupon climbed up to a high place and threw himself down, causing his own death. When the Sages saw what he had done, they said,[2] "It is forbidden for a man to walk four cubits without [his] tefillin."

According to the Sages,[3] one who is suspected of something that he has not done is assured of reward, as the Sages have said, "R. Jose said: May my portion be with him who is suspected of something which he has not done. And R. Papa said: They suspected me myself of something which I had not done."[4] But this applies only on condition **107b** that this suspicion which is cast upon him cease, and that people do not continue to discuss it, "even for one hour."[5] If, however, it does not cease, and the slander and suspicion against him continue for more than this length of time; or[6] if it ceases solely by order of the authorities or of someone whose power to punish is feared; or if the suspicion is revived after it has ceased not out of fear of the authorities, [the aforementioned rule] does not apply. Unless indeed there are involved in it [personal] enemies, opponents, and adversaries—[in that case], even if this suspicion

1. The source of the following story is B. Ber 23a.
2. Cf. B. Suk 28a.
3. The source for this paragraph is B. MḲ 18b.
4. Cf. B. Shab 118b.
5. This phrase (in Hebrew in H) is characterized by Obermann (p. 124, n. 17/18) as "a (misleading) gloss," since in the source the time limit is "a day and a half." Cf. Abramson, p. 421.
6. H has *wa-lā*, "and not"; cf., however, Obermann, p. 124, n. 19.

lasts for a number of years, nevertheless the victim of it is assured of reward, inasmuch as these [enemies of his] would [persist in] maligning him even after he has been found innocent of that suspicion and not guilty of having done anything wrong. It is this distinction **108a** that is referred to in the Talmudic refutation of the interpretation of the verse *They were jealous also of Moses in the camp, and of Aaron the holy one of the Lord* (Ps. 106:16)—"everyone of them was jealous of Moses with reference to his own wife."[7] The [Talmudic] answer is, "In this case it was done out of [sheer] hatred."[8] And R. ᶜAḳiba said, "Whosoever suspects the innocent will suffer affliction in his own body."[9]

[SOME SAYINGS OF R. JOSE]

R. Jose was the author of several apt sayings which have been gathered together in the Talmud.[10] Among them are the following: He said, as cited heretofore, "May my portion be with him who is suspected of something which he has not done."[11] And he said, "May my portion be among those who recite the complete Verses of Song[12] every day," meaning the Psalms recited each day before prayer. And he said, "May my portion be among **108b** those who carry out the [obligation of eating] three Sabbath meals," meaning out of their fervent desire to honor the Sabbath, glorify it, and rejoice in it. He said also, "May my portion be among those who recite the afternoon prayer at the standstill of the sun,"[13] meaning just before

7. Cf. B. Sanh 110a.
8. Cf. B. MḲ 18b.
9. H adds in Arabic: "that is to say, Whosoever accuses a person who is innocent is punished in his body." Cf. B. Shab 97a; Yoma 19b. [Abramson (pp. 421–22, 491) suggests that "R. ᶜAḳiba said" is a scribal error for "it is said further on," which reading indeed appears in a Genizah fragment.—LN]
10. For the source of the following sayings, cf. B. Shab 118b.
11. H adds in Arabic: "that is to say, Would that my lot were with him who is suspected yet is innocent of it."
12. Selected Psalms and cognate Biblical passages serving as meditation before morning prayer.
13. *Dimdume ḥammah*, when the sun appears to be standing still or silent. Rashi interprets this as meaning red glow, at either dawn or sunset.

sunset. And he said, "May my portion be among those who die of intestinal disorders,"[14] that is those who die of diarrhea, since most virtuous men come under this description. And he said, "May my portion be with those who die on their way to perform a religious duty."[15] This last saying involves details which need not be specified here. And he said also, "May my portion be with those who welcome the Sabbath in Tiberias," meaning those who hasten to receive the Sabbath upon themselves **109a** and cease work in daylight on Friday, because Tiberias is situated in the lowland,[16] "and with those who let the Sabbath depart in Sepphoris," meaning those who rest and do no work until early on the night of Sunday, because Sepphoris is situated in the highland,[17] as the Sages have said, "Sepphoris is perched on top of a mountain."[18] He said further, "May my portion be with those who cause [their disciples] to sit down in the house of study, and not with those who cause [their disciples] to stand up in the house of study," meaning with him who hastens [early] to come to the house of study, thus censuring him who says, "It is evening; I shall now cut short [my] lecture." That is why in our beloved house of study, on the Sabbath, you will observe that I, [Nissim], do not cut short my lecture until one of my disciples says to me, "It is evening"—only then do I stop, unless indeed the time for the afternoon prayer is approaching and I fear that it may be missed, in which case I stop **109b** even if I am not told, for study is not greater than prayer, in our judgment. R. Jose said also, "May my portion be with those who collect charity, not with those who distribute charity," since the latter often distribute it to the undeserving in preference to the deserving.

14. Rashi says that the suffering involved effects atonement for one's sins.

15. H adds in Arabic: "that is to say, With him who intends to perform a commandment and does perform it, and as a consequence of doing so dies."

16. The Sabbath begins earlier in Tiberias, which is situated in the deep valley of the Sea of Galilee and on the east side of high mountains.

17. Sabbath ends later in Sepphoris, which lies on one of the ridges of the mountains of Galilee.

18. Cf. B. Meḡ 6a.

R. Jose[19] took pride in the fact that he had never looked at his circumcised member, and that the ceiling of his house had never seen the [inside] seams of his shirt, because of his great modesty, for he never took off his girdle [but pulled his shirt over his head without turning it inside out].[20] Nor would he ever engage in conversation and look behind him, for he would not repeat anything the repetition whereof might give him ground to fear anyone. For it is he who transmits lies and calumnies that always looks behind him, fearing that someone else might overhear him; he who transmits the truth, on the other hand, desires **110a** that everyone should hear him. He also took pride in the fact that he had never contradicted the opinion of his friend or companion, saying, "I myself know that I am not of priestly descent, but if one of my companions said to me, 'You are a priest,' I would ascend the dais[21] and spread out my hands [in priestly benediction]."

We have likewise found[22] concerning our radiant master[23] R. ᶜAḳiba, while he was in prison, that when his servant brought him food together with some water, the jailer would let him take in only a little water, saying, "We are afraid he might use it to break through [the prison wall]." R. ᶜAḳiba thereupon chose to disregard his thirst and used that small amount of water to wash his hands [before eating], in order not to violate the ordinance [instituted] by his companions, saying, "It is better that I die by my own hand than that I transgress the opinion of my companions." **110b** Indeed one of the proverbs of Bar Mari[24] reads: "If your companion [calls you

19. The following paragraph is based on B. Shab 118b.

20. He pulled it up over his head while sitting in bed, so that he remained covered as much as possible.

21. *Dukkān*, literally "shop," here obviously referring to the Hebrew *dukan*, the platform from which the priests pronounce the benediction.

22. The source for the following paragraph is B. Er 21b.

23. Note the use for R. ᶜAḳiba of this title, usually reserved for Moses. Cf. above, pp. 22–23, where Moses and R. ᶜAḳiba are compared.

24. H has here "Ben Sira," which is obviously an error. Translation according to HY; cf. Obermann, p. 128, n. 1/2.

an ass], get [a pack-saddle]."[25] And when Rabba asked Rabba bar Mari,[26] "Do we find in Scripture any indication of this proverb?", he replied, "Yes, *And he said, Hagar, Sarai's handmaid*, etc. (Gen. 16:8)—when the angel called her *handmaid*, she answered, *from the face of my mistress Sarai* (*ibid.*)." The Sages likewise have said, "Rabba asked Rabba bar Mari, What is the source of the popular proverb, 'If your companion calls you an ass, put on a pack-saddle'? He replied, [The source is] *And he said, Hagar, Sarai's handmaid.*"

[CHOOSE GOOD MEN FOR YOUR FRIENDS]

One should not make light[27] of proverbs, since they are rooted in both Scripture and tradition. Just as [people say], "A man should associate himself only with those who are like him, and join only those who are of the same kind," so does the holy Torah indicate [the same thing]: *So Esau went unto* **111a**
Ishmael (Gen. 28:9); and so do the Prophets: *And there were gathered vain fellows to Jephthah* (Judg. 11:3); and so do the writings of the virtuous, *Every fowl dwells with its like* (Sir. 27:9). Likewise the Mishnah says, "That which is attached to unclean is unclean, and that which is attached to clean is clean;"[28] and so does the Baraita, "It is not for nothing that the starling follows the raven, but because he is of the same kind."[29] One should, however, seek out a good companion and should defer to his judgment, especially if the attraction is mutual; if not, one should leave him alone, as the Sages have said, "Rabba asked Rabba bar Mari, What is the source of the popular proverb, 'If you call out to your friend and he does not answer you, knock down a high wall and throw it over him'? [He

25. HY has: "bray like an ass," but see further on. Hirschberg (p. 72) translates H's text (which seems to be corrupt) "Your companion knows better [than you]."

26. The source for this discussion is B. BḲ 92b. [Hagar had previously behaved contemptuously towards her mistress, Gen. 16:4.—LN]

27. [Probably read *fa-lā yatahāwan.*—LN]

28. Kel 12:2.

29. B. Ḥul 65a.

replied], It is written, *Because I have purged thee,* **111b** *and thou wast not purged* (Ezek. 24:13)," meaning, if you call out to him, and he does not answer you, and [even] turns his back to you,[30] do not inquire about his welfare [ever again]. Many of the proverbs in the Talmud may be illustrated by such proof-texts, and I will not go into further detail in this matter.

30. [For *wa-arthā* probably read *wa-irtadda.*—LN]

CHAPTER [XXVII]

[NATHAN DĔ-ṢUṢIṮA (THE HALO BEARER)]

The Sages say[1] that there was a man, very well-to-do, named Nathan the Halo Bearer, who fell in love with the wife of a poor man, an extremely beautiful and comely woman. His infatuation with her was so intense that it led to his becoming seriously ill. The physicians said, "He will not recover from his illness unless she sleeps close to him," but the Sages ruled, "Let him die, just so this does not come to pass." The physicians then said, "At least let her speak to him from behind a curtain," but the Sages once more ruled, "Let him die **112a**, just so this does not come to pass." So his sickness went on for a long time.

Now the woman's husband had many debts, which he was requested by his creditors to repay, but since he possessed nothing he was confined in prison, whereat his wife stayed awake at night spinning, and in the morning went [to market] to sell [her handiwork], buy bread for him, and bring it to the prison. His imprisonment continued for so long a time that he was seized with distress, and one day he said to her, "Wife, you know that whosoever saves one soul from death is as though he had kept alive many souls.[2] As for me, my stay in this prison has been prolonged, and you see my condition, the distress that has befallen me, and the great sorrow in which I find myself. Arise therefore and go to Nathan the Halo Bearer, [and implore him] to give you [money to pay off at least] some of my indebtedness, so that you might arrange my affair with it **112b** and get me out of this prison." She replied, "Husband, [you speak] as if you were unaware of what had happened to me on his account, of the great sorrow

1. There is no clear Rabbinic source for this story, which, however, was known in early times, cf. Tosafoṯ to B. Shab 56b. It also has interesting Islamic parallels; cf. Thaᶜlabī, *Qiṣaṣ al-Anbiyāʾ*, p. 220.

2. Cf. B. Sanh 37a.

and illness that had befallen him, and of the riches that he had sent to me and that I did not accept from him. He is still ill in spirit and sick in body on my account, and every day his messenger comes to me but I give him no answer. So how fitting would it be for me to go to him and make such a request of him? Had you realized [all this], you would not[3] have made such a proposal to me. But the length of your stay in prison has caused you to lose your senses." She then left him and went off to her house, where she remained for three days without going to [visit] him.

On the fourth day she said, "I will go and see whether he is still alive or not," and having gone [to the prison] **113a** found him near death. When he saw her, he said to her, "God Most High will demand of you what is my sin that you desire me to die, in order that you may marry So-and-so." She replied, "Husband, divorce me and let me go, but do not make me beholden to him." He retorted, "Is this not [exactly] what I have just said to you, that you desire to marry him and leave me to die?" At this she cried out [bitterly], and sprinkling dust upon her head, said, "This husband [of mine] bids me, Go and commit adultery to get me out of prison!" When he saw her in such a state, he said to her, "Go then and leave me, until such time as God Most High may vouchsafe me deliverance." So she went away, entered her house, and began to reflect upon the distressful condition of her husband in prison. Whereupon her compassion for him grew greater than before, and having perfected **113b** her intent toward God Most High, she implored Him to deliver her from sin and preserve her from error, and then betook herself to Nathan the Halo Bearer.

When his slaves saw her, they hastened to their master, saying, "Hannah is at the door!" He replied, "If this is true, I will set all of you free, and moreover deal generously with you," [and ordered] a maidservant who knew her to go out to her and bid her enter. So she came in and stood before him,

3. Missing in H; restored by Obermann (p. 131, n. 1/2) from HY.

and when he raised his eyes and saw her he almost fainted. But he arose for her and said, "My lady, what brought you [here]? Perhaps you have some need that we can fulfill?" She replied, "Yes." [He said],[4] "State your need." She replied, "My husband is imprisoned for debt, and I would like you to advance me one hundred dinars to redeem him therewith, **114a** and you will attain a [high] degree [of merit] by this [good deed]." He immediately ordered several purses to be brought before her and bid her take out of them as much as she wished. He then said to her, "It is not hidden from you how deeply I am in love with you. Do now accede to my entreaty, and restore me to life." She replied, "Here I am before you. Do with me as you wish. But I must tell you that here and now is the moment when you can earn for yourself the hereafter. Do not forfeit your reward and recompense by making me forbidden to my husband. Do not waste much to gain little, the everlasting to gain the fleeting. Reflect upon the consequences, for God Most High will requite and reward you [if you choose wisely], and you will attain everlasting bliss. **114b** Observe those who have preceded [you] and have indulged their fancy, and how they came to regret it. This is the moment—earn with it for yourself the requital of everlasting bliss. It is within your power to attain this with the smallest thing."

When the man heard her plea, his heart grew soft, and he rose to his feet and humbled himself before God Most High, asking Him to subdue his passion and to set him on the path of goodness, to help him in accomplishing this, and to accept his repentance, forgive his sins, and pardon his errors. And God Most High, Receiver of the penitent, answered him, and his passion broke away from him. Nathan then said to her, "Depart from me in peace for your home, and redeem your husband with this sum, until such time as God Most High may grant you a livelihood [sufficient to repay me]; if not, you shall be released from this debt." So Hannah went to her

4. Missing in H.

husband, redeemed him from prison, and told him about what had happened to them. Doubt, however, now entered his heart, and he thought that Nathan had had his way with her and that she was hiding **115a** this from him.

The Sages say that one day R. ᶜAḳiba was sitting looking out from a dormer window in his house, when he saw a man riding a horse and bearing upon his head something like a lantern shining brightly like the sun. He called out to some of his disciples, saying, "Who is this?" They replied, "It is Nathan the Halo Bearer, the whoremonger." He asked, "Do you see something upon his head that shines?" They replied, "No." He said, "I would like you to bring him to me." So Nathan was brought before R. ᶜAḳiba who said to him, "My son, I saw a great light upon your head as you were moving along, and I have no doubt but that you are one of the people of the hereafter, meriting great requital and immense reward. Nevertheless I wish you would tell me what you have done in this world to earn **115b** this great distinction. Let me know everything that has happened to you." Nathan then told him everything that had happened to him, and R. ᶜAḳiba was filled with great wonder and awe at Nathan's steadfastness in abandoning lawlessness and returning to rewarding conduct, and he said to him, "This is what I had expected of you, and I have no doubt but that you have earned this light, which the Lord of the worlds has made to shine upon you, only because you had done this great deed. This is [your reward] in this world—how [much more] in the hereafter? Now take my advice, and let me set you down [here] and teach you Torah." Nathan did so and sat before him studying, and it was only a short time before he reached a high degree in learning and sat by the side of R. ᶜAḳiba in **116a** the seat of honor.

One day Hannah's husband passed by R. ᶜAḳiba's academy, and seeing Nathan the Halo Bearer sitting with him in the same seat, asked one of the disciples what had brought him to this high rank. The disciple told him everything that had happened to Nathan, whereat the man's heart was reassured and his spirit was eased and relieved of the doubts that had beset him on account of his wife. He then went back to his wife, kissed her upon her head, and said to her, "Forgive me for doubting [you] in my heart, and for keeping away from you all this time. It is only today that I saw this man sitting with R. ᶜAḳiba in his seat. I asked how he had reached this [distinction], and was told the facts of the matter. I now ask God Most High to reward **116b** and requite you with the best requital. I had indeed been in grievous error on your account, until God Most High delivered me from it with what I saw today."

[HOW TO OVERCOME THE INCLINATION TO EVIL]

It is therefore obligatory for the believer to consider the consequences [of things] and not to indulge his fancy, so that he might be saved. On the contrary, he should be eager to do that which endures, and energetic in earning that which neither ceases nor is cut short, namely the reward of the hereafter. He should renounce that which would earn for him great pain and bring upon him distressing punishment. He should reflect that this is like [the case of] a person who[5] eats honey mixed with deadly poison—let him not delight in this sweetness, for it will pass in the shortest time, while the deadly poison will remain. By my life, he who overcomes [his desire] is a mighty man, as the Sages have said, "Who is a mighty man? He who overcomes **117a** his Inclination [to evil]."[6] Let it suffice for you that because of this Inclination's intensity and great power its Creator Himself has called it Inclination to evil, [as the Sages have said,[7] "So powerful is the Inclination to evil][8] that even the Holy One Himself, blessed be He, [forgiving though He is, yet] has called it evil, as it is said, *For the inclination of man's heart is evil from his youth*, etc. (Gen.

5. Reading with Ḳ (Abramson, p. 494) *anna dhālika ka-man.*
6. Ab̲ 4:1.
7. Cf. B. Ḳid 30b.
8. Missing in H, and restored from source and HY. Cf. Obermann, p. 134, n. 26.

8:21)." And the Sages have said further,[9] "By seven names has the Inclination to evil been called: The Holy One, blessed be He, called it evil. Moses called it foreskin, as it is said, *Circumcise therefore the foreskin of your heart*, etc. (Deut. 10:16). David called it unclean, as it is said, *Create me a clean heart, O God*, etc. (Ps. 51:12)—indicating that there is [also] an unclean [heart, inspired by the Inclination to evil]. Solomon called it enemy, as it is said, *If thine enemy be hungry, give him bread to eat; and if he be thirsty, give him water to drink* (Prov. 25:21)—meaning, teach it Torah, and God Most High will deliver it into your hand. Isaiah called it stumbling block, as it is said, *Take up the stumbling block out of the way of My people* (Isa. 57:14b). Ezekiel called it stone—*I will take away the heart* **117b** *of stone out of your flesh, and I will give you a heart of flesh* (Ezek. 36:26). Joel called it hidden, as it is said, *But I will remove far off from you the hidden one*, etc. (Joel 2:20)—that is, the Inclination to evil which is hidden in a man's heart." How many are its names, and how immense its havoc, were it not for the help of God Most High vouchsafed to those who seek to be saved from it and to break it away from the disciples of the Sages.[10] Most of its enmity and power is [directed] against them, as the Sages have said, "And against the disciples of the Sages above all others." Indeed, as a scholar's learning increases, so does its power increase, as the Sages have said, "A certain old man taught Abbaye: Whosoever is greater [in learning] than his companion, his Inclination [to evil] is likewise greater [in power]."

The Creator Most High has commanded us to study Torah whenever we feel that the Inclination [to evil] is about to overpower us, for **118a** it is this that weakens it, as the Sages have said, "My son, if that ugly thing should meet you, drag

9. The entire passage is quoted from B. Suk 52a.

10. This sentence is defective in H. The first word *fa-lā* is emended by Obermann (p. 135, n. 17/19) into *fa-lawlā*, to which he adds: "[man would not be able to withstand it]," on the basis of a similar sentence in the Talmudic source from which the previous quotation is taken. [Rather read *illā* for *fa-lā*, which makes the addition unnecessary.—LN]

it to the house of study, and even if it be [made of] stone, it will dissolve,[11] as it is said, *Ho, everyone that thirsteth, come ye for water*, etc. (Isa. 55:1), and it is said, *The waters wear the stones* (Job 14:19). And if it be [made of] iron, it will break into pieces, as it is said, *Is not My word like as fire, saith the Lord, and like a hammer that breaketh the rock in pieces?* (Jer. 23:29)." And the Sages have said further, "The Holy One, blessed be He, said: I have created the Inclination to evil, and I have created Torah as seasoning for it. If you will busy yourselves with Torah, you will not be delivered into the Inclination's hand."[12] In another place they have said, "So long as Israel busy themselves with Torah and with deeds of loving-kindness, their Inclination [to evil] is delivered into their hands."[13] **118b** In still another place they have said, "God Most High told our master Moses to say to the angels: Is the Inclination to evil present among you that you are in need of Torah?"[14] And R. Simeon ben Laḳish said, "Man's Inclination [to evil] grows in strength over him every day, as it is said, *The wicked watcheth the righteous, and seeketh to slay him.*[15] *The Lord will not leave him in his hand, nor suffer him to be condemned when he is judged* (Ps. 37:32–33)."[16]

God Most High will aid one against the Inclination to evil only when He sees him[17] studying Torah and knows that it is his intention to seek to flee from it and from disobedience, and to be saved from it. As for one whose desire He sees inclining toward acts of disobedience, He will leave him **119a**

11. B. Suk 52b, Ḳid 30b; i.e., overcome the evil Inclination by study of Torah.

12. B. Ḳid 30b. H adds in Arabic: "that is to say, God Most High created the evil Inclination and created Torah; and if one continuously busies oneself with Torah, the Inclination is kept away from that man."

13. B. AZ 5b.

14. B. Shab 88b–89a, and elsewhere. [The angels are said to have been opposed to the giving of the Torah to Israel; cf., e.g., YJS, *13:1*, 121 ff.—LN]

15. H adds in Arabic: "that is to say, The wicked never ceases to seek to injure the righteous."

16. B. Suk 52b, Ḳid 30b. H adds in Arabic: "but God does not deliver the righteous into the hands of the wicked, nor let him win his wish for him."

17. So Ḳ (Abramson, p. 496).

in his present condition, for were He to divert him from it, this would constitute constraint, and consequently denial of impending reward and punishment. God will therefore leave him to the evil of his choice, so that after having satisfied his desire he will receive punishment therefor, as the Sages have said, "To him who comes to defile himself, one should open the way; to him who comes to purify himself, one should render assistance."[18]

The Sages have propounded a parable to [illustrate] this [aphorism], about a man who sells both naphtha and balsam oil. When a customer asks him [for naphtha, he tells him, "Take as much as you need," so that he himself would not have to handle it, because it is evil-smelling. But when a customer asks him for balsam oil],[19] he tells him, "Wait until I pour it for you into its glass container, so that we may both savor its fragrance."[20]

Observe therefore the multitude of our Lord's kindnesses toward us. Not only does He place before us the path of life, but [21] He also helps us to [follow] it in order to save us from
Gehenna. It is as the Sages have said in the Talmud,[22] **119b**
"Hezekiah said: What is the meaning of the verse, *Yea, He hath allured thee out of straitness* (Job. 36:16)? Come and see that the way of the Holy One, blessed be He, is not like the way of flesh[-and-blood. The way of flesh-and-blood] is to allure his companion from the paths of life to the paths of death, whereas the Holy One, blessed be He, allures man from the paths of death to the paths of life, as it is said, *Yea, He hath allured thee out of straitness*, that is, out of Gehenna whose mouth is strait, in order that its smoke should be confined within it. You might perhaps say that just as its mouth is strait, so is all of it strait—[not so], for the verse goes on to say, *Into a*

18. B. Yoma 38b.

19. Missing in H, and restored by Obermann (p. 137, n. 16) on the basis of HY and source. [For Ḳ's variant, see Abramson, p. 496.—LN]

20. B. Yoma 38b–39a.

21. [For *illā wa-yuʿinunā* Ḳ (Abramson, p. 496) has *ḥattā yuʿinunā*.—LN]

22. B. Men 99b–100a.

broad place, where there is no straitness (*ibid.*), and it is said elsewhere, *Yea, for the king it is prepared, deep and large* (Isa. 30:33). You might perhaps say there is no firewood therein—[not so], for the verse goes on to say, *The pile thereof is fire and much wood* (*ibid.*). You might perhaps say this [deliverance] is the sole reward therefor—[not so], for the verse goes on to say, *And that which is set on thy table is full of fatness* (Job 36:16)."

120a The wise one, [Solomon], has warned us not to indulge our appetites nor to abandon the scrutiny by our intellects of the outcome of this pleasure, for though it may produce a little sweetness it also involves great bitterness, as it is said, *For the lips of a strange woman drop honey, and her mouth is smoother than oil* (Prov. 5:3), and the next verse reads, *But her end is bitter as wormwood, sharp as a two-edged sword* (Prov. 5:4).[23] Woe unto him who submits to his Inclination [to evil] and is deceived [by it], as the Sages have said, "Woe unto him whose Inclination [to evil] lies in wait for him,"[24] and others have said, "Woe unto him from His Creator, [and] woe unto him from his Inclination."[25]

Therefore one must be on guard against **120b** his Inclination [to evil], for it lies in ambush against a man until it throws a noose over him and jerks him [off his feet], before it overcomes him and gains mastery over him,[26] as the Sages have said, "At first the Inclination [to evil] resembles a thread as thin as a hair, but in the end it is as thick as a cart rope, as it is said, *Woe unto them that draw iniquity with cords of vanity, and sin as it were with a cart rope* (Isa. 5:18)."[27] The more a man in-

23. H adds in Arabic: "that is to say, Her result is more bitter than colocynth, and is like a sharp sword."

24. No Rabbinic source found for this. For Obermann's conjecture about the possible Sufi origin of this phrase, see p. 139, n. c/9.

25. B. Ber 61a (variant, B. Er 18a). H adds in Arabic: "that is to say, Woe unto him whose Inclination makes him obey it, and whose Creator then punishes him."

26. Text of H, obviously corrupt, emended according to Ḳ (Abramson p. 498).

27. B. Sanh 99b (variant, B. Suk 52a). H adds in Arabic: "that is to say, Woe unto him whose fancy entices him, because at first it is like a spider's web, but the more he nurses it the more it grows in power over him like a thick rope."

dulges it, the more its power over him grows, as the Sages have said, "Man has a small organ; when he satisfies it, it is hungry, and when he starves it, it is satisfied."[28] I ask God Most High to keep the Inclination [to evil] away **121a** from us.

Observe then this virtuous man[29] and the sore affliction and illness with which he was stricken, yet when he reflected upon the consequences[30] [of misconduct] and made things easier upon his soul, they became easier. Had he earned nothing [thereby] but deliverance from punishment, it would have been enough for him; all the more so seeing that he attained thereby abundant reward and lasting bliss. Behold therefore the honor and the learning which came to him in this world, aside from what was set apart for him in the hereafter. What lucrative merchandise,[31] and how greatly profitable! How can one fail to desire it?

[GOOD DEED'S REWARD AND TRANSGRESSION'S PUNISHMENT]

Indeed a man must know that there is such a sin as might cause him to forfeit all the good deeds[32] that he had done, just as we believe that he whose good deeds **121b** outweigh his evil doings will be deemed worthy of a reward; indeed that even if the two balance each other, he will likewise be deemed worthy of a reward, and the punishment due to him will be remitted. For it is the custom of our Lord Most High, out of the abundance of His kindnesses, to be forgiving, as the Sages have said,[33] "The school of Hillel say: *Abundant in goodness* (Exod. 34:6)—that is, He tilts [the scales] toward goodness." If, on the other hand, a man's evil doings outweigh his good deeds—even if by only one—he is entitled to no reward at all

28. B. Sanh 107a (variant, B. Suk 52b). [Referring to the organ of generation.—LN]

29. Referring back to Nathan dĕ-Ṣuṣita.

30. [Obermann's emendation (p. 140, n. 18) *al-ʿawāqib* is confirmed by Ḳ (Abramson, p. 498).—LN]

31. [So Ḳ: *fa-hiya tijārah* (Abramson, p. 498).—LN]

32. [So Ḳ: *qad takūn khaṭīʾah . . . min al-ḥasanāt* (Abramson, p. 498).—LN]

33. B. RH 17a.

and earns only punishment. That is why[34] the Sages have said,[35] "A man should always consider himself as though he were half guiltless and half guilty. If he then performs [even just] one more good deed, happy indeed is he, for he has thereby tilted the balance toward his own guiltlessness," since by earning [the merit of] that one good deed he has caused the remission for himself of the punishment due to him **122a** for all of his evil deeds, and has become one of the company of the righteous and the virtuous, deserving of great reward and lasting bliss. Contrariwise, "If[36] he commits [even just] one more transgression, woe is unto him, for he has tilted the balance toward his own guiltiness, as it is said, *But one sinner destroyeth much good* (Eccl. 9:18b)," meaning that with that single evil deed he has earned punishment and has canceled all the good deeds that he had performed to his own merit. And even if that one sin were to cause him to forfeit no more than an equal amount of reward, or even less, he should desire even this little [amount of reward] and guard himself against doing anything that would cause him to forfeit it; all the more so if this sin should cause him to forfeit much reward—what benefit and what usefulness would there be in that?[37] As the Sages have said,[38] **122b** "For what is there for a man in food which leads [him] to many disputes, or in drink which leads him to many worries, or in clothing which causes him shame, or in an impure thought that causes him pains, or in a sweet moment that brings upon him a horrible kind of death, or in a sin that causes him to forfeit many merits?" And they have said also,[39] "What benefit is there for him in transgressions, seeing that they are like fire touched to flax?"

34. [So Ḳ: *wali-dhālika* (Abramson, p. 498).—LN]
35. B. Ḳid 40a–b.
36. B. Ḳid 40b.
37. For a discussion of R. Nissim's deviation here from the traditional attitude, see Hirschberg, p. 80, n. 12.
38. *Bet ha-Midrash*, 2, 121.
39. No Rabbinic source is found for this quotation; cf. Obermann, p. 142, n. b/27, for a discussion of its possible origin.

As for those sins that are major,[40] and are like fire [touched] to clothing, like a sword [struck] against the neck, like an arrow [shot] at the horseman, like a snare [entangling] the feet, like deafness [affecting] hearing, like demotion from high rank, and like reduction[41] to low esteem after glory and honor—all of these may be derived from Scripture, as **123a** it is said, *Can a man take fire in his bosom, and his clothes not be burned?* (Prov. 6:27);[42] and also, *Till an arrow strike through his liver*, etc. (Prov. 7:23a); and also, *The way of the wicked is as darkness, they know not at what they stumble* (Prov. 4:19);[43] and also, *But her end is bitter as wormwood, sharp as a two-edged sword* (Prov. 5:4); and also, *Their ears shall be deaf*, etc. (Micah. 7:16b); and also *For a harlot is a deep ditch*, etc. (Prov. 23:27); and also *All the horns of the wicked also will I cut off; but the horns of the righteous shall be lifted up* (Ps. 75:11), meaning that as the wicked are destroyed, the state of the righteous is exalted. All these Scriptural proof verses were excerpted not by **123b** me but by my late father.[44] Any intelligent man who examines carefully and meditates seriously upon all that I have mentioned [can hardly go astray, as the Sages have said, "Any bashful man][45] will not easily sin."

[THE WAYS OF PENITENCE]

Since God Most High is aware of the proneness of some people to engage in disobedient acts, He has made penitence available to them as a refuge for him who would betake him-

40. Obermann suggests that these similes may be based on *Bet ha-Midrash*, *2*, 122. [*Al-jasīmah*, literally "corpulent," emended by Obermann (after HY) to *li-jismihi*, "that are to one's body like fire," etc.—LN]

41. [For *kal-zawāl* presumably read *kal-ḥawāl*.—LN]

42. H adds in Arabic: "this is said by way of simile, 'If a man pours fire into his bosom, his clothes cannot but be burned.'"

43. H adds in Arabic: "that is to say, The way of the wrongdoers is as darkness, they know not at what they stumble."

44. HY has here: "I, Nissim, have not made these interpretations myself; they were made by my father, my teacher, the Chief Rabbi." Cf. Hirschberg, p. 81, n. 16; Obermann, pp. 143–44, n. 31/32.

self thereto; provided, however, that his penitence satisfies four conditions.[46]

The first condition is the discontinuance of the disobedient acts in which he is engaged, as it is said, *Let the wicked forsake his way, and the man of iniquity his thoughts; and let him return unto the Lord, and He will have compassion upon him, and to our God, for He will abundantly pardon* (Isa. 55:7).[47] Proof of his having discontinued [disobedience] consists in his being able to associate with the person in whose company he had previously committed an act of disobedience [without repeating the same act], from which it would then be evident that he had indeed discontinued and repented what he had been doing, as the Sages have said in the Talmud,[48] "What is the definition of a penitent? R. Judah said in the name of Rab: [One who has an opportunity to transgress once, and then again, and is saved from it, is absolved. R. Judah added: It must be] with the same woman, in the same place, and for the same length of time." This [last stipulation] is not an essential one, and is merely a matter[49] of happenstance; and under [all] other circumstances, so long as he has discontinued what he had been doing,[50] [his penitence is valid]. For this stipulation would imply that people must follow the penitent to make certain that he has fulfilled this [particular requirement], which is why I have not made this stipulation a prerequisite. On the other hand, so long as he has not discontinued [his disobedience], his penitence is not valid. The forefathers **124b** have pro-

45. Missing in H, and restored by Obermann (p. 144, n. 36) on the basis of HY. Cf. B. Neḏ 20a.

46. Compare with the Muslim version of three principles of penitence, al-Ghazālī, *Iḥyā*ʾ, *4*, 25 f.

47. H adds in Arabic: "that is to say, Let the evildoer discontinue the transgression in which he is engaged, and a man his thought and what he is intending to do, and let him return **124a** to God, and He will have mercy on him, for He will show him abundant pardon and forgiveness."

48. B. Yoma 86b.

49. [For *in* presumably read *amr*.—LN]

50. Large lacuna in Ḳ (Abramson, p. 500). [Presumably read *taraka mā kāna yaʿmal*.—LN]

pounded ten parables concerning the penitent, which our master Saadiah has explained in his Commentary,[51] and I will therefore not cite them here.

The second condition is that the penitent must show profound regret of the sins which he had previously committed, as it is said, *Surely after that I was turned, I repented; and after that I was instructed, I smote upon my thigh; I was ashamed, yea, even confounded, because I did bear the reproach of my youth* (Jer. 31:19).[52] And the Sages have said,[53] "Whosoever acts [wrongfully] and then shows contrition, will be forgiven."[54] **125a** Man cannot refrain from penitence if he reflects upon the enormity of his sins and the multitude of his evil deeds, and [realizes that] penitence will bring him forgiveness for all that he had misdone.

Thus you learn from the story[55] of Ben Durdaya[56] how he worshiped idols for twelve years and left no harlot without fornicating with her—his tale is long, and I will not cite it at length, nor is there any need to explain it [here]. Yet when he reflected upon the consequences, and looked into all the acts of disobedience which he had committed, and all the pleasures which he had attained, and [realized] that he had earned thereby nothing but sins, intense regret overcame him

51. Obermann and Hirschberg suggest that the reference is to Saadiah's *Sefer hag-Galuy*, ed. Harkavy (Berlin, 1891), pp. 176–77. Obermann (p. 145, n. a/b) suggests that R. Nissim is referring to ten parables found in various places in Rabbinic literature which were expounded by Saadiah. [Abramson (p. 500, n. 15) refers to Saadiah's *Amānāt*, 5th discourse (ed. S. Landauer, [Leyden, 1880], pp. 168 ff.; tr. Rosenblatt, YJS, *1*, 209 ff.), where the penitent is the last of the ten categories of man's virtues and vices, and must fulfill four conditions of penitence (Landauer, p. 177; Rosenblatt, p. 220).—LN]

52. H adds in Arabic: "that is to say, After a man's return, he is sorry; after he acknowledges and understands the punishment [due him], he slaps his face in shame and embarrassment for what he had done in the beginning."

53. B. Ber 12b.

54. H adds in Arabic: "that is to say, If a man commits an error and is then sorry, God Most High will forgive him for it."

55. The source for this paragraph is B. AZ 17a.

56. H adds here: "all that he had done," which Obermann considers a dittography from the preceding line

of all that had come to pass. And so he rested his head between his knees and wept bitterly until he died, **125b** whereupon a voice came forth from heaven proclaiming that his penitence had been accepted, his sins forgiven, and his errors pardoned, and that he had become one of those who have earned the reward of the hereafter, as the Sages have said, "A heavenly voice came forth and said, '[Rabbi][57] Eleazar ben Durdaya has been accepted as a penitent, and he is now among the people of the hereafter.' Thereupon Rabbi [Judah] wept and said, 'There are those who attain their world[-to-come] in a single moment. Happy are the penitent, for not only are they accepted, but they are also called Rabbi.'"

The third condition is the pledge that the penitent will not return to any of his previous misdeeds, as it is said, *Asshur shall not save us*, etc. (Hos. 14:4), meaning that [if] you pledge that you will not repeat your acts of disobedience and will not **126a** [continue to] rely on the king of Assyria to save you, your penitence will be accepted, as it is said thereafter, *I will heal their backsliding, I will love them freely; for Mine anger is turned away from him* (Hos. 14:5). So long, however, as he does not pledge to cease reverting [to sin], and is confident that upon having sinned [again] he will again repent of what he had misdone, his contrition is imperfect and his repentance is invalid, as the Mishnah puts it,[58] "He who says, 'I shall first sin and then repent,' will be granted no time to do repentance."[59] **128b, line 1** Thus also, if he sins, and is confident that the [next] Day of Atonement will bring him pardon for that sin, it will bring him no pardon at all, as the Mishnah puts it,[60] "[He who says], 'I shall sin, and the [next]

57. Omitted in H but found in HY and in the source. The title is an important point in the story, being a sign of the degree of acceptance of his penitence. Cf. Obermann, p. 146, n. 36; Hirschberg, p. 82, n. 25.

58. Yoma 8:9 (cf. Ab̲ 5:18).

59. At this point the copyist of H seems to have been misled by some misplaced leaves in the prototype from which he was copying. Obermann's rearrangement of the material is followed here; cf. his note, p. 147, n. 25.

60. Yoma 8:9.

Day of Atonement will bring [me] atonement [for it],' the Day of Atonement will bring no atonement [for him]." And the Sages have said further,[61] "[Even though Rabbi (Judah) taught that the Day of Atonement atones for all sins, repented and unrepented], it is different when he relies upon this," meaning that the Day of Atonement will not wash him clean of that sin, if he committed it out of reliance upon the Day of Atonement, saying, "Why should I worry? I will commit this error—behold, the Day of Atonement is approaching, and on it [all] my errors will be forgiven." They will not be forgiven. And Ben Sira has said on this subject, *Count not upon forgiveness, that thou shouldst add sin to sin. And say not, His mercies are great, He will forgive the multitude of mine iniquities; for mercy and wrath are with him, and His indignation abideth upon the ungodly* (Sir. 5:5–6).[62] If, however, **129a** he offers his pledge, and does not have it in his soul ever to return to anything of what he had been misdoing, and if thereafter he sins [again] and again repents, this repentance will be accepted from him, because his first repentance was complete and wholehearted, and he was merely induced to pay heed to the Inclination to evil on a subsequent occasion, and did sin, and repented of this sin also. Therefore this repentance of his [too] will be accepted; indeed, even if he repeatedly wavers between contrition and acts of disobedience, he will be forgiven in the first instance [for all his previous sins], according to this condition.[63]

The fourth condition is [the penitent's] seeking forgiveness from his Lord, and imploring and beseeching Him to forgive him for what he had misdone, and to pardon him for his previous errors, as it is said, **129b** *Take with you words,* [*and return unto the Lord*] (Hos. 14:3), and again, *And turn unto the Lord your God, for He is gracious and compassionate, long-suffering,*

61. B. Yoma 87a.

62. See also Saadiah, *Sefer hag-Galuy*, pp. 176–77. Cf. Hirschberg, p. 83, n. 28.

63. For this explanation cf. also Saadiah, *Amānāt*, ed. Landauer, p. 179, tr. Rosenblatt, p. 223.

and abundant in mercy, and repenteth Him of the evil (Joel 2:13).[64] Included in this [entreaty] must be admission before his Lord [of his sins] and humbling [of himself], **126a, line 8** in order to subdue his spirit. It is similar to what the prophets had done, one of whom said, *And pardon our iniquity and our sin, and take us for Thine inheritance* (Exod. 34:9); and another said, *We have sinned with our fathers, we have done iniquitously, we have dealt wickedly* (Ps. 106:6); and still another said, *I was ashamed, yea, even confounded*, etc. (Jer. 31:19). That is why **126b** the Sages have imposed upon us the obligation of confession [of sins].

If the sinner's penitence includes all these four conditions, it is complete, and he becomes worthy of pardon and deserving of reward.

[STATUS OF THE PENITENT]

The penitent should not think that his status[65] in the hereafter will not be high; on the contrary, it will be higher and loftier than the [status of] the righteous, as the Sages have said, "In the place where penitents stand, not [even] the perfectly righteous can stand."[66] For the perfectly righteous man had not become accustomed to taking pleasure in forbidden things, so that righteousness and abstention became second nature to him, since he knew nothing else. The penitent, on the other hand, had tasted forbidden delights and had become accustomed to them; therefore, having abandoned them and desisted from them, he has earned a great reward, since it is obvious and clear that one who has become used **127a** to something finds it [more] difficult to abandon it. Do you not see how, in our own day, villagers eat for the most part barley bread, without [even] any seasoning? Had God Most High

64. H adds in Arabic: "that is to say, Seek out from among yourselves words and admonition and return unto God, your Lord, for He is merciful, kind, long-suffering, abundant of grace and beneficence, and forgiving of sin."
65. [For *tawbatuhu* read *darajatuhu* (Abramson, p. 516).—LN]
66. B. Ber 34b; B. Sanh 99a.

made it obligatory upon us[67] to eat barley bread, the reward of kings, who are not used to eating it, would have been greater than the reward of those [like us] who are used to it.

The Sages have propounded two parables about this.[68] The first[69] is that of a man who bought two [lean] cows and took care to feed and water them well, until they became fat cows and grew used to their place, so that their owner would go away and leave them at the trough. One day one of them ran away to the wilderness and remained there a long time, until she [finally] returned to her place and her companion, of her own will, **127b** after [her owner] had despaired of [recovering] her. He rejoiced greatly over her and was glad to have her back, and increased her feed, drink, and grooming. She thus gained greater favor with him than the other one, because she had returned after he had given her up.

The other parable[70] is that of a man who bought two saplings, which he planted, watered, and tended. One of them bore fruit, but the other did not, and he grieved about it. Several years later, the other one, too, brought forth fine fruit, and he rejoiced over it [more than he did over the first one].[71] Even so the status of the penitents in the hereafter is higher than that of the righteous.

[SAYINGS OF THE SAGES CONCERNING PENITENCE]

The Sages have said on this subject,[72] "Great is penitence, for it brings healing to the world, as it is said, *Return, ye back-*

67. [For *irtaḍā* read *iftaraḍa* (Abramson, p. 516).—LN] H has: "of them," but Obermann (p. 150, n. 27) suggests reading "of us," as in HY. [Abramson's text omits "of them."—LN]

68. This introduction presupposes a Rabbinic source for the two parables, which has not yet been found; cf. Obermann, p. 150, n. b; Hirschberg, p. 85, n. 31 (misprinted 30; cf. Corrigenda, p. 119).

69. Obermann compares this parable to Luke 15:4 ff., the parable of the lost sheep.

70. Cf. Ginzberg, *Genizah Studies, 1*, 202; Hirschberg, p. 84, n. 31 (misprinted 30).

71. [So HY (Obermann, p. 151, n. 22). Abramson (p. 517): "very much, more than he did over the one which bore fruit immediately."—LN]

sliding children, I will heal **128a** *your backslidings. Here we are, we are come unto Thee* (Jer. 3:22)."[73] And they have said also, "Great is penitence, for it reaches up to the Throne of Glory, as it is said, *Return, O Israel, unto the Lord thy God, for thou hast stumbled in thine iniquity* (Hos. 14:2)."[74] And they said further, "Great is penitence, seeing that for the sake of a single individual who has done penance, the Holy One, blessed be He, forgives the whole world." Moreover,[75] repentance is accepted from a man even [as late as] one moment before his death, as it is said, *Thou turnest man to destruction,*[76] *and sayest, Return, ye children of men* (Ps. 90:3). **129b, line 7** Furthermore,[77] most people have the knowledge of their life-span hidden from them, and do not know the time of their departure from this world, and it is therefore incumbent upon them to hasten their repentance, lest the sinner should decease while still in his sin and consequently be punished in the hereafter. For the more a man hastens [to repent], the better for him **130a** and the more abundant his reward. That is why the Mishnah states,[78] "Repent one day before your death," so that a man would be all his life in the state[79] of repentance, especially seeing that it prolongs a man's life, as the Sages have said,[80] "Great is penitence, for it lengthens a man's days and years, as it is said, *And when the wicked turneth from his wickedness . . . he shall live thereby* (Ezek. 33:19)."[81]

72. B. Yoma 86a–b.

73. H adds in Arabic: "that is to say, Return, O ye who have been unruly, so that I may heal your sickness—meaning, in consequence of the sincerity of their repentance."

74. H adds in Arabic: "that is to say, Return, O Children of Israel, to God your Lord, for you have become disgraced by your sins."

75. P. Ḥaḡ 2:1, 77c.

76. [So AV; JV: *contrition.*—LN]

77. The three following sentences are from B. Shab 153a.

78. Aḇ 2:10.

79. [For the indistinct *quds* read *ḥāl* (Abramson, p. 517).—LN]

80. B. Yoma 86b.

81. H adds in Arabic: "that is to say, If the evildoer turns back from his [evil deeds], his life will be long."

How great is the loving-kindness of God our Lord,[82] seeing that He did not create the illness until [after] He had created the cure, for penitence is reckoned among the "seven things[83] created prior to the creation of the world, as it is said, *Before the mountains were brought forth, or ever Thou hadst formed the earth and the world, even from everlasting to everlasting, Thou art God, Thou turnest man* **130b** *to destruction*,[76] etc. (Ps. 90:2–3)." I implore Him Most High to place us among those who are worthy of eternal bliss, as His saintly one, [David], had implored Him, saying, *Thou makest me to know the path of life, in Thy presence is fullness of joy, in Thy right hand bliss for evermore* (Ps. 16:11).[84]

Were it not for my fear of being long-winded, I would have mentioned the categories of penitents and of those who are punished in the hereafter, their standings in regard to reward and punishment, and the duration of their chastisement, as mentioned by the Sages in the Talmud.[85] I will, however, with the help of God Most High, mention this in another work.[86]

82. The following sentence is based on B. Meḡ 13b.

83. B. Pes 54a.

84. H adds in Arabic: "that is to say, I ask Thee, O Lord of the worlds, to show me the path of life, so that great joy everlasting shall be my share."

85. For example, B. Shab 152a–153a.

86. Nissim's *Mĕgillaṯ Sĕṯarim*, Hirschberg, p. 86, n. 38. Cf. Introduction, p. xxii, and Abramson, pp. 179–360.

CHAPTER [XXVIII]

[CITRONS AS REMEDY]

I shall now return to my main subject. Know—may God aid you and enable you **131a** to perform good deeds—that our masters have told[1] of a man who had two sons, one of whom, unlike the other, was eager to do good and loved acts of charity, even though he was poor. The other was the opposite of this, even though he was rich. When the Festival of the Hosannas[2] came around, the poor son's wife said to him, "Husband, take this dirham and buy something with it for your children to sustain themselves with during the festival." He took the dirham, and as he went off, he met the communal leader[3] who asked him, "Do you perhaps have something for alms to the poor?" He replied, "Yes," and gave him the dirham. Fearing to return to his children without anything, he went to the synagogue, where he found some citrons which the children had thrown away after they had left the synagogue **131b**, subsequent to the recitation of the Hosannas. He picked up enough of them to fill his girdle, and went to the seashore, where he found a ship sailing to the king's city—which was near his[4] city—whereupon he boarded it and sailed with the ship's company to the [capital] city in less than two hours.

Now the king had been stricken with an illness of the stomach and was told, "Nothing will avail you nor will you be relieved except by the citron of the Jews, over which they pronounce a blessing." While his servants were searching for it, they came upon the poor son who had disembarked from the ship, and asked him, "Do you perhaps have anything

1. Source for the following story: Lev. Rabbah 37:2, 106b.

2. The Festival of Hoshaᶜna Rabbah ("the Great Hosanna"), which falls on the seventh day of Sukkot (Festival of Tabernacles).

3. *Firnās* (Hebrew *parnas*); HY and source have: "alms-collectors."

4. Literally "their."

to sell?" He replied, "[I] am a poor man—I have nothing with me to sell, nor anything [else] of use to you," but they looked [at him more closely], and behold, he had what they were looking for and what the king wanted. When the man was brought before the king, **132a** the latter ate one of the citrons, and forthwith the illness from which he suffered ceased to affect him. So the king ordered the man's girdle to be filled with dinars in payment for the citrons, and said to him, "Ask a favor, if there be anything you need, so that we may grant it." He replied, "I wish the king would command someone to take me back to my place, and let a proclamation be made in my town that everyone is to come out to meet me." The king accordingly ordered him to be returned to his place and a proclamation to be made to the people of his town to come forth to meet him, and this was done. All the people came out to meet him, including his brother, who set out to sea [in a boat to reach him first], but as he was on the point of meeting him, his boat overturned, and he drowned before reaching him and died. The man then disembarked from the ship with high honor and great glory and went to his brother's house **132b**, where he took hold of all his possessions, and his circumstances became eased. His wife thereupon said to him, "God indeed doth nought but bestow many favors! What brought you to this estate?" So he told her all that had happened to him, and as time went on, so did his wealth increase and so did he multiply good deeds, and he continued to prosper for as long as he lived, until his death.

CHAPTER [XXIX]

[THE DIRHAM THAT BROUGHT BLESSING][1]

Eleazar of Ṣiṣiṯ Bebai[2] was also noted for great charitableness and openhandedness, and whenever the alms-collectors met him he would give them everything he had on him, until [finally], whenever they saw him from afar, they would hide from him in order that he should not see them. One day, as he was leaving his house with a dinar in his hand to buy **133a** a silver bracelet for his daughter—the day of her wedding to her husband was drawing near—he saw the collectors from afar, but they did not see him. When he drew near to them, they fled from him, but he kept following them until he overtook them, and said to them, "I adjure you by God Most High to tell me what you are now [collecting] for." They replied, "For an orphan boy whom we have married off to an orphan girl, and we now wish to buy them some things which they cannot do without, such as clothing and the necessary equipment of vessels." So he gave them what he had in his hand, saying, "These have precedence over my daughter," and leaving nothing with him except a dirham which was tied up in the tip of his girdle. Therewith he bought some wheat, came back with it to his house, placed it in a storeroom[3] that he had, and went off. His wife asked her daughter, "What **133b** did your father buy today?" She replied, "Whatever he bought he dumped in the storeroom." [So she arose to look in the storeroom],[4] and behold, it was filled with wheat. When her father came in in the evening, she said to him, "Come and see what God Most High has given us!" He then said to her, "This is [meant for] alms. You have only a share therein, the same as the share to be taken by [each one of] the poor in Israel."

1. Source for the following story: B. Ta 24a.
2. Source has: Eleazar of Birta (Obermann, p. 156, n. 3/4).
3. [So source; H has *mustarq*[*ā*?], "attic, elevated storage space (?)."—LN]
4. Restored by Obermann (p. 157, n. 1) from HY.

CHAPTER [XXX]

[INTERPRETATIONS OF LETTERS]

It is said about Abbaye[1] that he loved almsgiving and was eager to do good. When he saw the alms-collector, he would follow him until he could give him [all he had with him], for he was well-to-do. After a period of time, however, his wealth slipped away and nothing remained to him except a plot of land and a cow. One day R. Eleazar, R. Joshua, and R. ᶜAḳiba came to the place **134a** on [the business of] alms for the poor, since they were about to collect for it. When Abbaye saw them, he entered his house, his face pale, and wept. He then said to his wife, "What shall I do? The Sages[2] have come to collect alms for the poor, and I have nothing to give them." She replied, "Do not worry. Go out, sell half of the plot of land, and give them the proceeds thereof." He did so.

It is said that when afterwards he went out to plow the remainder of the plot, the plowshare got caught in the ground, and the cow kept on walking until she broke the plowshare and fell, [injuring herself]. Abbaye thereupon took a hoe, dug up the spot, and found in it a great treasure containing a large amount of money, at which he exclaimed,

"It was for my prosperity
That my cow suffered injury."[3]

Observe then **134b** the eagerness of these virtuous men to be generous in almsgiving and in benevolence.

That is why the Sages have taught,[4] saying, "Why does the

1. The source of the following story is Lev. Rabbah, 5, 16a; P. Hor 3:7, 48a. In the sources the story is about Abba Judah or Abba Yudan.

2. H adds "of blessed memory"; probably added automatically by a scribe, although these Sages were still living at the time of the event reported; cf. Obermann, p. 157, n. 25.

3. This jingle-like phrase is in Hebrew in the text. H adds in Arabic: "that is to say, It was for my benefit that the plowshare broke and my cow fell."

4. B. Shab 104a.

front of the letter *gimel* face the back of the letter *daleṯ*?[5] Because he who dispenses (*gomel*) loving-kindness runs after the poor (*dallim*), [facing their backs]." They said also, "Why does the letter *ḳof* turn its back to the letter *reš*, and not its face? Because the Holy One (*haḳ-Ḳadoš*), blessed be He, said, 'I cannot bear to look at the wicked (*rašaᶜ*)'; and this is why the *ḳof* was left open and was not closed, so that should the wicked repent, he will find the gates of repentance open." Understand then what [mysteries] are hidden underneath these letters!

It is incumbent upon a man, therefore, not to take lightly even a single letter of the Torah, for underneath each letter thereof there are many meanings. Do you not see **135a** that there are some views, as taught by the Sages in the Talmud, the starting point of which is the addition of a single letter in the Scriptural text, as when they have said,[6] "[If this is said to be so], Scripture should have said *wĕ-yibbem* (*and perform the duty of a husband's brother*, Deut. 25:5); why then does it say *wĕ-yibbĕmah*, [the added letter *he* signifying *unto her*]? To indicate [the prohibiton of] both [the forbidden female relative and her co-wife]." They thus deduced an additional rule from the additional letter. Or as when they have said,[7] "[If] this is said to be so, Scripture should have said *u-ḇaᶜal* (*and marrieth*, Deut. 24:1); why then does it say *u-ḇĕᶜalah*, [the added letter *he* signifying *her*]? To indicate both [that a woman may be acquired in marriage by sexual intercourse, and that an Israelite bondsmaid cannot be so acquired]." Here too they have deduced a rule from the additional letter. [Or as when they have said],[8] "If this is said to be so, Scripture should have said *loʾ taḳol* (*Thou shalt not revile* [*God*], Exod. 22:27); why then [did it use the intensive form] *loʾ tĕḳallel*? To indicate [the prohibition of reviling] both [God and judge]." Or

5. H: *dal*, either a mistake for the Hebrew *daleṯ* or a (deliberate) misspelling of the Arabic *dāl*.

6. Cf. B. Yeḇ 8a–b.

7. B. Ḳid 9b.

8. B. Sanh 66a–b.

as when they have said,[9] "Is it then said 'and branches'? Is it not said just *branches* (Lev. 23:40)?"[10]—[and so forth], as we have explained it and the meaning of it in "The Book of the Law of the Lulab"[11] which I have composed.

The believer must hold it to be true that there is not a single additional letter in the Torah that does not have an [additional] significance **135b**, all the more so an [additional] word, and even more so an [additional] verse. He must not go astray as did Manasseh, [king of Judah], son of Hezekiah, about whom the Sages have said in the Talmud,[12] "*But the soul that doeth aught with a high hand*, etc. (Num. 15:30)—this refers to Manasseh son of Hezekiah, who used to sit and expound [Scriptural] narratives to prove them worthless, saying, 'Did Moses have to write *And Lotan's sister was Timna* (Gen. 36:22b); *And Timna was concubine to Eliphaz*, etc. (Gen. 36:12); *And Reuben went in the days of the wheat harvest and found*, [etc.] (Gen. 30:14)?' Thereupon a heavenly voice came forth and said to him, *Thou sittest and speakest against thy brother, thou slanderest thine own mother's son. These things hast thou done, and should I have kept silence? Thou hadst thought that I was altogether such a one as thyself, but I will reprove thee, and set the cause before thine eyes* (Ps. 50:20–21). [And of him it is stated] in post-Mosaic Scripture,[13] *Woe unto them that draw iniquity with cords of vanity*, **136a** *and sin as it were with a cart rope* (Isa. 5:18)."

I think I ought to explain [here] what the Sages have said about this matter, in order not to deprive my book of any [possible] usefulness. They have said[14] that Timna was a daughter of royalty, as it is said, *the chief of Lotan* (Gen. 36:29), and every chief was a king [in all respects], except that he did not wear a crown upon his head. Now when she wanted to

9. B. Suk 34b.

10. The absence of the conjunction "and" in this case and its presence in the case of the myrtle and willow that follow is taken to mean that while the last two must be tied together, the first need not.

11. Cf. Introduction, p. xxii, and Abramson, pp. 157–176.

12. B. Sanh 99b.

13. *Kabbalah*, literally "tradition," the part of Scripture following the Torah.

14. B. Sanh 99b.

enter into the faith of Israel, she was unable to find a way to do so, because the Patriarchs—I mean Abraham, Isaac, and Jacob—would not accept her. So she went forth and became a servant to Eliphaz son of Esau, saying, "For me being a servant to this people is better than being a chieftainess to any other people," or as the Sages have put it,[15] "Be thou a tail unto lions, and be not a head unto foxes." From her descended Amalek who waged war against Israel, which was a punishment **136b** upon Israel from God Most High, because notwithstanding that she wanted to enter into the faith, they would not accept her. That is why the [aforecited] verse was incorporated [in Scripture], so that we should know of this [affair], and so that whenever a person wishes to enter into our faith, we should accept him.

As for the verse[16] *And Reuben went*, [etc.] (Gen. 30:14), its purpose is to teach us that he did not regard robbery as lawful and would not seize anything owned or possessed [by someone else], but rather took only what was permitted to him to take and what was allowed. He therefore left alone pomegranates, grapes, and apples, which were subject to ownership and were thus forbidden, and took permitted mandrakes because they were allowed, or as the Sages have put it,[17] "This shows that the righteous do not extend their hands to commit robbery." It is therefore incumbent upon us to learn a lesson from this and be warned of it.

Since I have mentioned what the Sages have said about these verses **137a**, we shall also explain it [by] what is written in another place in the Talmud,[18] in order to enlarge the usefulness [of this book] and increase the reward.

[VERSES WHICH ARE ESSENTIAL PARTS OF THE TORAH]

"R. Simeon ben Laḳish said: There are many verses which

15. Aḇ 4:15.
16. Source for the following paragraph; Gen. Rabbah, 72, 280a–b; cf. Saadiah, *Sefer hag-Galuy*, p. 175.
17. B. Sanh 99b, and elsewhere.
18. B. Ḥul 60b. Cf. also Saadiah, *op. cit.*, p. 173.

seem fit to be burned—like the books of the heretics[19]—but are really essential parts of the Torah. Thus, *And the Avvim that dwelt in villages*, etc. (Deut. 2:23)—of what use to us is the writing down of this verse? The Sages have explained the usefulness of it, namely that it tells us of the fact that as for the treaty which Abraham had made with Abimelech, when the latter said to him, [*Swear unto me*] . . . *that thou wilt not deal falsely with me, nor with my son, nor with my son's son*, etc. (Gen. 21:23), the Israelites did not abrogate it, but rather confirmed it. Now the Avvim were descendants of Abimelech, as it is said, *The five lords of the Philistines . . . also the Avvim* (Josh. 13:3), and dwelt in *villages as far as Gaza* (Deut. 2:23). **137b** Since we find that the Israelites had seized these villages and had settled in them, had Scripture not informed us that it was the Caphtorim who first seized these villages from the Avvim, we would have thought that the Israelites had abrogated the treaty. The verse thus tells us that the Israelites did not wage war against the Avvim.

The same applies to the verse *For Heshbon*, etc. (Num. 21:26), whose setting down serves to inform us of the fact that the Israelites did not violate the word of God Most High, *Be not at enmity with Moab*, etc. (Deut. 2:9). For they seized Heshbon from the hand of Sihon, [king of the Amorites]. Even though this city originally belonged to Moab, it was Sihon who had waged war against Moab and had seized it from their hand, whereat the Israelites were permitted to seize it [in their turn]. Had this verse not established this fact, we would have thought that the Israelites had seized Heshbon [directly] from Moab and had thus violated the prohibition of waging war against them **138a** or even approaching them[20] [in a hostile manner].

Should someone ask,[21] why did God Most High prohibit waging war against Moab, as it is said, *Neither contend with*

19. Reading *minin*; H has "Midian," while the source has "Sadducees," probably because of censorship; cf. Obermann, p. 162, n. 2. This clause is found in some MSS of the Talmud and not in others.

20. Cf. Jacob N. Epstein, in *Tarbiṣ* 2 (1930), 12–13.

21. Source for this paragraph: B. BḲ 38b, and elsewhere. Cf. Gen. 19:30–38.

them in battle (Deut. 2:9), while in regard to Ammon He has prohibited opposing them in any manner, warlike or other, as it is said, *Harass them not, nor contend with them* (Deut. 2:19), [the answer is that] the Sages have said that inasmuch as Lot's elder daughter had called her son Moab, [meaning] "This son that I have borne is by my father," and was not ashamed of [revealing] this fact, God Most High forbade only the waging of war against Moab. In the case of Lot's younger daughter, however, who had named her son, [the forefather of Ammon], euphemistically Ben Ammi, [meaning, "The son of my people"], God did not permit opposing them in any manner, or as the Sages have put it, "The Holy One, blessed be He, does not withhold reward even for a decorous expression."

For this reason did the Sages enact a prohibition, saying,[22] "One should not send forth an unseemly word out of his mouth, **138b** for Scripture itself employs a circumlocution of eight letters rather than send forth an unseemly word out of its mouth. R. Papa says nine [letters]. Rabba says ten. Rab Aḥa bar Jacob says sixteen." All of these [counts of letters] are based on [the negative words in] *Of beasts that are not clean* (Gen. 7:8), *That is not clean by reason of that which chanceth him by night* (Deut. 23:11), and [*For he thought*], *Something hath befallen* [*him, he is not clean*], etc. (1 Sam. 20:26). And they said also in another place,[23] "Rab Ḥanan bar Rabba said: Everyone knows for what purpose a bride enters the bridal chamber; but whosoever utters an unseemly word [about it], or defiles his mouth by uttering an obscenity—even if a decree of seventy years of good fortune has already been sealed [for him], it will be changed to ill fortune." It is even forbidden to listen to such indecencies, as the Sages have said,[24] "Why are a man's **139a** fingers tapered like pegs? So that should a man hear something unseemly, he might put his finger in

22. B. Pes 3a.
23. B. Keṯ 8b; variant, B. Shab 33a.
24. B. Keṯ 5b.

his ear."[25] And they have said also,[24] "R. Ishmael says: Why is the ear all hard, while [its] lobe is soft? So that should a man hear something unseemly, he might fold the lobe into the ear," in order not to hear what is forbidden to be heard.

Scripture supplies a similar indication[26] to us in the verse, *Which Hermon the Sidonians call* [*Sirion*, *and the Amorites call it Senir*] (Deut. 3:9), which tells us that the [alternate] names of the [same] mountains of the Land of Israel were Senir and Sirion, thus informing us that these nations named their castles and their cities after the names [of landmarks] of the Land of Israel, because of its high **139b** status with them, "to teach you how beloved the Land of Israel is to the nations of the world."

And they have said[26] further concerning the verse *And as for the people*, *he removed them city by city* (Gen. 47:21), that by removing the Egyptians from city to city the lord Joseph intended that they should not rebuke his brothers for being perpetual transients in their cities, since a person blamed for something would not attribute the same thing to someone else, or as the Mishnah puts it,[27] "It has been taught that R. Nathan says: A defect that is in you, do not attribute it to your companion, or as people are wont to say, If there is a hanging in a person's family record, he should not say to his companion, String up this fish," meaning that if a person's relative had been hanged upon the scaffold, he should not say to his companion, "String up this fish with your hand." This interpretation is the one given **140a** in some academies; there are also other interpretations, but the meaning of the Mishnah is [in any case] that he who has a fault should not blame his companion for the same thing.

In like manner[28] have the Sages interpreted names. Why

25. H adds in Arabic: "that is to say, Why are a man's fingers shaped like pegs? So that if he hears what is not permitted, he may put his finger in his ear."

26. B. Ḥul 60b. Cf. Saadiah, *Sefer hag-Galuy*, p. 177.

27. B. BM 59b. HY omits the reference to the Mishnah. The citation is from the Baraita.

28. Source for this paragraph: Tanḥuma, *Ḳoraḥ*, 12 (cf. Num. Rabbah 18, 152b).

did Abraham name [his son] Isaac? Because in the name Isaac (*Yṣḥḳ*) the letter *yoḏ*, [whose numerical value is ten], stands for Abraham's ten[29] trials; the letter *ṣaḏe*, [whose numerical value is ninety], stands for Sarah's ninety years[30] when she gave birth to Isaac; the letter *ḥeṯ*, [whose numerical value is eight], stands for the eight days of circumcision,[31] since Isaac was the first to be circumcised on the eighth day [after birth]; and the letter *ḳof*, [whose numerical value is one hundred], stands for Abraham's age of one hundred years when Isaac was born.[32] The same applies to Jacob (*Yᶜḳḇ*): the letter *yoḏ* corresponds to *And of all that Thou shalt give me I will surely give the tenth unto Thee* (Gen. 28:22); the letter *ᶜayin*, [whose numerical value is seventy], corresponds to *Thy fathers went down into Egypt with threescore and ten persons* (Deut. 10:22); the letter *ḳof* corresponds to **140b** the one hundred letters with which his father [Isaac] had blessed him, from *So God give thee* to *And blessed be every one that blesseth thee* (Gen. 27:28–29), not counting the Divine Name nor [the words] *thy mother's sons*, since he did not need them in view of the preceding *Be lord over thy brethren*. As for the letter *beṯ*, [whose numerical value is two], it indicates that Jacob will inherit both worlds.

Indeed, even in the Mishnah the Sages are particular about an added or subtracted letter. For example, they have asked,[33] "Did we learn *nizoneṯ* ('is to be maintained'), or did we learn *han-nizoneṯ* ('one who is maintained')?", or[34] "Did we learn *ᵓeno muᶜaḏ* ('is not forewarned'), or did we learn *wĕ-ᵓeno muᶜaḏ* ('but was not forewarned')?", the Talmud going into particulars as to how the passage should be understood. In other instances the transmitter [of the Mishnah] swears that it was

29. Cf. Aḇ 5:3. The ten trials are enumerated in ARN 33 (YJS, *10*, 132).
30. Cf. Gen. 17:17.
31. Cf. Gen. 21:4.
32. Cf. Gen. 21:5.
33. Keṯ 11:1; B. Keṯ 95b. Referring to a widow's right to be supported out of her deceased husband's estate.
34. BḲ 4:2; B. BḲ 37a. Referring to an animal whose owner was thrice forewarned, and is thereafter fully liable for any further damage caused by it.

transmitted thus-and-so, thus making any [discussion of] particulars unnecessary. For example, the Sages have asked,[35] "Did we learn *paṯ* [*ḳiṭniṯ* ('bread made of pulse') or *paṯ wĕ-ḳiṭniṯ* ('bread and pulse')?", whereupon R. Ḥisda swore that the correct reading was *paṯ*][36] *wĕ-ḳiṭniṯ*, with a long letter *waw*, shaped like the shovel [with which bread is placed] in the oven, or as the Sages have put it, "R. Ḥisda said to him: **141a** By God, the *waw* is necessary, as [long as] a [ship's] rudder (*murdĕya*ʾ) on the [river] Librut." Some have interpreted *murdĕya*ʾ to mean a sail yard, called *kahwār* in the language of Iraq.[37] But the correct interpretation is that it is the wooden instrument with which the carder cards a strip of cotton by striking it.[38] There are many instances like this [in the Talmud], which I will not mention at length.

Thus[39] also did God Most High say, *For it is no vain thing for you* (Deut. 32:47), meaning that there is not a single letter in the Torah but that it is necessary. Indeed, even if it is not a letter but only a mark underneath it, it has its uses. Thus, if we should inquire about the mark, [a large inverted letter *nun*], which stands in the section [beginning with] *And it came to pass, when the Ark set forward* (Num. 10:35–36), both at the beginning and at the end of the section, as did the Sages by asking why this section was marked with these marks, [the answer is] to inform us that this is not its place **141b**, and that its proper place is in [the chapter on] the [tribal] banners (Num. 2), since it is clear and evident that the proper place for it is there. The reason for its being placed here is to separate the two punishments. The first punishment is [implied in] *And they set forward from the Mount of the Lord* (Num. 10:33);

35. BM 7:1; B. BM 87a.

36. Bracketed words missing in H and restored by Obermann (p. 167, n. 2) from HY.

37. [Persian *kahwārah, gahwārah*, "cradle, swing," here evidently a swinging sail yard. For Torrey's interpretation of this whole passage, see Obermann, pp. lvii–lviii.—LN]

38. Hirschberg, p. 92, n. 17, gives the full text of this difficult passage in HY.

39. The following discussion is based on B. Shab 115b–116a.

the Sages said, "This teaches that on that day they turned away from the Lord,"[40] and they said further, "There is no doubt that punishment was meted out to them for this, even though Scripture does not expressly say so." The second punishment is [implied in] *And the people were as murmurers,* etc. (Num. 11:1).

Observe therefore and understand these sublime [hidden] meanings—how many more such there are, which remain undiscovered and are not truly known. *The law of the Lord is perfect, restoring the soul;* [*the testimony of the Lord is trustworthy*], etc. (Ps. 19:8)—"The Torah may be trusted to testify in behalf of them that study it."[41] Happy is he who is so privileged, as it is said, **142a** *Happy is the man that findeth wisdom, and the man that obtaineth understanding* (Prov. 3:13).

40. Cf. B. Ta 29a.
41. B. Yoma 72b.

CHAPTER [XXXI]

[THE LORD IS FAITHFUL IN REPAYING]

I will now return to the subject of this book. A certain Sage is reported to have said:[1] I used to know a man of the people of Palestine who had several children and a wife, but lived in this world in great destitution. Now it happened that I had to journey to Iraq and stay there for some years, and when I returned to the place I found him in the most perfect and comfortable state as to his material circumstances[2] and his livelihood. So I said to him, "I would like you to tell me how you attained this condition and how you acquired this wealth." He replied, "I was a plowman in [other people's] fields when you left me, and we maintained ourselves with what I would receive as my wages **142b**, together with whatever vegetables and other produce I would pick, using the leftovers to defray [other] living expenses. One day, while I was carrying on my work in one of the fields, a person of pleasant demeanor and handsome appearance stopped by me and said, '[My good] man, you will live in this world for seven years in great comfort and abundant wealth. Now do you prefer to have it soon or in your old age?' I thought that he was an astrologer looking for a fee from me for what he had told me, so I replied, 'I do not believe in the stars, and I have nothing to give you. Depart from me in peace!' He went away. The next day, behold, he came back, repeating to me what he had said to me the previous day, and I likewise gave him the same answer as I did **143a** then. When he returned to me a third time, I said to him, '[My good] man, you must not divert me from my work. You see my destitute condition—I have children who look forward to what I bring them. Do not sin on my account.' He replied, 'I have thrice addressed my question to

1. Source for this story: Yalḳuṭ Ruth 607, 1043.
2. Reading with Obermann (p. 169, n. 5) *dunyāhu* for *dīnihi*, "in his religion."

you. If you lend credence to me, let me know your choice—it will be better for you. [As for me], I will take nothing from you, either sooner or later.' His words made such an impression upon me that I said to him, '[My lord], please give me time until tomorrow, for I have someone whom I must consult in this [matter].' He replied, '[God] bless you.'[3]

"When I returned to my wife, I told her everything that the man had said to me, and that the matter was thus-and-so, and she said, 'Tell him, What is near is better than what is far.' I replied, 'Wife, **143b** is not old age a better and preferable time? I will then be unable to work, nor fit for hard labor.' She said, 'Husband, tell him what I told you, for it is more fitting. God Most High makes His choice unbeknownst to you. He will [surely] extend his favor to you at the time of your old age.' When I arose [to my work] in the morning, behold, the man had come back. He asked me, 'On what did your minds agree?' I replied, 'My lord, what is near is better than what is far.' He said, 'Arise and go back to your house, and leave [the work] that is in your hand, for your Creator has visited you with His mercy and has bestowed upon you His favors and His gifts.' So I returned to my house, reflecting upon my affair and saying [to myself], 'What assurance do I have of the truth of this promise, and how can I enter my house with empty hands, stripped of my daily wages **144a** and work, my family unable to find sustenance with which to maintain themselves?'

"While I was thus reflecting, I reached my house and was met by [my wife] who had come out to meet me, and when she saw me, she said to me, 'Come in and see the favor of our Lord, and what He has given us.' I entered my house and found it filled with good things and great and copious wealth, whereat our joy waxed abundant and our rejoicing great, and we gave thanks to God Most High for what He had bestowed upon us. My wife thereupon said to me, 'Take the advice that I am about to give you, and you will prosper.' I replied, 'I

3. [A pious way to signify consent.—LN]

did not disobey you in the beginning, and I will not disobey you in the future.' She said, 'Go to the market place and buy for yourself a manservant able to read and write.' I followed her advice, **144b** and [having purchased the manservant], put him in charge of the administration of charitable expenditures, commanding him to give to each person what he was entitled to—one used to riding would be given a mount, and one used to a manservant would be given a manservant. We then sat eating and drinking, going out only to the synagogue in the morning and in the evening, and [for any other purpose] that would earn a reward for us, until the seven years came to an end.

"When they came to an end, thieves entered our house and seized everything that was in it, so that nothing of what we had acquired was left for us. I then said to my wife, 'Did I not tell you that it was better for me to defer [God's] favor until the time of old age? What about our present condition? What shall we do now that we are known among the people as favored [with wealth]? I am grown old and laden with years, **145a** and can no longer do the work I used to do.' She replied, 'Husband, do not worry nor grieve. Take out your ledgers,[4] see what you have given to the poor, and let me know it.'"

When[5] this was reckoned up, it came to a large sum of money that had been given out in alms. Thereupon the woman fasted for three days, and then stood up humbling herself before her Lord and saying, "O Lord of both worlds, Thy saintly one, [Solomon], has said that whosoever wishes to lend unto the Lord a goodly loan, should give alms to the poor.[6] Now Thou, O Lord of both worlds, art faithful in repaying—repay therefore our loan.'"

4. [Reading with Torrey (Obermann, p. 171, n. 27) *dafātiraka*. The text has *bi-fāthirika* (Arabic *fāthūr*, "money tray").—LN]

5. In this paragraph the speaker is the Sage.

6. Cf. Prov. 19:17, *He that is gracious unto the poor lendeth unto the Lord.* Obermann cites also Koran 2:245 (246), "Who is he that will lend to God a goodly loan?", which has the same Arabic wording as here. Hirschberg (p. 95, n. 3) rejects the Koranic source, which does not speak of almsgiving.

The man continued: "That night I saw in a dream the same man who had originally come to me, and he said, 'God Most High has heard your wife's prayer, and will bestow upon you, out of what you have given out in alms to the poor, enough for you to live **145b** comfortably until the day of your death; and moreover the principal thereof will be kept for the two of you until the [future] world of recompense. When you awake in the morning, dig in such-and-such a place, and you will find there a great treasure containing a large sum of money.' When I awoke from my sleep, I informed my wife of the dream, betook myself to the place which the man had told me about, dug therein, and retrieved the money from it. And now we are as you see us, going out nowhere except to perform a deed that would earn a reward, or to the synagogue, or to [do other deeds of] righteousness. I have enough goods for us to live on, myself and my family, until we die."

And so, [continued the Sage], I praised God Most High who delivers from every distress, and I gave thanks to Him for His graciousness and kindness, and for His requiting His saintly ones and those who fear Him, for He will not let the wages of those who do good be wasted,[7] as it is said, *And showing* **146a** *mercy unto the thousandth generation of them that love Me and keep My commandments* (Exod. 20:6; Deut. 5:10).

7. Cf. Koran 9:121, "Verily God suffereth not the reward of the righteous to perish."

CHAPTER [XXXII]

[KING SOLOMON'S THREE COUNSELS][1]

A tale is told also of three brothers who were [living] in the land of Babylon during the reign of Solomon son of David. They came to him to ask him for a favor, but he said to them, "It is not proper for me to give you anything by way of alms. Hire yourselves out to me for one year for three hundred dinars." They did so. [At the end of the year], when they were about to depart, the youngest said to the eldest, "If we tell people that we were with Solomon son of David, they will ask, 'What did you learn of his wisdom?' What shall we say?" So [the youngest brother] returned and said to Solomon, "Master, I desire something. Give me leave to speak about it." Solomon gave him leave, and he continued, "I have been thinking **146b** that when I return to my city and say, 'I have been [with] Solomon,' the people will ask me, 'What did you learn of his wisdom?' What shall I answer them?" Solomon replied, "You have done your work and have received your wages. What you demand [now] is more precious than gold and silver," as it is said, *For the merchandise of it* (*of wisdom*) *is better than the merchandise of silver, and the gain thereof than fine gold* (Prov. 3:14).

The man thereupon said, "I would prefer to return the three hundred dinars and learn [instead] something of my master's wisdom that will be of benefit to me, so that when I relate it[2] in his name I may boast about it among the people." To which Solomon replied, "Each benefit will cost you one hundred dinars," and the man agreed. Then Solomon said, "When you reach a village past the time of the afternoon

1. This story, found in *Bet ha-Midrash*, *4*, 148–150, is not included in any edition of HY. The version given here is incomplete, omitting a major element, the use made by the young man of the advice given him. See below.

2. i.e., the wisdom.

prayer,[3] do not leave it [on that day] for any [other] place; when you come to a river, be the last of all **147a** the people to cross it; and do not reveal your secret to a woman, [not even[4] to your own wife." So the youngest brother immediately asked leave to mount his horse and hurried after his brothers. When he reached them, they said to him, "What have you learned?" He replied, "I learned what I learned."[5] He then traveled on with his brothers for nine hours until they reached a place which was suitable for making camp. The youngest brother said, "This is a good place to spend the night, since it offers water, firewood, and grass to pasture our horses. If you agree, let us spend the night here, and at dawn, if God grants us life, we shall go on our way in good order." His brothers, however, replied, "Fool, when you gave away (our) money and bought words therewith, we realized that there is no wisdom in you. We can still travel eight more miles before nightfall, yet you say we should stop here!" He said to them, "Do as you wish. As for me, I shall not stir from here." So they went on their way, while he remained there and proceeded to chop wood, made a fire, and built a shelter for himself and his animal, but let the horse graze until evening, when he gave it some barley, and he and his beast ate, and then he lay down to spend the night in safety.]

[His brothers meanwhile continued traveling until evening, but were unable to find pasture for their animals or wood for fire. A heavy snow fell on them, until they died of the intense cold, whereas the youth was protected from the snow by the shelter, the fire, and the food and drink. At dawn he set himself in order, mounted his horse, and resumed the road to follow his brothers, only to find them dead. When he saw

3. *Al-ʿaṣr*, one of the five daily prayers incumbent upon Muslims, corresponding to the Jewish *Minḥah* prayer, which may be recited at any time in the afternoon, before sunset.

4. The continuation of this story, as found in *Bet ha-Midrash* (above, n. 1), is reprinted by Hirschberg (pp. 96–97). It differs in some details from the text in H.

5. Meaning "I prefer to keep it to myself."

them, he fell upon them weeping, then took their money, buried them, and went on his way.]

[The sun came up and the snow melted, so that the rivers overflowed, and he was unable to cross the river (in front of him); he therefore immediately dismounted and set himself to wait until (the water) would recede. As he walked along the riverbank, he looked at the other side and saw there menservants of King Solomon leading two pack animals laden with gold. They called out to him, "Why don't you cross?" He replied, "Because the river is overflowing." Nevertheless they began crossing over, but when they entered the river, it swept over them, and they died. The youth waited until the water receded, then crossed over, retrieved the gold, and went on to his home in safety.]

[When his brothers' wives saw him and asked him about their husbands, he replied, "They are about to learn wisdom." He then proceeded to buy up fields and vineyards, build a palace, and acquire cattle and property, but when his wife asked him, "My lord, tell me, where did you get all this money?", he became angry with her and gave her a severe beating, saying, "What right do you have to ask such a question?" Nevertheless she cajoled him again and again until he told her everything. Once, as he vexed his wife, she began to shout, saying, "It is not enough for you that you killed both your brothers—you want to kill me too!" When his brothers' wives heard this about their husbands' death, they went straightway to the king and lodged a charge against him. The king immediately ordered him brought before him and ordered his execution. As the executioners were taking him out to slay him, he said to them, "I pray you, give me leave to speak my piece before the king." They forthwith led him before the king, whereupon he fell upon his face and said, "My lord, I am one of the three brothers who served you for thirteen years[6] in order to learn wisdom. I am the youngest (of them, the one) who returned the gold pieces in exchange

6. *Sic!* Above, p. 164: "one year."

for your wisdom, and the wisdom which you imparted to me did indeed save me in the past."]

[The king immediately recognized the truth of the matter and said, "Fear not. The money which you took from your brothers and from my menservants was rightfully yours. The wisdom which you acquired and which saved you from death in the past, (will now save you also) from these two women.[7] Now go and rejoice with your wife!" At that same moment Solomon said, *How much better is it to get wisdom than gold!* (Prov. 16:16).]

7. The text has "this woman," meaning his wife, which does not fit what follows.

CHAPTER [XXXIII][1]

THE QUERIES PROPOUNDED BY THE MEN OF SERENDIB[2]

These were the sixty philosophers in Serendib[3] who lived in the time of Nahum the man of Gamzu.[4] The king of Persia sent for [the wise men of] Israel, had them brought before him, and asked them, "Is there one among you who can silence these philosophers?" Nahum the man of Gamzu replied, "I will go to them and silence them, but on one condition." The king asked, "What is it?", and Nahum replied, "I want to have with me sixty ships, a jar, and a chain; and command the sailors to take their orders from me." The king granted him his request, and he set out until he reached Serendib.

He then left the ships and the men at the seashore, while he himself went up to [the city],[5] **147b** where he inquired about the house of the philosophers, but no one dared guide him [thereto], until he came upon one person, a seller of [sheep's] heads[6] who was roasting them. So he accosted him, saying, "I want you to sell me the first head that comes up out of the oven." [When the seller agreed], he asked him, "How much is it?" The seller replied, "So-and-so much," whereupon he paid him the price. When the seller then thrust his hand [and

1. No Rabbinic source is known for the whole of the following narrative. Of its five episodes, however, three are based on Rabbinic sources, where they appear as independent stories, not about Nahum the man of Gamzu.

2. Source for the following story: B. Beḵ 8b–9a; ascribed to R. Joshua ben Ḥananiah.

3. The medieval name for the island of Ceylon, to which, according to Muslim legend, Adam was sent after his expulsion from Paradise.

4. For other tales attributed to him and for the origin of his name, see above, Chaps. IV–V.

5. Some word is missing here in H ("the city, the place, the island"). Cf. Obermann, p. 174, n. 28.

6. H has "*rawwās*," literally "head butcher, or dealer," i.e., a butcher specializing in heads of sheep; cf. Hirschberg, p. 98, n. 2*; J. Sauvaget, in *Bulletin d'Études Orientales 12* (1947–48), 38–39.

part of his head] into the oven [to pull out a sheep's head] and straightened up, Nahum seized hold[7] of his head and said, "This is what I bought—the first head to come up," and the seller acknowledged his right to it.[8] Nahum then asked him, "If I release you from my hand, will you show me the house of the philosophers?", to which the seller replied, "[If I do], we will both be slain." Nahum said to him, "I will tell you what to do. Put a bundle of fodder upon your head, and when you reach the door [of their house], shake your head, so that some of the leaves will drop off at the door." **148a** The seller did so, and Nahum the man of Gamzu came up and stood at the door, calling to the doorkeeper, "Inform the scholars that a scholar has come to [see] them." The doorkeeper accordingly obtained permission to let him in, and Nahum entered, and raising his head, saw them sitting in three rows. Afraid to show preference to some over the others, he said, "Peace be upon you, O lower ones, upper ones, and middle ones," then greeted again the upper ones, the middle ones, and the lower ones, and [so forth], citing [each row] first as well as last. After he had completed his greetings, they being thus unable to criticize him [for lack of respect to any row], they asked him what he wanted, and he replied, "Will you attend a circumcision?"[9] They answered in the affirmative, but said, "Not before we ask you ten questions. If you come out of them [successfully], we will be bound to go with you." He replied: "Ask!"[10] They then proceeded to ask him as follows: (1) **148b** "What is the highest point of the universe?" He replied, "The [ground of the] Temple [in Jerusalem]."[11] They

7. [For *lazima* read *akhadha*.—LN]

8. [For *fa-wajaba lahu dhālika* presumably read *fa-akarra lahu bi-dhālika*.—LN]

9. In Muslim society the parties given to celebrate circumcision were often very lavish affairs. To refuse an invitation to such an event would have been a grave insult; cf. *EI*[1], *s.v. khitān.*

10. Of the ten questions cited below, only seven occur in the Rabbinic sources; numbers one, three, and ten are not found there, and number seven differs considerably.

11. Cf. B. Zeb 54b; "the Temple was higher than . . . all lands."

asked further, "How do you know this?" He replied, "Because the waters of the Flood did not cover it."[12]

(2) "What is the center of the universe?" Again he replied, "The Temple." They asked further, "How do you know this?" He replied, "Come and let us measure the world."[13]

(3) "Which is farther, from heaven to earth or from east to west?"[14] He replied, "From heaven to earth is farther." They asked further, "Whence do you know this?" He replied, "Because if you look at the sun [at midday], its size is like that of a round cake of bread, but as it draws near the earth [at sunset] it grows larger."

(4) "If a chick dies inside the egg, how does its soul go out?" He replied, "Out of the same place where it came in, thence it goes out."

(5) "When salt is about to spoil, with what shall we salt it?" He replied, "With the afterbirth of an elephant."

(6) "A field grown with **149a** knives, with what shall we harvest it?" He replied, "With horns of asses."

(7) "Take this handmill and cut a shirt for us from it." He replied, "[First] take some of it and spin it into threads, and weave them loosely together."[15]

(8) "We want you to build for us a house in the air." He replied, "[First] bring the stones and tools for me to where the work is to begin, and it will be built."

(9) "This well outside the house—move it inside the house." He replied, "[First] take this [pile of] bran and twist it into ropes for me, so that I may pull the well with them."

(10) "The earth displaced by the stake—where does it go?"

12. For this phrase, cf. Song Rabbah 4, 25a; Gen. Rabbah 33a. The legend regarding the Flood not covering the Temple is applied in Islamic lore to the Kaaba; cf. A. J. Wensinck, *The Idea of the Western Semites concerning the Navel of the Earth* (Amsterdam, 1916), p. 22.

13. Cf. Louis Ginzberg, *Legends of the Jews* (Philadelphia, 1946), *5*, 14 f.

14. Cf. B. Tam 31b–32a. The question as phrased in H is impossible: "Which is farther, from heaven to earth or from earth to heaven?"

15. This question is found in this form in Ahiqar, Arabic version, 7:17–18; Syriac version, 7:20; English translation in *Apocrypha*, *2*, 765–66.

He replied, "To the same place where a woman's virginity goes."[16]

They then said to him, "Now we are bound to go with you—come, let us go." He replied, "You are men of learning. I therefore want to take you along one by one, but do you yourselves determine **149b** which one of you is worthy of being the first." He thereupon took them along one by one, brought each one to one of the ships, and said to the sailors, "Cast off!"—for fear lest, if he should take them [all] in the same vessel,[17] they should conceive an evil design and overpower it. So that, this being the case, Nahum joined only one [of them] in one of the ships, and the two of them traveled until they came to a place in the sea called "the Pool that swallows water," or in Hebrew "Swallowing waters."[18] His ship merely skirted the place, while he drew a jarful of water from it. They then continued their journey until they reached the city of the king, whereupon Nahum informed him that the philosophers had arrived and brought them before him. The king asked them, "How did [his] cunning gain mastery over you?", to which they replied, "Once [God's] judgment is decreed, eyesight is struck **150a** blind."[19] The king then turned to the Israelites, [saying], "Is it not written in the Torah, *Whoso sheddeth man's blood, by man shall his blood be shed*, etc. (Gen. 9:6)? These now have slain a number of people—what should the judgment be?" Nahum the man of Gamzu replied, "Let us sentence them to nothing more than that they should fill this large jar with water, on condition that they eat no food until after it is full, and to begin with I will bring a small jar [of water] and pour it in." The philosophers agreed to this, and he brought the same jar that was filled out of the "Swallowing waters" and poured it into the large jar. Now each time they brought sixty small jars [of water] and poured

16. No Rabbinic source is found for this question. Cf. n. 10, above.

17. [*Mawḍiʿan* is evidently a misreading of *markaban*.—LN]

18. Cf. Eccl. Rabbah 1, 3b; Gen. Rabbah 34, n. 2.

19. An Arabic proverb; cf. Freytag, *3*, 508, no. 3048 (variant 3047).

them into the large jar, the [swallowing] water would swallow the [poured] water. They did not cease bringing water and pouring it into the large jar in order to fill it, **150b** yet it did not become full. Finally they were taken from the king's gate to the sea [and cast into it], and thus all of them perished. The king thereupon asked the Israelites, "Since such wisdom exists amongst you,[20] why did your kingdom cease?" They replied, "Had our kingdom [not] ceased, you would not be king."

[NAHUM'S WISDOM][21]

Nahum the man of Gamzu was set up [as judge], and one day they found a man of Israel committing adultery with one of their [Gentile] women. They brought both her and him to the judge and said to him, "We found them doing thus-and-so," to which Nahum replied, "Proclaim about him as follows: These are the wages of him who is found [lying] with an animal." The man retorted, "Do not proclaim about me [that I lay] with an animal, for it was with one of you [humans] that they found me. But I know that they [the Gentiles] are [no better than] asses **151a** to you, which is why they have appointed [an ass like] you as judge." The judge said to them, "After you finish taking testimony against him, [and his guilt is established], bring him back to me." When they brought him back to him, he seized a staff and slew him with it, saying, "Whosoever cometh to slay thee, do thou slay him first."

When word[22] of this reached the king and his companions, they said to him, "We cannot submit to you when you appoint over us a man to whom we are [no better than] asses." The king replied, "Whatsoever woman surrenders herself to a

20. Almost literal translation of the phrase in B. Giṭ 56b, and elsewhere; cf. Obermann, p. 178, n. 18/19.

21. Source for the following paragraph (with some deviation from the original): B. Ber 58a (ascribed to R. Shila).

22. The following two paragraphs are not found in the source. Obermann (p. 179, n. a) suggests that they were invented by whoever combined the various independent Aggadic stories into the continuous narrative of this chapter.

man who is not permitted to her, is to us indeed [no better than] an ass, without a doubt." They said again, "We cannot accept [this]," and the king went on, "[In that case] we fear that if there should come before you a [case requiring] discriminating judgment, you will be unable to render a decision about it; we therefore [continue to] need them [the Jews], their [keen] judgment, and their [fine] intelligence." At this the former judge among them said, "Reappoint me, and should you thereafter find yourself in need of them, **151b** kill me." So the king dismissed Nahum the man of Gamzu, and reappointed their own judge to administer justice.

Nahum the man of Gamzu then went to his wife and said to her, "Go back to your father's house." She replied, "What is the reason [for my dismissal]?" He said, "The king has dismissed me, [and I now have no income]." She replied, "My father does not desire your wealth—he desires your learning and your [high] standing with God Most High. [Besides], how can the Jews spare you?" He said to her, "I, too, do not desire your beauty—I am desirous only [of the fact] that you are the daughter of a learned and meek man." He then asked her, "Do you perchance have some of your father's wisdom?", and told her [the details] of the matter. [She replied], "Tomorrow I will go and get your position back for you, as well as have him who was appointed in your place beheaded."

152a The next day[23] she called her son, took him along, and went to the king's gate, where she announced, "I seek the protection of God Most High and of the king." When she was brought before the king, she proceeded to say, "May God prolong the king's life! I am a Jewish woman. I had a husband, but he died and left me a manservant who would work all summer. I would take his earnings to sustain myself therewith through the winter, and I would flay [some of] his skin to make garments for my children. Now I have been forcibly deprived of my manservant, he has been beheaded,[24]

23. Source for this paragraph: B. BB 58a.
24. [Reading *ghuṣibtu . . . wa-ḍuribat raqabatuhu.*—LN]

and his skin has been flayed. Thus my manservant is being used, yet I am not being paid his wages." Her story having thus been presented to the king, he summoned his [new] judge and said to him, "Examine [the record of] this case and declare judgment **152b** upon it." When the judge read it, he said, "There is no such thing in the world. It must be one of the tricks of the Jews." The king asked him, "If we call the Jewish judge and he rules otherwise, what shall we do?" The judge replied, "Have me beheaded." So the king summoned Nahum the man of Gamzu and gave him the story, and after he read it, he smiled and said, "O king, I never saw anyone more witless[25] than this woman. This is her plea: She had a date palm—that is the manservant. She would take its produce and fruit and store it to feed her children. As for its skin, these are its branch stumps[26] from year to year; she saved its twigs to warm herself and her children therewith all winter. These are the garments. Her words "I have been forcibly deprived," **153a** [meaning] of her palm tree, signify that it was cut down—that is the manservant's beheading. The flaying of his skin is the stripping of the palm tree and [the use of] its wood, [with no compensation] paid to her—that is [what is meant by] the skin. The [trunk of the] tree has been made into a conduit pipe through which water irrigates the gardens. She is now demanding rental for her tree, and its price before [it was cut down]." The king thereupon said, "Let this [Gentile] judge be beheaded, and let Nahum the man of Gamzu be restored to his station." And so it was done.

25. [The context seems to require the opposite, "crafty, guileful"; perhaps *ajhal* is a misreading of a hasty naskhī *akyad*.—LN]

26. [Which are broad and thick.—LN]

CHAPTER [XXXIV]

[THE ABANDONED GIRL]

The story is told in the name of a certain scholar, that there were once two brothers.[1] As the end of one of them drew near, [he grew apprehensive that his daughter might marry unsuitably, so he instructed][2] his brother about it, saying, "Brother, I am about to depart on my way. Now I have this female child who possesses **153b** sufficient wealth to sustain her in this world and to supply her needs. I ask of you to let this girl be under your hand, to raise her, and not to marry her off except to one who possesses [knowledge of] Torah." The girl owned the house in which she dwelt, as well as fertile fields, gardens, and [other] sown lands yielding produce for her, by her father's grace,[3] and he left her also one hundred dinars. Then he deceased and departed on his way.

After a month had passed, [his brother] said to himself, "Is it not said in our Holy Writ, *I have been young, and now am old; yet have I not seen the righteous forsaken, nor his seed begging bread* (Ps. 37:25)? Let me therefore test this verse with this girl." So he said to her, "My daughter, know that your father said to me, 'I have a kinsman in one of the cities beyond the sea'; **154a** I would like you to meet him," to which she replied, "My lord, do as you wish." He then took the girl along and they both boarded a ship and sailed for twenty days, until they reached one of the cities beyond the sea. They both disembarked and walked on, until they reached the Street of the Perfumers, whereupon he said to the girl, "Sit here, while I return to the ship, for I have forgotten something there; I

1. No Rabbinic source has been found for this story.

2. A phrase has dropped out and has been supplied by Obermann, p. 182, n. 25/26.

3. [Indistinct in H, and so restored, *minan abīhā*, by Obermann; more probably, and more in accord with the context, read *mā yakfīhā*, "sufficient for her needs."—LN]

will come back." So the girl sat there, while he went back to the seashore, found a ship on its way to return, boarded it, and sailed away.

When the girl became aware [of his overlong absence], she nevertheless continued to wait patiently[4] until sunset, but did not see him [again]. She then put her sleeve over her face [in sorrow] and wept bitterly, and people gathered **154b**
around her, asking her, "What is the reason for your weeping? Do you lack expense money?" She replied, "My weeping is caused by an uncle [of mine], who was with me but has left me and went down to the sea, and I have not seen him since." So the [Gentile] elders who were in the street said to her, "Know that night is now fallen, and we cannot go off and leave you alone in the street. Come therefore with us and stay with the womenfolk of one of us until morning. Perhaps your uncle has lost his way, and when he comes back we will turn you over to him." She replied, "I cannot do so, inasmuch as I am a Jewess." Just then the qadi and the market inspector[5] happened to pass by, and hearing her words inquired, "Is there not a Jew in the market place?" They replied, "Yes, there is." So a Jew was brought up . . .[6]

4. So emended by Obermann (p. 183, nn. 13–14), and translated accordingly by Hirschberg (p. 103).

5. [In Arabic *muḥtasib*, an official who not only enforced law and order in the market places but also supervised public morals and controlled the town watch.—LN]

6. Here H ends, "a Jew" being the catchword of the next leaf, which, with whatever followed, is missing. Cf. Obermann, p. 183, n. 7.

LIST OF ABBREVIATIONS

Tractates of Mishnah, Tosefta, and Talmud

Aḇ	ʾAḇoṯ	Ḳid	Ḳiddušin
ARN	ʾAḇoṯ dĕ-Rabbi Naṯan	Kil	Kilʾayim
AZ	ʿĂḇoḏah Zarah	Mak	Makkoṯ
BB	Baḇa Baṯra	Meḡ	Mĕḡillah
Beḵ	Bĕḵoroṯ	Men	Mĕnaḥoṯ
Ber	Bĕraḵoṯ	MḲ	Moʿeḏ Ḳaṭan
Beṣ	Beṣah	Neḏ	Nĕḏarim
BḲ	Baḇa Ḳamma	Pes	Pĕsaḥim
BM	Baḇa Mĕṣiʿa	RH	Roš haš-Šanah
Dem	Dĕmai	Sanh	Sanheḏrin
Ed	ʿEḏuyyoṯ	Shab	Šabbaṯ
Er	ʿEruḇin	Soṭ	Soṭah
Giṭ	Giṭṭin	Suk	Sukkah
Ḥaḡ	Ḥăḡiḡah	Ta	Taʿăniṯ
Hor	Horayoṯ	Tam	Tamiḏ
Ḥul	Ḥullin	Yeḇ	Yĕḇamoṯ
Kel	Kelim	Zeḇ	Zĕḇaḥim
Ket	Kĕṯubboṯ		

B. prefixed to the name of a tractate indicates a reference to the Babylonian Talmud; P. indicates a reference to the Palestinian (Jerusalemite) Talmud; and Tos a reference to the Tosefta (ed. Zuckermandel, Pasewalk, 1880; 2d ed., Jerusalem, 1937). Otherwise the reference is to tractates of the Mishnah.

BIBLIOGRAPHY

(including abbreviations)

I. Manuscripts and Early Printed Editions

1. Judeo-Arabic
   H—MS Harkavy, published by Obermann, *q.v.*
   Ḳ—MS Ḳāfiḥ, published by Abramson, *q.v.*
2. Hebrew
   HY—MSS and early printed editions (1519–1746) of Hebrew versions of the Judeo-Arabic original.

II. Books

Abraham ibn Ḥasdai, *Barlaam and Josaphat*, trans. Joseph Jacobs, London, 1896.

Abraham ibn Ḥasdai, *Ben ham-Meleḵ wĕhan-Nazir*, ed. A. M. Habermann, Tel Aviv, 1950.

Abrahams, Israel, trans, *The Book of Delight*, Philadelphia, 1912; *see also* Ibn Zabarah.

Abramson—Abramson, Shraga, *Raḇ Nissim Gaʾon, Ḥamišah Sĕfarim* (R. *Nissim Gaon Libelli Quinque*), Jerusalem, 1965; *see also* Ḳ, above.

Apocrypha—*The Apocrypha and Pseudepigrapha of the Old Testament*, ed. R. H. Charles, 2 vols., Oxford, 1913.

ʿ*Aruḵ*—Nathan ben Jehiel of Rome, *Aruch completum*, ed. A. Kohut, 8 vols., New York, 1955; *Additamenta*, by S. Krauss, vol. 9.

Berechiah han-Naḳdan, *Mišle Šuʿalim*, ed. A. M. Habermann, Jerusalem, 1945–46; *see also* Hadas, Moses.

Bet ha-Midrash—Jellinek, Adolph, ed., *Bet ha-Midrash*, vol. 1–4, Leipzig, 1853–57; vol. 5–6, Vienna, 1873–77.

Bialik, H. N., and J. H. Ravnitzky, *Sefer ha-ʾAggaḏah*, Tel Aviv, 1935.

Blau, Joshua, *The Emergence and Linguistic Background of Judeo-Arabic* (Scripta Judaica, V), Oxford, 1965.

Brinner, *Chronicle*—Ibn Ṣaṣrā, Muḥammad ibn Muḥammad, *A Chronicle of Damascus, 1389–1397*, ed. and trans. W. M. Brinner, 2 vols., Berkeley, 1963.

Derenbourg, Joseph, ed., *Deux versions hébraïques du livre de Kalilah et Dimnah*, Paris, 1881.

Dik. Sof.—Rabbinovicz, Raphael N., *Dikduke Sofĕrim*, 16 vols., Munich and Przemysl, 1867–97.

Dozy—Dozy, Reinhart, *Supplément aux dictionnaires arabes*, 2 vols., Leyden, 1881.

*EI*²—*Encyclopaedia of Islam*, New edition, Vols. 1–, Leyden, 1960–.

Epstein, Morris, ed., *Tales of Sendebar: An Edition and Translation of the Hebrew Version of the Seven Sages*, Philadelphia, 1967.

Exempla—Gaster, Moses, *The Exempla of the Rabbis*, London, 1924.

Fakkar, Rouchdi, *At-Tanûḫî et son livre: La déliverance après l'angoisse* (Institut français d'archéologie orientale, Recherches, XXIV), Cairo, 1955.

Freimann, Aaron, *Union Catalog of Hebrew Manuscripts and Their Location*, 3 vols., New York, 1964.

Freytag—Freytag, G. W., *Arabum proverbia*, 3 vols. in 4, Bonn, 1838–43.

GAL—Brockelmann, Carl, *Geschichte der arabischen Litteratur*, 2 vols., Leyden, 1936–42; and Supplement, 3 vols.

Gaster, Moses, *The Maᶜăśeh Book*, 2 vols., Philadelphia, 1934.

Genizah Studies—Ginzberg, Louis, *Genizah Studies in Memory of Dr. Solomon Schechter*, 3 vols. (Texts and Studies of the Jewish Theological Seminary of America, VII–IX), New York, 1928.

al-Ghazālī, *Iḥyāʾ*—al-Ghazālī, *Iḥyāʾ ᶜulūm al-dīn*, 4 vols., Cairo, 1316/1899.

Ginzberg, Louis, *The Legends of the Jews*, 6 vols.; *Index*, by B. Cohen, Philadelphia, 1946.

Hadas, Moses, trans., *Fables of the Jewish Aesop*, trans. from the Fox Fables of Berechiah han-Nakdan, New York, 1966; *see also* Berechiah han-Nakdan.

Hirschberg—Nissim ben Jacob ibn Shāhīn, *Ḥibbur Yafeh mehay-Yĕšuᶜah*, (Sifriyyat Mĕkorot, 15) trans. H. Z. Hirschberg, Jerusalem, 5714/1953.

Ibn Saᶜd, *Ṭabaqāt*—Ibn Saᶜd, *al-Ṭabaqāt al-Kubrā*, 9 vols., Leyden, 1904–40.

Ibn Zabarah, Joseph, *Sefer haš-Šaᶜšuᶜim*, ed. Israel Davidson, New York, 1914; *see also* Abrahams.

JE—*The Jewish Encyclopaedia*, ed. I. Singer, 12 vols., New York, 1901–06.

Kalonymos ben Kalonymos, *ʾIggereṯ Baʿăle Ḥayyim*, ed. Y. Toporovsky, Jerusalem, 1949.

Löwy, Adolf, *Die Tugend- und Sittenlehre des Talmud*, Vienna, 1890.

Noy, Dov, ed., *Folktales of Israel*, Chicago, 1963.

Obermann—Obermann, Julian, ed., *Studies in Islam and Judaism: The Arabic Original of Ibn Shāhīn's Book of Comfort* (Yale Oriental Series, Researches, XVII), New Haven, 1933; *see also* H, above.

Pfeiffer, Robert H., *Introduction to the Old Testament*, New York, 1941.

Saadiah, *Amānāt*—Saadiah ben Joseph, *Kitāb al-Amānāt wal-Iʿtiqādāt*, ed. S. Landauer, Leyden, 1880; tr. S. Rosenblatt (Yale Judaica Series, I), New Haven, 1948.

Saadiah, *Sefer hag-Galuy*—Saadiah ben Joseph, *Sefer hag-Galuy*, ed. A. Harkavy, Berlin, 1891.

Schechter, *Saadyana*—Schechter, Solomon, ed., *Saadyana, Geniza Fragments of Writings of* R. *Saadya Gaon and Others*, Cambridge, 1903.

Sefer ham-Maʿăśiyoṯ—Halpern, Mordecai ben Ezekiel, *Sefer ham-Maʿăśiyoṯ*, 2 vols., Tel Aviv, 1965.

SER—*Seder Eliyahu Rabba*, with *Seder Eliyahu Zuṭa*, and *Pseudo-Seder Eliyahu Zuṭa* (*Tanna de-Be Eliyahu*), ed. M. Friedmann, Vienna, 1902.

SEZ—*Seder Eliyahu Zuṭa*, *see* SER.

STwA—*Seḏer Tannaʾim wĕ-ʾAmoraʾim*, ed. Z. H. Filipowski, with *Liber Juhasin*, Frankfurt, 1924; *see also* Yuḥasin.

Sherira—Sherira Gaon, *ʾIggereṯ* R. *Sherira Gaon*, ed. A. Heiman, London, 1914.

Singer, Isaac Bashevis, *Elijah the Slave: A Hebrew Legend Retold*, trans. from the Yiddish by the author and Elizabeth Shub, New York, 1970.

Soncino Talmud—*The Babylonian Talmud*, trans. . . . under the editorship of Rabbi Dr. I. Epstein, 18 vols., London, 1935.

Tanḥuma—*Midrash Tanḥuma*, ed. S. Buber, Wilno, 1885.

al-Tanūkhī, *Faraj*—al-Tanūkhī, *Kitāb al-Faraj baʿd al-Shiddah*, 2 vols., Cairo, 1955.

al-Thaʿlabī—al-Thaʿlabī, *Qiṣaṣ al-Anbiyāʾ*, Cairo, 1348/1929.

Tishby, I., and J. Dan, *Hebrew Ethical Literature* (in Hebrew), Jerusalem, 1970.

Wensinck, A. J., *The Idea of the Western Semites concerning the Navel of the Earth*, Amsterdam, 1916.
Yalkuṭ—Simeon of Frankfurt, *Yalkuṭ Shimᶜoni*, Wilno, 1898.
YJS—Yale Judaica Series.
Yuḥasin—Zacuto, Abraham, *Sefer Yuḥasin*, *see* STwA.

III. Articles

Abramson, S., "Letters by Geᵓonim," *Tarbiṣ 31* (1961–62), 191–213.
Abramson, S., "ᵓImre ḥoḵmah we-ᵓamre ᵓinše," *Minḥah li-Yĕhuḏah*, J. L. Zlotnik Jubilee Volume, ed. S. Asaf, Jerusalem, 1949, pp. 20–38.
Abramson, S., "R. Joseph Rosh ha-Seder," *Kirjath Sepher 26* (1949–50), 72–95.
Asaf, S., "Ancient Book Lists," *Kirjath Sepher 18* (1941–42), 274.
Baneth, David H., "Ḥăluḳaᵓ dĕ-Rabbanan, Ḥibbur Yafeh min hay-yešuᶜah, and a Mohammedan Tradition," *Tarbiṣ 25* (1957), 331–36.
Baneth, David H., Review of Obermann, *Kirjath Sepher 11* (1935), 349–57.
Epstein, Jacob N., "Collecteana from Sefer ham-Mafteaḥ of Rabbenu Nissim," *Tarbiṣ 2* (1930), 1–26.
Goitein, S. D., "A Letter by Labrat ben Moses ben Sighmar, Dayyan of al-Mahdiyya, about R. Nissim, 'Renewer of the Faith,'" *Tarbiṣ 36* (1966), 59–72.
Goitein, S. D., "New Information about the Negidim of Kairouan and about R. Nissim," *Zion 27* (1962), 11–23.
Harkavy, A. A., "Ḥăḏašim gam yĕšanim," *Festschrift zum achtzigsten Geburtstage Moritz Steinschneider's*, Leipzig, 1896, Hebrew section, pp. 9–24.
HUCA—Hebrew Union College Annual.
Lieberman, Saul, "Sin and its Punishment: A Study in Jewish and Christian Visions of Hell," *Louis Ginzberg Jubilee Volume*, New York, 1945, pp. 249–70.
Lieberman, Saul, "Tiḳḳune Yĕrušalmi," *Tarbiṣ 5* (1933), 97–110.
Margoliouth, D. S., "Notes on the Sefer hag-Galuy Controversy," *Jewish Quarterly Review 13* (1901), 155–58.
Mĕgillaṯ Sĕtarim—Poznanski, S. A., "Liḳḳuṭim min Sefer Mĕgillaṯ Sĕtarim," *Haṣ-Ṣofeh le-Ḥoḵmaṯ Yiśraᵓel, 5–6* (1921–22), 177–93, 294–301, 329–50.

Obermann, J., "Ein Werk agadisch-islamischen Synkretismus," *Zeitschrift für Semitistik 5* (1927), 43–68.

Obermann, J., "The Sepulchre of the Maccabean Martyrs," *Journal of Biblical Literature 50* (1931), 250–65.

Obermann, J., "Two Elijah Stories in Judeo-Arabic Transmission," *Hebrew Union College Annual 23:1* (1950–51), 387–404.

Plessner, M., Review of Hirschberg, *Tarbiṣ 24* (1954), 469–72.

Poznanski, Samuel A., "Anše Ḳayrawan," *Festschrift zu Ehren des Dr. Harkavy*, St. Petersburg, 1908, pp. 175–220.

Poznanski, Samuel A., "Schechters Saadyana," *Zeitschrift für hebräische Bibliographie*, *7* (1903), 107–13, 142–47, 178–87.

Rappaport, S. I., "Tolĕdoṯ R. Nissim bar Yaᶜăḳoḇ we-ḳoroṯ sĕfaraw," *Bikkure ha-ᶜIttim 12*, 5592/1831, 56–83.

Sauvaget, J., "Décrets mamelouks de Syrie," *Bulletin d'Études Orientales 12* (1947–48), 5–60.

Schloessinger, Max, "Nissim ben Jacob ben Nissim Ibn Shahin," *Jewish Encyclopaedia 9*, 315–16.

Scholem, G., "The Paradisiac Garb of Souls and the Origin of the Concept of *Ḥăluḳaᵓ dĕ-Rabbanan*," *Tarbiṣ 24* (1956), 290–306.

Schwab, Moïse, "Les manuscrits et incunables hébreux de la Bibliothèque de l'Alliance Israélite Universelle," *Revue d'Études Juives 49* (1904), 74–88, 270–96.

Vajda, G., Review of Abramson, *Revue des Études Juives 125* (1966), 422–26.

Wiener, Alfred, "Die *Faraǧ baᶜd aš-Šidda*-Literatur," *Der Islam 4* (1913), 270–98, 387–420.

GLOSSARY

Baraita

an extraneous Mishnah, containing a Tannaitic tradition not included in the Mishnah, but cited in the Tosefta, the Gemara, or the Midrash

Citron (*ʾeṯroḡ*)

the citrus fruit traditionally taken to be *the fruit of the goodly trees* (Lev. 23:40), hence one of the four species used in the observance of the festival of Tabernacles

Exilarch (*reš galuṯa*)

title borne by the lay head of the Jewish community in Babylonia (later Iraq) from at least the Parthian period (ca. 140 C.E.) down to the Mongol conquest of Baghdad in the middle of the 13th century. Traditionally the exilarchs were of Davidic descent and represented the Jewish community at the court of whoever ruled over Iraq

Fringes (*ṣiṣiṯ*)

tassels attached to the corners of four-cornered garments worn by men, in fulfillment of the Biblical commandment in Num. 15:37–41 and Deut. 22:12

Haḇdalah lamp

the light (usually a candle) used together with wine in the religious ceremony marking the end of the Sabbath or a festival, emphasizing the "distinction" (*haḇdalah*) between the sacred day and the following profane day

Kĕṯubbah

"marriage writ," a document, usually written in Aramaic, detailing the financial and other obligations of the husband to his wife. The signing and public reading of the *kĕṯubbah* are among the significant acts of the Jewish wedding ceremony

Lulaḇ

the palm branch, which is one of the four species of plants used in the celebration of the festival of Tabernacles. The other three are the citron, the willow, and the myrtle

Mezuzah

a small parchment scroll containing the Biblical verses Deut.

6:4–9, 11:13–21, placed in a case which is affixed to the doorpost of a Jewish home

Minḥah
the afternoon prayer service, one of the three daily services of the Jewish liturgy

Prince (*naśiʾ*)
under Roman and Byzantine rule until the 5th century C.E., a descendant of Hillel the Elder who was recognized as the political head of the Jews of Palestine. He presided over the Sanhedrin, fixed the calendar, and ordained scholars. After the lapse of the institution in Palestine, the title persisted and spread to other lands during the Middle Ages

al-Shām
the Arabic name of Syria, which until the 20th century encompassed Palestine as well. In the *Ḥibbur* it is used generally to refer to Palestine, the Land of Israel

Sukkah
"booth, hut," the temporary structures covered with twigs and branches, used by Jews during the festival of Tabernacles (*Sukkoṯ*) in memory of the huts used by the Children of Israel in the desert; cf. Lev. 23:42 f.

Tanna (pl. *Tannaʾim*)
the name given to the Sages from the period of Hillel the Elder (1st century C.E.) to the completion of the Mishnah by the end of the next century

Tefillin
usually translated "phylacteries," two black leather boxes containing the Scriptural passages Exod. 13:1–16, Deut. 6:4–9, 11:13–21, tied to the left arm and to the head during morning prayers on all days of the year except Sabbaths and Scriptural holy days

Three Sabbath Meals (*šaloš sĕʿuḏoṯ*)
the custom of eating three meals on the Sabbath day is considered a positive commandment by the Sages. The third meal, often eaten jointly in the synagogue on Saturday afternoon, may not commence before the time of the *Minḥah* service

Torah
"teaching, doctrine, instruction"; *the* Torah is the Pentateuch and the law set forth therein. Torah (without the definite article) signifies the whole corpus of Jewish traditional law from the Bible to the present day

SCRIPTURAL REFERENCES

GENESIS

1:1, 86
2:1, 86
7:8, 155
8:21, 131, 132
9:6, 171
16:4, 125
16:8, 125
17:14, 113
17:17, 157
19:30–38, 154
21:4, 157
21:5, 157
21:23, 154
27:28–29, 157
28:9, 125
28:22, 157
30:14, 152, 153
34:20, 105
36:12, 152
36:22b, 152
36:29, 152
47:21, 156

EXODUS

4:22, 29
13:21, 70
20:6, 163
20:12, 17, 18
20:23, 30
21:26, 29
22:19, 30
22:27, 151
33:13, 36
34:6, 136
34:9, 143
34:14, 29

LEVITICUS

1:1, 88
15:28, 34
22:28, 31
23:40, 152
26:44, 95

NUMBERS

2, 158
10:33, 158
10:35–36, 158
11:1, 159
15:30, 152
15:38, 41
15:41, 42
21:26, 154
24:11, 56
25, 107

DEUTERONOMY

2:9, 154, 155
2:19, 155
2:23, 154
3:9, 156

JOSHUA

JUDGES

1 SAMUEL

2 SAMUEL

2 KINGS

ISAIAH

JEREMIAH

EZEKIEL

HOSEA

JOEL

OBADIAH

MICAH

HABAKKUK

ZECHARIAH

PSALMS

PROVERBS

JOB

LAMENTATIONS

ECCLESIASTES

ESTHER

DANIEL

2 CHRONICLES

Apocrypha

SIRACH

JUDITH

New Testament

LUKE

Koran

INDEX

A. PERSONS

B. NATIONS, SECTS

C. PLACES

D. WORKS MENTIONED IN THE TEXT

E. RABBINIC SOURCES QUOTED

Tractates of the Mishnah are listed in their textual sequence, whether referring to Mishnah, Tosefta, Babylonian or Palestinian (Jerusalemite) Talmud. Abbreviations preceding names of Biblical books or following them will be found in the Bibliography.

Mishnah and Tosefta

MINOR TRACTS

AGGADIC MIDRASHIM

TOSAFOṮ